THE

SOCIALIST REGISTER 1976

THE
SOCIALIST REGISTER
1976

EDITED BY
RALPH MILIBAND
and
JOHN SAVILLE

Merlin Book Club

THE MERLIN PRESS
LONDON

First published in 1976
by The Merlin Press Ltd.
2—4 West Ferry Road
Sufferance Wharf, Isle of Dogs,
London E.14.

Printed by
Whitstable Litho Ltd.,
Whitstable, Kent.

PREFACE

Most of the essays in this thirteenth volume of *The Socialist Register* are concerned with the upheavals which made 1956 so traumatic a year for the left in general and for the Communist left in particular. The intention of this Symposium is clearly not to recall in tranquillity the events of twenty years ago: it is rather to contribute, in the tradition which the *Register* has established for itself, to the clarification of issues and problems of crucial importance to the socialist movement. John Saville describes how he and E.P. Thompson, in defiance of the leadership of the Communist Party, gave voice to a new opposition with the publication of what, in 1957, became *The New Reasoner*. Malcolm MacEwen and Margot Heinemann, from different points of view, recall the impact of the Khrushchev speech to the XXth Congress of the C.P.S.U. on the British Communist Party; and the two interviews which follow these articles also describe the reception of that speech by the French and Italian Communist Parties. Mervyn Jones surveys the main events of 1956; and Bill Lomax provides a detailed account of the little-known Workers Council of Greater Budapest in November 1956. Ken Coates reviews critically a recent compilation on *The Left in Britain;* and Ralph Miliband explores further the present limitations of the British left, and suggests that it should now "move on". His article extends an argument which has appeared in earlier volumes of the *Register,* and to which articles in future volumes will undoubtedly return.

In Part II of the volume, Laurence Harris and Ben Fine set out the main issues in a long-standing debate on Marxist economic theory; and Hal Draper and Anne Lipow present some important texts, never published in English before, on the controversial issue of "Marxist Women versus Bourgeois Feminism".

*   *   *

We wish once again to express our warm thanks to our contributors and to our translators, Anthony and Françoise Strugnell. We also gratefully acknowledge the helpfulness of Martin Eve, our publisher. As in the case of previous volumes, we must stress that the views expressed by any of the contributors to this volume are not necessarily shared by the others, or by the Editors.

R.M.
J.S.

July 1976

TABLE OF CONTENTS

PART I : 1956 AND AFTER

PART II

PART I

THE TWENTIETH CONGRESS AND THE BRITISH COMMUNIST PARTY*

by John Saville

I

No one in Western Europe could have foreseen the extraordinary events of 1956 in Eastern Europe.[1] The year opened with the general belief that the cautious de-stalinisation which had begun with Stalin's death in the Spring of 1953 would continue. In Yugoslavia—a useful yardstick by which to measure changes in Soviet policy—a trade agreement had been signed in October 1954, and about the same time Tito's speeches began to be factually reported. During 1955 there was a continued improvement in diplomatic and political relations, with a visit of the Soviet leaders to Belgrade in May—in the course of which Khrushchev put all the blame for the bitter dispute between the two countries upon Beria—an accusation that was soon to be extended to cover most of the crimes of the later Stalin years. Inside the Soviet Union the principle of collective leadership was increasingly re-affirmed, and the cult of the individual increasingly denounced. Stalin was not yet, however, named as at least part villain of the piece. Indeed a Moscow despatch from Alexander Werth of the *New Statesman* (28th January 1956) suggested a certain rehabilitation of Stalin's reputation in the closing months of 1955. However, the 20th Congress was soon to define 'the Stalin question' in very certain terms.

The 20th Congress of the Communist Party of the Soviet Union met towards the end of February 1956. All the world's communist parties sent their leading comrades as fraternal delegates; from Britain these were Harry Pollitt, general secretary; George Matthews, assistant general secretary; and R. Palme Dutt, vice-chairman of the Party and its leading theoretician. The reports of Khrushchev and Mikoyan emphasised the 'negative' effects of the cult of the individual and the absence of collective leadership—'for

---

*I must make it clear that Edward Thompson, with whom I worked closely and continuously throughout 1956 and subsequent years, has not seen this article in draft. The fault is mine. I wrote this essay so late before the publishing deadline that no one, save my co-editor, saw it before it was sent to the printers. I much regret that Edward Thompson did not see a draft; but readers may comfort themselves with the thought that this article is only the beginning of the historical documentation and analysis of this period. *J.S.*

1

approximately twenty years' said Mikoyan. Khrushchev denied the inevitability of war and Mikoyan accepted that in the past Soviet foreign policy had at times been responsible for increasing tension. The public speeches, therefore, emphasised and underlined the fact of de-stalinisation and it was now abundantly evident that the 'mistakes and errors' of the Stalin years were responsible for the repressive acts which had outraged opinion outside the Soviet Union and for which the world communist movement had acted for so long as apologists. It was, however, the speech of Khrushchev at the secret session on the last day of the Party Congress that provided the explosive material of 1956. Foreign delegations were excluded from the secret session, but it later became clear that at least an edited version of Khrushchev's speech had been made available to foreign Communist Parties during the month or six weeks which followed the ending of the Congress. It is also clear that some foreign delegates, Togliatti and Thorez, for example, knew about the secret speech and its content before they returned home, or soon after; and it would be interesting to know whether this was also true of members of the British delegation. Pollitt and Dutt are dead, but George Matthews, who was much younger, is still an active Party functionary, and the question ought to be addressed to him. There is no doubt at all that leading members of the British Party knew the main facts of the Khrushchev secret report by the middle of April at the latest (see below for a comment on Pollitt's article of 21st April) and they then took up the attitude that Thorez adopted (for which see the interview published in this volume.)

The lid was certainly intended to be kept tightly shut within the British Party, but elsewhere, and above all in the Soviet bloc countries of Eastern Europe, events moved very quickly. During March and April there were announcements of the 'rehabilitation' of leading Communists who had been executed in the years after 1948—among them Rajk in Hungary and Kostov in Bulgaria. As early as March 4th Walter Ulbricht (then East German vice-premier) said in a speech reported in *Neues Deutschland* that Stalin had done 'severe damage to the Soviet State and the Soviet Communist Party' and on 17th March he elaborated these statements and added that the 'myth' of Stalin as a military leader of genius had been developed by Stalin himself. One of the earliest published summaries of Khrushchev's secret speech seems to have been by Jercy Morawski, one of the secretaries of the Polish United Workers Party, in an edition of the Polish Communist paper *Trybuna Luda* for 27th March. In the Soviet Union itself the attacks on Stalin developed by stages, and it was not until 28th March that *Pravda*, in a sharp attack on Stalin, mentioned him by name. On the 2nd April the Russian Academy of Agricultural Sciences ordered the re-publication of the works of N.I. Vavilov (who disappeared during the war and was believed to have died in a Siberian labour camp in 1942). On the 9th April Trofim Lysenko (a name well-known in the West in the first post-war decade) resigned as president of the Academy of Agricultural Sciences.

The British Party took things along slowly and cautiously. According to the testimony of Malcolm MacEwen in this volume there was a stream of letters to the correspondence columns of the *Daily Worker* after the publication of the speeches at the Open Sessions of the 20th Congress, but by the 12th March the editor, J.R. Campbell, declared the discussion closed and rounded it off with an article on 15th March. On 17th March George Matthews wrote in *World News*—the only weekly journal the Party published—on the political significance of the Soviet Congress. His commentary was based entirely upon the published speeches of the Russian leaders, and his analysis was corn for the faithful. The conditions of war, or the threat of war, had produced an abnormal situation in which 'some normal practices were bound to be affected'. Moreover, crisis situations offer opportunities in which 'an enemy of the people', namely Beria, although he was not mentioned by name, could do 'enormous damage to the Party and the people'. But all was now well: 'the mistakes have been recognised and put right. . . as was clear from the Congress, an exceptionally healthy situation exists within the Party, with the fullest operation of inner-Party democracy'. Matthews emphasised the general point about Stalin that was being made at this time: 'Nor is it the case that criticisms of Stalin and of the cult of the individual mean that his great positive services to the Soviet Union and the cause of Socialism, especially during the life-and-death struggles of the Second World War, should be denied'.

It is not known whether Matthews knew the content of Khrushchev's secret speech at the time he wrote this article, which presumably would be early March; but it was not long before it became known to leading members of the British Party. MacEwen reports that the main facts of the speech began to be available to the *Daily Worker* staff from about the middle of March; and the international specialists of the Party could hardly be unaware of the ferment that was growing in Eastern Europe. *World News* on 31st March republished a long extract of the report that Togliatti had made to the Central Committee of the Italian Communist Party. His report, more detailed and much more sophisticated than George Matthews' account, did much to encourage speculation and discussion among the British Party.

The overwhelming majority of the active members of the British Party were, however, still wholly concerned with domestic matters. The 24th National Congress took place at the end of March. The Political Resolution and the Discussion Statement for the Congress was published in *World News* on 28th January 1956 and from this time until the end of March the correspondence columns were entirely devoted to comments from Party members; and throughout April instead of correspondence there were selected contributions from the discussion in the Congress itself. None of these reports related to the important questions raised by the 20th Congress; and it was not until the first of two articles by Harry Pollitt (*World News,* 21st April 1956) that the British Party were given a summary of Khrushchev's secret speech. Pollitt, it should be noted, gave no indication that his article was based upon a text of the secret speech, and he completely omitted the specific details that made the impact of Khrushchev's speech so shattering: the fact, for instance, that 1,108 delegates to the Soviet Party Congress of 1934—out of a total of 1,966, including Central Committee members—had been arrested by 1938 (and almost all of them done to death, it could be added). But the greater part of what Pollitt wrote would either be new to his readers or they would not understand its full implications. Certainly to those who were already questioning and discussing the implications of the 20th Congress, Pollitt's article was further confirmation of the urgent need for a full debate within the Party.[2] Pollitt himself had a second article in *World News,* 5th May in which he attempted, within the context of his own narrow, unimaginative and basically sectarian assumptions and understanding, genuinely to answer the questions of how Stalinism came about. Its serious weakness was that it was couched in personal rather than social/political terms.

There was still no sustained discussion of the main issues of the 20th Congress in the British Party press, and those who tried to get letters published, failed. In *World News* the first letters touching upon the 20th Congress appeared in the issue of 12th May, but it was not until the following week that a long letter from myself was published which set out, in some detail, the issues that required serious argument. This was the one and only letter I ever had published in *World News* during 1956. A second attempt a month later was rejected on the grounds that I had already had 'one crack of the whip', and after that I tried no more.

The context of my letter to *World News* was a growing appreciation of the dimensions of the moral/political problem that confronted Communist Parties everywhere. But most members of the British Party were not in my own privileged position, with access to good libraries, time to read, and a group of acquaintances within the Party, with similar advantages, and with whom I exchanged facts and ideas. Who in the British Party, for example, knew that on 14th April the American *Daily Worker* reported its acceptance of the facts about the destruction of Jewish culture in the Soviet Union after 1948, and the deaths of many Soviet Jewish intellectuals? The paper went on to express 'strong dissatisfaction that the Soviet leaders have not offered any explanation'. How could the overwhelming majority of the British Party know what had been written in the American press? Most only read the British Party's publications, their trade union journal and their local newspaper. And how would they become aware of the fact that two days after the American statement, Molotov and Mikoyan attended the Independence Day celebrations at the Israeli Embassy in Moscow; the first occasion ever that Soviet officials had been present. And even if some of the evidence had become known, how did one put the jig-saw together? The British Party Press provided very few facts and offered no clues.

Pollitt's article on 21st April must have been written about the same time as R. Palme Dutt's 'Notes of the Month' in the May issue of *Labour Monthly*. Dutt's statement was headed 'The Great Debate':

> 'What are the essential themes of the Great Debate? Not about Stalin. That there should be spots on any sun would only startle an inveterate Mithra-worshipper. Not about the now recognised abuses of the security organs in a period of heroic ordeal and achievement of the Soviet Union. To imagine that a great revolution can develop without a million cross-currents, hardships, injustices and excesses would be a delusion fit only for ivory-tower dwellers in fairyland who have still to learn that the thorny path of human advance moves forward, not only with unexampled heroism, but also with accompanying baseness, with tears and blood. . .'

To a growing minority of the Party membership who were becoming outraged at the lack of response of the leadership to the revelations of the 20th Congress, these words of Dutt's were a provocation; and such was the clamour against him (in letters to *Labour Monthly*) that Dutt published a statement in *World News* (2nd June) acknowledging his unfortunate treatment of the problem and promising that the June 'Notes of the Month' would be more 'helpful'. They were not, for what Dutt offered was only a more sophisticated apologetic. One incidental comment revealed that summaries of Khrushchev's speech 'have been made available' (p. 251) although these were never published, and as far as my present research goes, this is the only reference to them before the publication by the American State Department early in June of a complete version of the speech. It was published by the *New York Times* on 5th June and in Britain by the *Observer*, who gave their whole issue of 10th June to the speech, to the fury of many regular readers, who missed on this Sunday their book reviews, bridge and gardening columns. The speech, which went to 26,000 words, was also published by the *Manchester Guardian* in a booklet of 33 pages.

The publication of the secret speech did not lead to an intensified discussion in the communist press in Britain. The first reference in *World News* to the publication of Khrushchev's speech was on 30th June when the journal printed the statement of the Political Bureau of the *French* Communist Party published on 19th June. Apart from the now obvious reluctance of the British Party leadership to encourage a serious discussion, the Party had just launched a campaign for working-class unity. This had been a major theme at the 24th Congress in March, and on 9th June Emile Burns opened with a specially commissioned article for *World News*. A few days later John Gollan published a pamphlet *End the Bans*, and the discussion on unity henceforth became central to the Party's propaganda. It was a bizarre episode. The leaders of the Soviet Union had themselves made nonsense of the uncritical and unswerving support given to every turn and twist of Soviet policy over the previous decades; Eastern Europe was in ferment with the Poznan riots at the end of June presaging the more bitter events of the autumn; there was a growing minority within the British Party who were demanding recognition of the developing moral and political crisis within the Party because of the Khrushchev revelations— and the British Party leaders apparently remained oblivious to the issues involved, and as became known later, deliberately suppressed much of the critical correspondence they were receiving. There was no absolute ban on such material. What happened was that letters on the 20th Congress were included as just one more item in a broad selection of differing interest with the unity theme being dominant. Edward Thompson managed to get an article in *World News* on 30th June—'Winter Wheat in Omsk' which brought a reply from George Matthews in the same issue; but by this time it had already become clear that no serious debate was ever going to be permitted. It was the growing realisation of this fact that led Edward Thompson and I to begin to plan the publication of a discussion journal, and in mid-July there appeared the first issue of *The Reasoner*.

II

The Reasoner was a duplicated journal of 32 pages, with a quotation from Marx on its masthead: 'To leave error unrefuted is to encourage intellectual immorality'. It sold for two shillings. The first number contained two editorials, the first 'Why We are Publishing' and the second 'Taking Stock' which developed further the political arguments which for us represented the crisis within the Communist Party. These were followed by a long article on Democratic Centralism; Edward Thompson's reply to George Matthews (see above) which had been submitted to *World News* but rejected; three (solicited) letters, since this was a first number; and three documents, two from America. The first of these was a letter from Steve Nelson to John Gates of the American *Daily Worker*, congratulating him on the frank editorial on the Rajk case (published on 2nd April); the second a statement by the editorial board of the American communist Jewish organ, *Jewish Life* (June 1956) expressing their horror at the annihilation of Jewish culture in the Soviet Union in the late 1940s; and the third, a translation of a long article in *Nowa Kultura*, the weekly journal of the Union of Polish writers. The translation was made by a good comrade and friend, Alfred Dressler, who taught at the University of Leeds and whose tragic death occurred a few years later.

Edward Thompson and I were historians. He was an extra-mural lecturer at the University of Leeds—although he lived at Halifax and that was the area where most of his classes were; and I was an economic and social historian at the University of Hull. We were both very active in our own party branches and Edward was on the District Committee of the Yorkshire region. I had been a party member since 1934, and Edward from about 1940. We were also members of the Communist Historian's group which had been meeting regularly since the end of the war, and which included a number of quite outstanding intellectuals who have since become well-known. Some in 1956 were already well on the way towards establishing an international reputation. As I wrote to Edward Thompson later in the year (29th November):

> ... It is, I think, significant that of all the intellectual groups in the Communist Party, the historians have come out best in the discussions of the past nine months—and this surely is due to the fact that over the past decade the historians are the only intellectual group who have not only tried to use their Marxist techniques creatively, but have to some measure succeeded. The interesting thing is that the writers as a group have been much more confused—a quite different situation from that in the Eastern countries—and it is precisely the creative writers who should have seen so much more clearly to the heart of things. Of what, otherwise, does their 'creativeness' consist?

Edward and Dorothy Thompson and I had been friends for half a dozen years before 1956, but we were not especially close friends at that time. We were in fact rather late in communicating with each other over the 20th Congress discussions, but once we made contact it soon became clear that we were of one mind in our insistence that if the British CP was to recover its self-respect, let alone the respect of the labour movement in general, it must encourage an honesty of discussion that would, undoubtedly, be painful to many. By about the beginning of June—and I cannot, from the records available, date the matter more precisely, we had agreed first, that the Party leadership were deliberately curbing and confining discussion, and second, that the most obvious way to force an open debate was probably to publish independently of the Party press. The key word was 'probably'. We were highly committed Party members who had come through the tough and difficult years of the Cold War—more difficult than is often appreciated—and we had personal experiences of those who had left the Party to cultivate their own gardens, or of those who had left to become, in our eyes, renegades. One of the original sins for Communist Party members was to publish criticisms of the Party outside the Party press, and in this context journals such as *Tribune* or the *New Statesman* were no different from any other periodical. We therefore conceived our own independent journal as in no way disruptive of the Party to which we belonged, or, to be more accurate, to which we had dedicated ourselves. At the same time we had both been emotionally, politically and morally shocked at the revelations of what Stalinism really meant, and as Communists and historians we saw clearly that we were obliged to analyse seriously the causes of the crimes which in the past we had defended or apologised for. And further, we argued that to take our proper place in the British labour movement demanded a thorough analysis and acknowledgement of past dogmatism and sectarianism. In the second editorial of the first *Reasoner,* we wrote:

> The shock and turmoil engendered by the revelations were the result of our general failure to apply a Marxist analysis to Socialist countries and to the Soviet Union in particular. The absence of such an analysis is an admission of naivety, or worse. This failure bred Utopianism, and encouraged attitudes of religious faith amongst us. When, as so often happened, there came a recognition of the gulf between myth and fact, the disillusion which followed turned in many cases to bitterness. Our irrational approach to the Soviet Union, and our hostile attitude towards those who were not prepared to accept our myths, have brought some Socialists to the point of doubting our integrity, have been a factor contributing to the disunity of the movement, and have helped to drive others into anti-Soviet attitudes dangerous to the cause of peace and Socialism.
>
> Certainly, the establishment of Soviet power is the greatest historical event of this century. From the moment of its foundation, the defence of the Soviet Union from the attacks of the capitalist world was rightly at the centre of working-class internationalism. The debt which all humanity owes to the Soviet people, the heroism of the Soviet people in the Second World War, can never be forgotten. But the balance sheet cannot be closed at this point. Our responsibility to our own Labour movement is no less heavy. To argue, as has so often been argued, that 'we do not believe (that) the interests of the British working class people conflict with the interests of the working class and people of other countries' (Gollan, *End the Bans,* p. 11) is to include the complexities of the real world within a platitude. Argument begins at the point where the phrase ends; and we must still interpret these interests in terms of political action. In practice, the interests of the British working-class have been interpreted in such a way that we have identified them with the acceptance of the foreign policy of the Soviet Union, and at the same time we have been indignant at accusations of blindly 'following Moscow'.
>
> The discussion cannot rest here, for the uncritical character of our public support for the Soviet Union was carried over into other fields. Certain recurring themes in the history of our party demand particular attention. One is the chequered history of Communist-Labour relations; another is the ever-present problem of our sectarianism and dogmatism; a third is the slow growth of a native Marxist tradition. . .

The first number of the *Reasoner* sold out in a few weeks, although it must be added that we only printed a few hundred to begin with (we reprinted) and we gave away a lot of free copies, for what we thought were good political reasons. We received close on three hundred letters by early August. The great majority of our correspondents supported our initiative, and we received much more evidence about the suppression of discussion in the Party press and the difficulties of obtaining a real debate in Party branches. Above all, we were urged to continue.

It was not to be expected that the Party leadership would allow this unusual event in the history of the Party to go unheeded or unchecked. The

Daily Worker had accepted our first advertisement, before the *Ressoner* was published, but our request to insert a further advertisement to the effect that further supplies of No. 1 had been reprinted, was refused. Bert Ramelson, now (1976) national industrial organiser, was then in charge of the Yorkshire District; and we were summoned to appear before a specially convened Sub-Committee of the District. For family reasons I was not able to attend, so I submitted a statement to the meeting on 10th August. Edward and I exchanged several drafts of this statement, and it is not clear from my files which draft was eventually sent. But none of them differs in any substantial way, and extracts are worth quoting to define our position at this time:

> ... It is necessary at the outset to emphasise that *The Reasoner* was conceived entirely in terms of the general interests of the Party. It is not, and we do not intend to allow it to become, a journal of faction. I am as firmly convinced as ever of the need for a Communist Party in Britain. Those who have sought to present it as an 'opposition' journal, aiming a destructive or factional attack upon the Party leadership, are entirely mistaken. This was clearly stated in our first issue.
>
> Why then did we publish? We did so for a number of reasons. In the first place we believed that—before we published—there was a crisis developing in the Party which was not being reflected in the Party press or in the statements and actions of the leadership. We know now, from the dozens of letters that we have received in response to our first number, that we had judged correctly. There is a ferment in the Party that reaches out to its four corners. Nor is the alleged division between intellectuals and industrial comrades borne out by our experience. One of the most interesting and significant aspects of the support we have received has been the positive welcome that industrial comrades have expressed.
>
> In the second place we published because we were of the opinion that there was a marked reluctance amounting to definite opposition on the part of those in control of the official Party press to analyse fully and frankly the consequences of the revelations of the 20th Congress. We could give many examples of the difficulties that comrades up and down the country have experienced in breaking into the Party press. The treatment of the now famous *Volkstimme* article, the subject of a recent letter by leading Jewish comrades in the *Daily Worker,* is an example known to wide sections of the Party. But there are many others. In this connection I would offer a quotation from R. Palme Dutt in 1929 when, with Comrade Pollitt, he was engaged in an internal Party fight for both a drastic change of policy and a sweeping change of the majority leadership. He said, and his words have a vivid relevance to the situation today:
>
> > '. . . the mistakes of the past two years have already cost us too much. The easy going attitude which is satisfied to "recognise" mistakes and pass on, without deeper analysis or drawing of lessons for the future, and with the inevitable consequence of repeating these mistakes in new forms must end. . . It is no longer sufficient merely to "recognise" a mistake after it has been pointed out, and pass on. It is necessary to draw out by the roots the *tendency* revraled by the mistake and brand it.'
>
> In the third place we published because we believed recent events have made it plain that without the right of free, open and unfettered discussion Communist parties will become victims of the disease of orthodoxy. . . In the fourth place

we published because we believed that the widespread discontent—vague, un-formulated, often very emotional—would harden in bitterness, frustration or anti-Party attitudes (depending on the individual concerned) unless some evidence of a new spirit was forthcoming.

We see no reason to stop publishing *The Reasoner;* to do so would be a defeat, not for us, but for the principle of full and frank discussion we are determined to establish. But, if this principle is safeguarded, we are willing to try and meet serious and reasonable objections; we would be glad to publish more contributions opposed to positions expressed in the last issue—a reply from George Matthews to the article of Edward Thompson, a critique of the article on democratic centralism, and so on. Edward knows my views on this, and has my authority to discuss with you any proposals of this sort you wish to bring forward. . .

We were both present at a meeting of the Yorkshire District Committee on 18th August which discussed the report of the Sub-Committee and our general position. The resolution below was adopted by 19 votes out of 21 present, with one vote against (Edward Thompson) and one abstention:

This District Committee asks Comrades Thompson and Saville to cease the publication of *The Reasoner.*

We told the District Committee that on grounds of principle, since no guarantee of open and free discussion had been given, we could not accept the instruction. On 26th August the District Committee held a further meeting, and a long resolution was passed by 15 votes to 5 with 2 abstentions. The resolution reaffirmed in stronger terms the instruction to cease publication, and referred the matter to the national executive. The Political Committee had already received a report of the first Yorkshire District Committee of the 18th August, and it requested Edward and me to attend a meeting prior to the September meeting of the EC. This took place on Friday 31st August at King Street (the London headquarters of the CP). Harry Pollitt was in the chair, and others present included John Gollan, the new general-secretary, R. Palme Dutt, and J.R. Campbell. The meeting began with a long statement from each of us in turn, and we then put forward some compromise proposals which Edward had already communicated in writing. Our statements, with one exception only, were summarised fairly in the 22nd September issue of *World News*. We made the now familiar points:

(1) there was a major crisis in the Party; (2) there was abundant evidence that critical letters etc. were being refused publication; (3) for democratic centralism to work there must be free and open discussion; (4) we were not engaged in factional activity. It was further alleged that we stated that we could not discontinue publication of *The Reasoner* because we had given pledges to others that we should continue. This was untrue, for at no time did we ask any one else to take decisions on our behalf.

The Political Committee members made a wholly constitutional reply to our points; and the publication of *The Reasoner* was considered entirely within the context of Party rules and regulations, the meaning of democratic centralism, and so on. It was a complete failure of minds to meet; on our side we wanted to discuss politics, what the crisis was about and why we needed a much more serious analysis of the 20th Congress; while the PC talked only within the narrow framework of Party organisation and the ways in which we had violated its rules. After three hours we adjourned for lunch and when we re-assembled we re-affirmed our decision to continue publication, arguing the same points that we had put forward to the Yorkshire District. We were asked to reconsider the matter further and to write to Pollitt individually prior to the September 8/9th meeting of the Executive. We drafted our letters on the train going home, and Edward's letter expressed our position:

5th September 1956

This is to confirm our statement at the conclusion of the special meeting of the Political Committee last Friday. We consider it to be the fundamental interest of the Party that the fullest and frankest discussion shall continue. Since you were unable to give us either assurances of effective guarantees that it shall continue in other forms, we regard it as a question of Communist principle to continue publishing *The Reasoner* and the second number is in active preparation.

The second issue of *The Reasoner* was published twenty-four hours before the September meeting of the Executive Committee which proceeded to 'instruct Comrades Thompson and Saville to cease publication of *The Reasoner*'. We had got our timing just right; the problem now was the third issue. If we published again, after the EC's clear instruction, we should be disciplined—expelled or suspended. We still saw the maintenance of the Party as crucial, although we were becoming more and more aware of the deadweight of the bureaucracy upon it. What we had not yet achieved was any certainty that free discussion would be permitted and even more important that the leadership could be brought to understand what the fundamental issues were. We had long discussions between ourselves— usually at Halifax, since Dorothy was nearly always involved; with our own comrades in Yorkshire; and we wrote almost daily to each other. Here is an extract from a very long letter I sent to Edward & Dorothy on 22nd September 1956:

'. . . in all our discussions on what is to be done, I take it that we are agreed that the determining factor is our estimate of what decision on our part will make the greatest political impact—unless you are prepared to argue that the Party is finished and nothing can be done with it, i.e. there is no hope of changing it from below. . . Whatever view we have of the leadership I take the line, and I believe Edward does too, that in the Party there are thousands of honest socialists. True that only hundreds are active; but the others would become alive, as we are always arguing.

Therefore, we have to consider the effect of what we do, not only upon those who are completely with us but upon those many more who are only half-way to our position—what I have always called the middle group. This middle group—who want discussion but who [are] still uncertain how it can be organised—who want new forms of democracy in the Party but who fear (rightly) the degeneration into a Labour Party type of organisation—this group is very mixed in social composition and outlook, and is much larger than our group of supporters. Many of this group are only now going through the kind of intellectual crisis that we passed through in March and April. . .'

By the beginning of October we had decided our line: to publish the third *Reasoner* and at the same time announce we were stopping further publication in what we conceived to be the best interests of the Party. We assumed that our action would have a disciplinary outcome—that we would either be expelled or suspended for a period, and that in either case we would appeal in order to keep the political issues alive. We were certainly by this time becoming increasingly disillusioned with the Party leadership, and were less and less sure that they would respond in any generous or positive way. We had had a further meeting in London with John Gollan and George Matthews and while, as always, they listened to what we had to say and the discussion was conducted in a civilised way, we were left in no doubt that until we stopped publishing there would be no consideration of our request for guarantees regarding an open Party Press. But we were still working within the framework of assumptions that had served us from the beginning, viz. that for the future of the whole Labour movement the democratisation of the Communist Party was urgent and necessary. As I wrote to a member of the staff of the *Daily Worker* on 4th October:

'. . . I want to make one point, and I hope that I shan't sound like Old Father Time himself. I would suggest that it would be wrong for you or anybody else to resign from the *Daily Worker* in the event of our expulsion. I think all of us have been so shockingly starry-eyed about the Party and believed that it is so very different from all other parties. In a number of crucial respects it is very different, not least in the self-sacrificing response it evokes from its members. But because we have set our sights too high and then for various reasons we miss the target we tend to throw in our hand (if you will excuse my mixed metaphors). What I am trying to say is that we must recognise that any party develops institutional structures, conditioned attitudes, a machine and a bureaucracy—and that the fight to reform always encounters hostility, opposition, trimming, verbal but no real agreement etc. In any party those who want a change must be both patient and impatient, tough and conciliatory, compromising and obdurate. Whatever happens the Party goes on and unless one believes there is really no hope, one should be prepared to accept defeat for the time being and continue to fight in perhaps less spectacular ways, always taking the long view. . .

Please believe me when I say that I am talking to myself as much as to you. It so happens that I dislike politics—and even more after the past few months—

and all I really want to do is to write history. What I have to keep telling myself is that this is exactly the kind of attitude that bourgeois society inculcates, and that in the end, if I accept it, it will and can only lead to stultification. Now my problem is not yours—but what I am trying to say is that I hope that you won't take any decision on the rebound—but at least postpone any decision for a few months. After all we may find surprising developments occur in the next six months—and in any case with Poland, Yugoslavia and the Italian Party, our Party here is going to find it increasingly difficult to remain unaffected. . .'

Surprising developments were, indeed, on the way. There is almost nothing in my correspondence up till this date about Suez, largely because we could all take our total opposition as agreed, and when the Anglo-French forces attacked Egypt it was just one more example—of a particularly monstrous, as well as absurd, kind—to which we had all become accustomed in the history of imperialism. But when the revolutionary disturbances began in Hungary at the end of October, reactions were quite different. Before the night of October when fighting began, it was already evident that widespread discontent was showing itself among the Hungarian people. 200,000 had attended the reburial of Laszlo Rajk at a time when the London Daily Worker was calling for 'no vengeance' against Stalinists who had been guilty of what became the standard phrase for massive injustices, torturings and killings: 'violations of Socialist legality'. Edward Thompson wrote a brilliant polemic in the third issue of The Reasoner against the approach of the Daily Worker during October towards both Hungary and Poland, where tensions were also considerable, and where the threat of Soviet intervention was also a reality.

We were writing and producing the third issue of The Reasoner during the second half of October. A long editorial which we printed at the back of the issue was dated 31st October, and Edward's article 'Through the Smoke of Budapest' which dealt with the first Soviet intervention in Hungary, was dated 1st November and published as a seven-page Supplement at the front of the number. The editorial was in part a comment on the EC resolution and statement published in World News 22nd September and in part a broad review of all the political issues involved in the original publication of our journal. We concluded with the statement that we were ceasing publication with this third number in order that the 'case of The Reasoner' should no longer be used as 'a diversion from the central issues of the discussion rights of the whole membership'. But throughout the editorial we emphasised the basic principle of free discussion for which we had been fighting, and that there were still no guarantees at all from the EC that the principle had been accepted. By this time we were, in fact, convinced that the Party leadership was too sgrongly conditioned by the history of the previous decades to be able to comprehend what the intellectual and moral ferment which The Reasoner represented was all about; but had not the Soviet intervention in Hungary occurred, we should certainly have continued to fight for democratic rights within the Party. The social basis of the discussion had broadened considerably by the date of publication of the third issue; we knew, for example, about the fierce debates among the journalists on the *Daily Worker*, and our second and third issues carried a cartoon by Gabriel, the famous *Worker* cartoonist. The point we kept emphasising to each other, and those with whom we were in contact, was that the realisation of the meaning of the 20th Congress took different forms for different people, and their time-span was also different. The longer the discussion went on, the more debate centred upon some, at least, of the basic principles with which we ourselves were concerned. John Mahon was chairman of the Commission on Inner-Party Democracy and his opening statement in *World News* on 1st September caused a considerable adverse reaction; and there are other examples that could be cited of events and episodes which suddenly made people see things differently.

The second and third issues of *The Reasoner* were a considerable improvement over the first. The range of our contacts had widened considerably, and we were now beginning to raise important questions— such as an honest account of history of the British Communist Party— which were part of our general argument for our moral and political rehabilitation as an integral part of the Labour movement. Then came the Russian attack on Budapest in the early hours of 4th November. This was how our last-minute editorial, agreed on the phone during the Sunday of 4th November, began:

> This final number of *The Reasoner* was planned several weeks ago; most of it was typed and duplicated before the events of the past fortnight in Poland and Hungary.
>
> Three days before publication, Eden launched his brutal aggression against Egypt. Every one of our readers will be fully occupied in organising protests and demonstrations of every kind, to end this war and to bring down the Government. Our first thought was to withdraw or postpone this number while the emergency lasts.
>
> But even while we considered, Soviet forces surrounded Budapest and, as we write these lines, we hear the tragic news of the attack on the city.
>
> Even the urgency of the Egyptian crisis cannot disguise the fact that the events of Budapest represent a crucial turning-point for our Party. The aggression of British imperialism is uglier and more cynical in degree than previous imperialist aggressions. But the crisis in World Communism is now different in kind.
>
> The intervention of Soviet troops in Hungary must be condemned by all Communists. The working people and students of Budapest were demonstrating against an oppressive regime which gave them no adequate democratic channels for expressing the popular will. The fact that former fascists and those working for the restoration of Capitalism joined the revolutionaries does not alter this central issue. The criminal blunder of unleashing Security Police and Soviet forces against these crowds provoked the mass of the people to take up arms, in the name of independence, liberty, and justice, against an oppression that was operated in the name of Communism. Those Hungarian comrades of ours who

were innocent of the corruptions and abuses of the Rakosi regime were placed in a horrifying and tragic dilemma. . .

In this crisis, when the Hungarian people needed our solidarity, the British Communist Party has failed them. We cannot wait until the 21st Congress of the CPSU when no doubt the attack on Budapest will be registered as another 'mistake'. The International Communist movement, and also the World Peace movement, must exert its full moral influence to effect the immediate withdrawal of Soviet troops from Hungary; at the same time demanding the neutralisation of Hungary and resisting all Western attempts to turn the situation to their military and political advantage. . .

We went on to urge all our readers, like ourselves, to dissociate themselves from the leadership of the British Communist Party in their support—which was unequivocal—of Soviet intervention in Hungary. For this, as well as for our publication of the third number of *The Reasoner*, we were suspended from membership of the Communist Party, and contrary to our intentions *before* the Hungarian intervention, we both resigned, believing that the Party was now wholly discredited. We were also highly conscious of the change in the internal situation within the Party. Had the Hungarian situation not happened, suspension from membership would have allowed us, and those who thought like us, to continue the fight for unfettered discussion within the Party. I put the matter in this way to a correspondent on 17th October, 1956:

You will know that the EC suspended us for three months and that we refused to accept this, and resigned. I am enclosing a copy of our statement. My position is briefly this: that as the result of our four months fight around *The Reasoner* it had become very clear that the leadership is Stalinist to a man and that it is going to be impossible to shift them. Had not Hungary occurred I was prepared to stay in and continue the fight so long as the ban on discussion was not complete—not so much because of any real effect upon the leadership that might result but only to help further the processes of new thinking that despite its limitations *The Reasoner* has undoubtedly encouraged. Now, however, it seems to me that the Party is hopelessly discredited and compromised and I see no future for it except as a militant industrial force on the factory floor. This doesn't mean that I believe people should come out without a fight—on the contrary. What I personally am urging is that those who are prepared to stay in should do so (many, of course, have lost all stomach for the internal Party struggle) but that no one should be under any illusion that the leadership is going to be shifted. Let me qualify my dogmatism, and say that I think it is improbable that the leadership will be shifted. They might be moved if the USSR performed a volte-face over Hungary for example. But on my present assumptions there can be only one reason for staying in, and that is to continue the discussion of new thinking in opposition to the Stalinist rigidity of King St. There are many many honest people who have only since Hungary woken up to what has been done in their names. The intellectual processes of revaluation develop at very different rates within different individuals, and it seems to me that it be very wrong not to appreciate this important fact. . .

The internal Party situation had indeed hardened. One of the reasons for

our decision to cease publication of *The Reasoner* was the growing
bitterness towards us. This was not a serious problem from our personal
point of view, although it was unpleasant; but continuation of independent
publication was undoubtedly getting in the way of a discussion of basic
principles. In particular anti-intellectualism within the Party was developing
fast: the most vociferous critics being usually other intellectuals. Hungary,
which was a traumatic experience, meant that ideas of accommodation
and compromise were no longer practicable. When a number of well-known
party intellectuals published a *Reasoner*-type letter in the *New Statesman*
(1st December 1956) they were each in turn addressed by John Gollan in
tough language of a kind never used to Edward and myself.[3] The debates
at the 25th Party Congress in the spring of 1957 exhibited a roughness and
sectarianism which was the product of the political agony that everyone—
Stalinists and anti-Stalinists—had experienced in the previous twelve
months. When Professor Hymie Levy made an impassioned speech at the
Congress attacking the leadership for having so misled the members of the
Party about the real situation in the Soviet Union, he was answered next
morning by a speech of great vituperation, in which the parallel was made
with the Bolshevik Party around 1905 who also lost many members: 'The
Russians, too, were confused by the backboneless, spineless intellectuals
who were turned in on their own emotions instead of using their
capabilities for rallying the Party'. The *Daily Worker* headlined this
stirring stuff as 'Revisionist Views Smashed'.

Some 7,000 or so members left the Communist Party during 1956. The
belief that most of these 7,000 were intellectuals is untrue, although
several hundred intellectuals did certainly resign. But from the evidence we
gathered at the time, there were a large number of resignations from
industrial workers, including trade union officials. 1956 is a main landmark
in the history of the British CP. There have been two periods in its history
in which its membership declined sharply. The first was spread over the
years 1929-32 when as a result of the frenzied sectarianism which followed
the directives of the 1928 Sixth Congress of the Communist International—
the 'social-fascist period'—both the membership of the CP and its political
and industrial influence were at the lowest point in the whole of the inter-
war period. At that time the number of intellectuals within the Party were
few, and it was the working-class membership that had declined so sharply.
In 1956, while those who resigned represented a cross-section of a now
more socially variegated membership, the large numbers of intellectuals
who left, almost all of whom had come through the Cold War and were
seriously committed to left-wing politics, meant a severe loss for the
future. There were, of course, other periods of decline: the change of
attitude towards the war in 1939; the Yugoslav question after 1948; the
Lysenko affair—but none achieved the impact that occurred in the early
1930s or in 1956. The crisis within the British Communist Party was grow-

ing throughout 1956 but was far from having reached a critical point by the middle of October: Hungary was responsible for that being achieved. Without Hungary the course of events might well have been very different, but that involves the large assumption that de-stalinisation in Eastern Europe could have occurred without an uprising from below. Most Stalinists in positions of power at whatever level of authority proved incapable of transforming themselves and their power structures except under the pressures from without. In Eastern Europe there has been no radical change of any kind; and in the Communist parties of the rest of the world the history of the next twenty years has been extraordinarily diverse, with Stalinism proving extremely durable and persistent in many places.

*   *   *

III

There will be a good deal more flesh on the bones when the complete story of 1956 is told. As I indicated at the beginning of this article, for reasons of time it has not been possible to allow Edward Thompson to see a draft, and this has meant that I have not felt it proper to quote from any of his many letters to me. Without his account the story is obviously incomplete, and he may well have a somewhat different analysis to offer from that which is made here. There is also a great deal of illuminating material in the large collection of letters we received following the publication of *The Reasoner,* and again, because I have not discussed the general issue with Edward Thompson, I have refrained from quotation.

Edward Thompson and I usefully supplemented each others' qualities. I should make it clear that at the time I was conscious that by myself I could not have carried through the publication of a journal like *The Reasoner*—I lacked both experience and editorial imagination—while I believed that Edward could have succeeded, provided that he was able to attract sufficient local labour for the many chores involved: in addition, that is, to the editorial side of things. I still think I was correct. But since we did join together, we made a useful, and somewhat tempestuous, working team. We never treated each other's ideas with a less critical approach than we accorded those belonging to anyone else, and we were on many occasions rude and rough in our comments. There never was a major issue, during the whole of *The Reasoner* period, on which we agreed from the beginning. We always had to argue and debate our tactics and our strategy, and whatever the pressures upon us, we always talked matters through. Naturally, there was an underlying respect and trust, predicated upon the recognition of each other's commitment to the cause of Socialism. Without that we should never have lasted; but with trust and affection we could be wholly candid and frank. One example of a not untypical exchange between myself and Edward is dated 15th October 1956, and relates to the third number of *The Reasoner:*

> . . . About the Harry Pollitt insert. No. Emphatically no. And for exactly the same reason, but with much more force that you argue for the removal of the comment about [Comrade X]. If [Comrade X], who hasn't really done anything for the working class movement in this country, will rally 'defensive emotions' to himself, how much more will it be with Harry. There's a difference in age here between you and me that is important. To me Harry is linked with Spain, anti-appeasement and the Hunger Marches. He's washed up now, but the affection for Harry is tremendous among my generation. And your additional comment would be considered much-raking of a type that would nullify the effect of the whole article. I feel all this very strongly although there isn't time to make it clear to you. So your comment can't go in. . .

Despite the political pressures, I find from our correspondence that we spent quite a lot of time explaining to each other where and why the other was wrong, or going wrong. Edward had some splendidly sustained polemics against me and he was always a good deal more able at literary and political argument than I was. The first drafts of editorials were usually his, for example; but since for reasons already explained I am not able to quote from his correspondence to me, the following extract from a long letter from me to Edward must suffice as an example for our personal/political dialogue. It was written after we had resigned from the Communist Party and when we were beginning to discuss seriously the launching of what became *The New Reasoner*. The date of the letter was 29th November 1956:

> I think a typewriter must have a peculiar effect upon you, because how you do rampage! Of the two long letters that you recently [have] written me, the first accused me of intellectual and moral arrogance and the second, a couple of days ago, of cultural philistinism. I certainly agree that what for shorthand purposes we have to call our culture vs politics approach is a very real one; but the assumptions from my side are not what you think they are. One reason is that in writing you always find two words where one will do, while I set down in a totally inadequate form what I think—and therefore get misunderstood. The fault is mine in this respect. And this is why there is no substitute for personal discussion.
>
> Let me come to this bleeding question of culture. Basically, I react so strongly against your general proposals on this side because I have no confidence in our people to produce what is needed. As far as I am concerned practically nothing worthwhile has been produced in the past decade. The important exception is Doris [Lessing] who has roots in a quite different environment and who has apparently been uncontaminated by Stalinist values. But who else would you mention by her side?. . . And at least part of the answer lies in the uncertainty of our moral values. Let us take yourself, for example, and your constantly expressed desire to write poetry. I ask myself why someone with the poetic urge doesn't write poetry, or at least not very much. You cannot surely believe that 'more time' on your hands, more leisure, would result in a flowering of the poetic impulse in yourself? There are some obvious answers, but here are you, with an integrity and an honesty fundamentally untouched by all the horrible things to which we have agreed in our name, unable to write worthwhile poetry. Maybe

you're not really a poet—I don't know—maybe you are a devastatingly good literary polemicist and historical writer that showed itself in your magnificent book on Morris. But for all the other literary characters—none of whom have your power and ability—I reserve judgement. . .

. . . I am *not* asking for a *Modern Quarterly* publication—nor a *Science and Society*. I am asking for an English Marxist *Esprit*—which to me is the best periodical afloat—and I am sending you three numbers so that you may look-see. Second, I cannot accept your suggestion of a dividing line between the editors—this would be unworkable. There is, as I see the editorial problem, no substitute for the painful business of hammering out an agreement. Third, I am quite prepared for a bloody great row on editorial matters at some point in the future—and by prepared I mean that naturally I don't want it but that it would not be unexpected. My personal predilection at the end of the third *Reasoner* was no more—I do want to get back to history—and I shall within a year—but I do feel, as you do, that there is a moral responsibility to go on. And it is a sign of our wretched times, isn't it, when one always feels one has to qualify expressions such as 'moral responsibility' with some such phrase as 'said unpompously' or words to that effect. I would be very happy to slide out and suggest Randall Swingler in my place—except that I don't think he would take my place. *You* do need someone who is prepared to belch and be earthy when you soar on your higher flights and you do also need someone with the physique and the psychological armour plating of a sergeant major. . .

We were both writing similar kinds of letters to our many correspondents who over the *Reasoner* period as a whole offered us much contradictory advice. It was partly this that forced Edward and myself to argue continually between ourselves in order to prevent our basic points of reference from being obliterated. We were, that is to say, involved in a constant process of political re-education, and the correspondence with others helped greatly to focus our minds on the principles we were endeavouring to define and act upon. There was also some gentle domestic pressure. My wife, who morally and politically sustained me throughout, and whose advice I constantly quoted to Edward, threatened to leave (*sic*) me if we did not publish the third number of *The Reasoner* (or so I wrote to a correspondent). Below is an extract from a letter I wrote to a very well-known Communist intellectual with whom I had, and have continued to have, a very friendly relationship. The date of the letter was 7th September and it came, therefore, just at one of the points of greatest pressure upon us:

Your letter. . . strikes me as the most able argument of the case against our position that has yet been put down on paper. I must apologise for what will be only a brief note, but after Edward has read it and returned it I will set out the situation as I see it. . .

There are so many things I take exception to in your letter—the whole approach to which is quite alien to anything that Edward or I or anybody else stands, that it is difficult to pick out isolated points. What you don't apparently assume, and here the whole of King St. appears to be with you, is that there is a bloody raging crisis in the Party. When you say that we 'are gravely willing to weaken the Party' you are missing two things—apart from a rather surprising misunderstanding of our point of view. First, that the Party has been gravely weakened already by the line of the leadership since the 20th Congress, and regardless of whether *The Reasoner* was published or not, resignations would have been considerable. You can't surely be ignorant of this, and you can't be unaware that the Party, from a political and intellectual angle, is hopelessly compromised unless it undertakes a thorough house cleaning. You may be. I note again with a good deal of surprise, that you have concentrated your published letters upon electoral matters, not unimportant I grant, but certainly not the crucial issues at present before us. So you may deny both the intellectual crisis and the political crisis—in which case, as we found with the PC, we are talking different languages. The second point you are missing arises out of the first. Why has *The Reasoner* stirred up all this passion? Surely it's nothing to do with two relatively unimportant intellectuals who have done something 'unusual' which, at any other time than the present, would have led immediately to expulsion. It—i.e. the ferment—is only explainable in terms of this crisis.

I gather that you would have had little to say against us if we had resigned quietly—like [Comrade X] for example; and I also understand that you will do the same thing if ever you come to the point when either you feel that you can make no further impact or you consider the Party is no longer necessary. Let me put this to you. Would there never be an occasion when, in the interests of Socialist principle, you would never bring yourself to the point of taking a public stand? Or is the argument of the unity of the party so powerful that come what may, principle must give way before it?

Frankly, I suspect that we shall continue to talk different languages. You write in terms of 'trump cards', 'bluff' and so on while we are talking about a crisis of ideas, the integrity and honesty of the party, our relations with the Labour movement and such things. There is no urgency in your letter and you imply that a push here and a shove there, and extra pages in *World News* is the sort of answer that will bring about the necessary and desirable changes in attitudes and approach. . .

IV

We brought the publication of *The Reasoner* to an end with the third issue mainly because we believed that its continuation would obscure the central issues of the discussion rights of the party membership. But there were other contributory factors. One, as noted above, was the bitterness that was developing against us. There was increasing personal hostility and there was no question that some members of the party leadership were deliberately emphasising the intellectuals versus industrial workers division that was supposed to exist over the political questions represented by *The Reasoner.* By September we were having to spend some time with our correspondents denying allegations about our personal ambitions, our publication of material without the consent of authors, and the dark sources of our finances. Bitterness increased sharply with the development of the Hungarian situation and Soviet intervention, and just about this time, at an aggregate meeting of my own Party branch, when I was present, *The Reasoner* group were described as 'running dogs of imperialism'. The mood of the party leadership hardened notably during the aftermath of crisis which followed the Soviet action in Hungary, and the possibilities for a strategy of de-Stalinisation were no longer practicable.

The physical pressures of actually producing our duplicated journal were, of course, not inconsiderable. Edward typed all the stencils—in a note to a correspondent I remarked that Edward had typed nearly 40,000 words on stencils for the second issue in a period of five days, and he similarly typed the whole of the longer third issue. At the same time he was, of course, exercising his editorial functions in laying out articles etc. in a coherent way. The stencils were then sent by post or by train to Hull where I duplicated them. I cannot now remember where the first issue was run-off, but for the more substantial second and third numbers I was able to use the office duplicator of a business friend whose premises were in the Old Docks' area of the Old Town. Since we planned the maximum output the stencils would take for the third and last number, the duplication of 1,500 copies of some 50 stencils took a fortnight's evening and weekend work. On the last weekend of 3rd/4th November, when we had to write an editorial by telephone, following the Soviet attack on Budapest, I duplicated Friday night, Saturday afternoon and evening, all day Sunday and through the night until 7 a.m. on Monday morning, I travelled by bicycle since we did not possess a car at that time, and the transport of the duplicated sheets to my home was always a difficult problem, involving many journeys. The sheets were laid out on a large table at my home, and put together and stapled by a dedicated group of volunteer labourers. Each copy was checked twice to ensure that pages were in correct order: first when all the sheets were collected together and second after stapling.

We financed ourselves from our own salaries but the burden was less than we had expected since we received dozens of donations, totalling, by the time the third issue was published, about £70. A part—the smaller part—of our own editorial expenses were therefore met, since we had relatively few bad debts on sales; and two shillings a copy was quite a high price in those days.

V

This is not the place for the subsequent history of the years of the New Left. By the spring of 1957 *Universities and Left Review* had published its first number, and Edward and I had brought out the first issue of the printed *New Reasoner*. Nearly three years later the two journals amalgamated to form the *New Left Review*.

Nor is this the place for a detailed review of the subsequent history of the British Communist Party. The Party suffered a severe membership loss in the year following Khrushchev's secret speech and, as already noted, while the social composition of those who left included many trade unionists and industrial workers, there was a large scale resignation of intellectuals. Many of these belonged to the generation of the 1930s and 1940s, and they undoubtedly represented a serious capital loss, although it was certainly not understood in this way for many years after 1956. Anti-intellectual attitudes hardened as a result of the trauma of 1956, and some of the intellectuals who remained within the Party were not unwilling to go with the stream. As Arnold Kettle explained to the delegates of the 26th Congress in 1959, the recruitment and acceptance of professional people is often a difficult matter:

> It is difficult not only because there are always certain obvious problems in winning over middle-class people to the side of the working class, but also because, as everyone knows, in the difficult days our Party went through in 1956-57, it was the intellectuals in the Party who were, as a section, the most influenced by revisionist ideas.
> We should not, as Marxists, be surprised by this. It is due basically to the class and social position of professional workers and to the fatal separation of theory and practice which class society has brought about.
> It would be very foolish for us to believe that most of the ex-Party revisionists, are wicked or insincere people.
> Their principal trouble is a persistent desire to have the best of both worlds, to have their cake and eat it—to retain the privileges of their position in bourgeois society while at the same time attacking bourgeois society and associating them-selves with the socialist movement.
> Our job is to convince them—through experience and argument—that Socialism is indeed the answer to their problems, their frustrations and their hopes. . .

The world has continued to change since 1956, and it is safe to assume that these words just quoted could not have been spoken in quite the same way during the past decade. Marxism in Britain is no longer the prerogative of the Communist Party—as it mostly was until 1956—and the processes of de-stalinisation have acted in Britain as elsewhere. In this area change has been slow and uneven but the long-term trend has meant a Communist Party different in a number of ways from that of 1956. The official reaction to the Czech events in the late 1960s, and towards the question of dissent within the Soviet Union, are among the indications that the spirit of Stalinism no longer exercises the baleful dominance it once occupied. John Gollan's recent article in *Marxism Today* (January 1976) entitled 'Socialist Democracy—Some Problems. The 20th Congress of the Communist Party of the Soviet Union in Retrospect' is a good measure of how far the British Communist Party has begun to accept new ideas as well as the length of the road it still has to travel. Gollan's summary of what happened within the British Party in 1956 (p. 28) is scandalously inadequate and misleading, and it continues the practice of the British Party in the suppression of un-pleasant facts and episodes in its own history. At the same time Gollan's article does show the extent of the change in ideas and understanding, even though it has taken twenty years to admit many things that were accepted facts in 1956. What Gollan does not however deal with seriously are precisely the central problems that emerged from the Khrushchev revelations. These are the nature and character of socialist democracy, its forms and institutions, and above all the ways in which freedom, democracy and socialism can be realised, and then maintained, as integral and living processes of social life. On the historical evidence it is exceedingly difficult to begin; but the even more difficult problem for the future, and one for which we have not yet produced a satisfactory answer, in theory, and certainly not in practice, is how to avoid the decline into degeneration and arbitrary government. Twenty years after Khrushchev's secret speech we have to admit that the realistic debate on socialist democracy has hardly begun.

NOTES

1. Documentation has been kept to a minimum. The account in the text is based on two groups of sources: first, the published files of the *Times*, the London *Daily Worker, Tribune, New Statesman, World News, Keesings*; and second the unpublished correspondence of Edward Thompson and myself and the many hundreds of correspondents who wrote to us during 1956.
2. The identification in the text of Pollitt's speech of 21st April with at least a version of Khrushchev's secret speech has not, I think, been made before. If I am correct, the culpability of the Communist leaders in Britain in terms of the deception of their own members is considerably increased.
3. The letter read: 'At its last meeting the Executive Committee considered your action in publishing, in company with other members of the Party, a letter in the non-Party press attacking the Party.
   It instructed me to write to you and inform you that such an action is unpermissible and will not be tolerated in future.
   You have the same rights as all other Party members to put your views on Party policy in your Party branch and in the Party press, and the Party cannot and will not give you the right to go outside the Party and make public attacks upon it.'

THE DAY THE PARTY HAD TO STOP

by Malcolm MacEwen

I began 1956, as I had begun every year since 1944, as a journalist on the *Daily Worker*. They were enjoyable and fruitful years, most of which I spent as Parliamentary Correspondent, but I also did many other jobs—foreign editor, reporter, feature writer, even war correspondent in Greece (but only after the war was over, as the *Daily Worker* was denied accreditation by the War Office while it lasted). For most of 1956 I was features editor, responsible among other things for the Readers' Forum. At the end of October I went back to the House of Commons to report the Suez debates when Peter Fryer, my successor in the press gallery, was sent to Budapest to cover the Hungarian uprising. I was a member of the editorial committee which met twice a day to discuss the content of the paper.

The British Communist Party had not the slightest inkling of the storm that was about to burst upon it. In the build-up for the 20th Congress of the Communist Party of the Soviet Union, which opened on 14th February, our Moscow correspondent, Sam Russell, wrote a series of glowing reports which we splashed on the front page under such headlines as 'Russia's Mighty Plan', 'Russia is ready for the 21st Century', 'Up, Up, Up Goes Soviet Production'. 'The Age of Plenty Dawns'. On the opening day Prof. J.S. Bernal, one of Britain's greatest scientists, who symbolised the influence of the Party and of Marxism among professionals and intellectuals, began a series of four articles on technical education, headlined 'The Know How of a New Era: Russia is Mastering It: So Must We'. He was not to know that within eight weeks his most distinguished colleague, Prof. J.B.S. Haldane, for long the contributor of the *Daily Worker's* excellent science column, would quit the Party and begin the trickle of resignations by intellectuals that would become a flood. Still less was the *Daily Worker* itself to know how prophetic was its own greeting to the 20th Congress on 'one of the great days of history'. It was, indeed a historic Congress, but not for the reasons *The Worker* advanced.

It is impossible to understand the reactions of journalists like Peter Fryer, Philip Bolsover or myself to the speech delivered by Khrushchev to the secret session of the 20th Congress on 25th February, (and leaked in Bonn on 16th March) unless one appreciates how revolted we were by British politics at the time. Bolsover had an article in January on the colonial repression in Cyprus, Kenya and Malaya, headlined 'An Empire Full of Gangsters', illustrated with pictures of handcuffed 'terrorists' over the question 'Bandits or Patriots?'. Peter Fryer, the Parliamentary Correspondent, whose despatches from Hungary the paper refused to publish in October-November, had an article in February exposing the hypocrisy of the Eisenhower-Eden 'Declaration of Faith' by drawing attention to the blatant racialism still being practised at that time in the Southern states of the US. When Archbishop Makarios was arrested and deported from Cyprus, I wrote an article attacking the Colonial Secretary Lennox-Boyd for declaring that Cyprus could 'never' be independent. We saw ourselves—you may think naively—as democrats, humanists, socialists, engaged in the struggle for a humane, free, socialist democracy, and to a considerable extent we still looked to the Soviet Union as a model. An immense amount of space was devoted week by week to Soviet events and Soviet policy statements. When Bulganin and Khrushchev visited Britain the *Daily Worker* led its front page with the visit on ten successive days, and it gave an immense coverage out of its limited space to the 20th Congress itself.

In fact, this uncritical adulation of the USSR had become a source of increasing irritation to several members of the editorial staff, whose confidence in the Soviet Union was being undermined by the earlier revelations of the Khrushchev regime. Having gone along with the Party 'line' on Yugoslavia, when the Yugoslav Party was expelled from the Cominform in 1948, I was profoundly shocked by the British Party's reaction to the 'rehabilitation' of Tito by Bulganin and Khrushchev in 1955. The implications of this event were profound, for the British CP had endorsed the original condemnation at hastily convened meetings, and, as a result, had expelled or driven out members who had asked for some independent evidence of the 'imperialism' of Tito and his Party. The British Party made no comment on the admission that it had acted on false information, and my own efforts to raise the issue in correspondence with Harry Pollitt, the General Secretary of the Party for the previous 27 years, and Emile Burns, head of propaganda, got nowhere. A letter which I sent to the Party weekly, *World News*, pointing out the implications for the trials of Rajk in Hungary and Slansky in Czechoslovakia, was not published. To this day the Party has remained silent on the implications of the Yugoslav affair for our own Party organisation.

Harry Pollitt and George Matthews, the Assistant General Secretary, went to the 20th Congress as fraternal delegates. But they were sent to speak at factory meetings on Saturday, 25th February when Khrushchev made his famous speech in a private session from which foreign delegates were excluded. They returned in total ignorance, proclaiming that the Soviet leadership had courageously laid bare the truth about the 'cult of individual', had put right the injustices, and taken the necessary steps to prevent any recurrence. So far as they were concerned, 'the cult of the individual' was a closed chapter, and British Communists should concentrate their minds on the 'real issues'—i.e. the Soviet peace policy and five-year plan.

But, even on the basis of the revelations already published, many Party members were unable to stomach passing off the 'mistakes' of Stalinism as 'the cult of the individual'. Letters on Stalin flooded into the *Daily Worker*, and I had the utmost difficulty (as Features Editor) in getting them published. The Political Committee of the Party had little choice but to allow a discussion, but it saw the forthcoming Party Congress at the end of March as an excuse for bringing it to an end. On 12th March J.R. Campbell declared the discussion on Stalin closed, and replied to the Forum letters on the 15th in an article in which he expressed his satisfaction that most of the letters had not indulged in 'exaggerated denigration of Stalin'. Yet within two days his entire position had been undermined. On March 16th the text of the secret Khrushchev speech, exposing Stalin as a mass murderer and torturer, had been leaked in Bonn. And on the following day the Hungarian Government announced the rehabilitation of Lazslo Rajk, the former Party secretary who had been shot after a trial that Derek Kartun had reported for the *Daily Worker*. I proposed at the editorial conference that we should publish a leading article on 'judicial murder', but Walter Holmes, our veteran columnist, dismissed the idea with 'who the hell cares about Rajk?', and Campbell rejected my proposal.

The readers' Forum had to be re-opened nevertheless, and the flood of letters became a torrent. But the line of Pollitt and his colleagues hardly changed. Although the suppression of the Khrushchev speech showed how far removed the Soviet Union was from restoring the essential safeguards of democracy, Pollitt declared his total satisfaction with the Soviet Party's handling of these events when he spoke at the 24th Congress of our Party on 30th March. The public sessions were drab and non-controversial, and there was no real political discussion, except on the issue of conscription.[1]

The issue of Stalin and the 20th Congress was debated in a heated secret session in which I tried to speak, but was not called. At the end the following statement was issued:

> 'The private session received the report [by Pollitt] and expressed full confidence in the Soviet Union, its people and the Communist Party of the Soviet Union. It expressed its conviction that the great perspectives for the advance of Communism as outlined in the whole policy of the 20th Congress would be fully realised.'

Inevitably, this bone-headed handling of the situation caused the situation inside the Party to get out of hand, particularly as still further revelations were made. Our correspondent in Warsaw, Gordon Cruickshank,

reported on 9th May the sacking of the Minister of Justice and the introduction of an Amnesty Bill in the Polish Seym that was expected to
release 30,000 prisoners from jail. The Party leadership had to move, and
on 16th May the Executive Committee accepted the resignation of
Pollitt on the ground of age (he was 65) and ill health, elected John
Gollan as General Secretary, and issued a long statement on 'The Lessons
of the 20th Congress of the CPSU'. This contained the apology and
complete retraction on Yugoslavia it could have made 11 months earlier,
and expressed 'shock at the number of those arrested in the Soviet Union',
but only made a mealy-mouthed allusion to the mass murders and tortures
by referring to the 'victims of deliberate provocations and fabricated
evidence'. The statement offered no further probing into the experience of
the Soviet Union or the People's Democracies, but it did concede the need
for an investigation of the British Party's internal democracy.

'A special Commission' (it announced) 'has been established to examine
the methods and the working of our Party Congress, its committees,
methods of discussion and election, criticism and self-criticism, and the
improvements of inner party democracy'. In fact, the Commission had not
been established. Its members were not appointed until July, and it did not
meet until September. By that time, the Party leadership was desperately
in need of a quick report. Poland was already on the verge of eruption,
following the Poznan riots in June. The world crisis over Hungary and
Suez in October and November intensified the internal Party crisis, and
therefore the leadership's desire to demonstrate that it had taken some
effective action to meet criticism. The publication of The Reasoner by
Edward Thompson and John Saville, and the action taken against them by
the Party, had provoked a major dispute about the genuineness of 'inner-
party democracy' on the established basis of 'democratic centralism'.

At the height of the Hungarian crisis, at the end of October, my own
sense of personal responsibility received a savage bayonet thrust by the
announcement that Edith Bone had been released from prison in Hungary.
Edith Bone was not a journalist, but she had gone to Hungary with an
understanding between herself and J.R. Campbell, the editor of the Daily
Worker, that she would be our correspondent in Budapest. I did not know
her, and was unaware of this arrangement. But it had been known to some
other members of the staff, in particular to Allen Hutt, the Chief Sub-
Editor, whose comment when Edith re-appeared was 'so old woman Bone's
turned up again'. Allen, who was a member of the EC, was not in fact an
inhumane or unsympathetic man. But like so many Communists of long-
standing he felt he had to demonstrate his political virility, his machismo,
by taking a hard, unyielding line. I was profoundly shocked, for it rapidly
became known, and was admitted by Campbell and Pollitt at the EC, that
during Edith Bone's disappearance they had several times 'inquired' about
her, and had received no satisfaction whatever from the Hungarian Party,

or Rakosi, its General Secretary. The inquiries were renewed after the rehabilitation of Rajk, but even then, when it had become obvious that Edith Bone, whether alive or dead, must have been a victim of the secret police, the British Party remained silent and did not even inform the members of the *Daily Worker* staff that one of their colleagues had been left to languish in jail for years without so much as a private protest or complaint, let alone the kind of public pressure that could have secured her release. It was all very well for Pollitt to say that 'unity' must be defended at all costs, but the costs had to be borne by the Edith Bones, not by the Pollitts who enjoyed innumerable trips and holidays in Eastern Europe.

As a Party member of some standing (I had been a member of the Central Committee in 1941-3 and a Parliamentary candidate in 1941 and 1950) and one of the best-known critics of the leadership I was invited to an extended, emergency; private meeting of the Executive Committee on 3rd November, when the Soviet Union was intervening to overthrow the government of Imre Nagy in Budapest. I brought to the meeting a statement, which I had drafted, signed by 16 members of the *Daily Worker* editorial staff—about half the total. The signatories included John Gritten (today news editor of the *Morning Star*), Gabriel (Jimmy Friel, our cartoonist), Cayton (our successful racing tipster), Llew Gardner, Leon Griffiths and Sheila Lynd. In it we said:

> 'the imprisonment of Edith Bone in solitary confinement without trial for seven years, without any public inquiry or protest from our Party even after the exposure of the Rajk trial had shown that such injustices were taking place, not only exposes the character of the regime, but involves us in its crimes. It is now clear that what took place was a national uprising against an infamous police dictatorship which disgraced the good name of Communism. The danger that fascist elements will attempt to gain control in the present state of disorder cannot affect our judgment that the people of Hungary had had enough, and resorted to arms to obtain freedom. The Government had the Soviet Union were wrong to attempt to crush the uprising. No Government which has forfeited the support of its people has the right to crush the people with foreign arms.'

I also brought with me to the meeting a copy of a service message received the previous day from Gordon Cruickshank, our correspondent in Warsaw, which provided an off-the-record comment on an appeal issued by the Central Committee of the Polish Workers' Party:

> 'The appeal intends to convey that the Polish Party considers that the major inflammatory factor in the Hungarian situation was the intervention by Soviet troops. Such an intervention in Poland, where the stage for it was all set, and where even the call was given, was stopped at the 11th hour by the Polish Party.
> Although the Party here is restrained and cautious in its public declaration, and is genuinely concerned to avoid a break with the Soviet Union, privately leading members express their point of view about the Soviet Party leadership

with considerable feeling. They clearly have little confidence in that leadership. They contend that their viewpoint is based on 10 years of almost entirely had experiences.

To understand Hungarian events, they maintain they have only to study Soviet methods in the Eastern democracies over the past years: their insistence that there is only one way to build Socialism—their way. Their insistence on the transference of their pattern to all departments of life, large and small; their insistence on the organisation of the Stalinist type of security police and the use of Stalin type methods.

The Polish and Hungarian events therefore must be seen not only as caused by economic adversity and misery but also as an irruption of accumulated resentment against what was felt to be the overbearing domination of the Soviet leadership—resentment which became hatred in some cases, and which has affected a number if not a majority of the best Socialist and Communist workers, making them a prey even to reactionary influences. Which is a tragedy indeed.'

The Debate at the EC, in which I took part, was tense, and highly emotional on both sides, but the result was never in doubt. The hard-line leadership easily carried the day, and a statement was issued which came down firmly in support of the Soviet intervention against the Nagy Government. A week later, I resigned from the *Daily Worker,* in protest against the suppression of Peter Fryer's cables.

It was against this background that the Commission on Inner-Party Democracy, which had been appointed in July, met first on September 11th, 1956. The chairman was John Mahon, the London District Secretary, a member of the Political Committee, and an inflexible Party functionary with limited imagination. The Commission consisted of nine members appointed by the EC and six by the Party regions. It was heavily overloaded with full-time salaried Party officials, of whom there were no fewer than 10, five of them members of the EC. Only one member was an industrial worker, Keven Halpin, a vehicle inspector, appointed by the EC, which also appointed two well-known critics, myself and Christopher Hill the historian (who is now the Master of Balliol). Of the six regional nominees, four were full-time Party functionaries, one (Joe Cheek) was a teacher, and one, Peter Cadogan from the SE Midlands, was not only a teacher but also a known critic of the Party leadership. The Party officials included Emile Burns and James Klugmann, who controlled the Party's propaganda, education and periodical services, William Lauchlan, a former industrial worker who was National Organiser, and Betty Reid, a tough-minded and able member of the central organisation department. She ran the Commission, and controlled its programme.

The composition of the Commission guaranteed that it would not reach any conclusions disturbing to the full-time professional leadership whose grip on the Party (as we showed in the minority report) was maintained by the self-perpetuating system of 'election'. John Mahon, the chairman, did not see his role as leading an investigation; he saw it as securing the defeat of the 'revisionists' who were critical of democratic centralism. A Party discussion in *World News* was opened by Mahon with an article which prejudged all the issues that the Commission was supposed to examine. We were also denied the time to conduct any serious investigation, and the shortage of time was then given as an excuse for not conducting a serious investigation. We were informed at our first meeting on 11th September that, although four months had passed since the decision to establish the Commission had been taken, our work had to be completed in just over two months. This deadline was extended by two weeks after the date of the special 25th Party Congress in May 1957—to which our report was to be submitted—had been announced. But this meant that, although nearly six months were allowed for publishing and debating our report, the Commission was given a totally inadequate period in which to do its job. We met for the last time on 6th December 1956.

At the outset Hill, Cadogan and myself, with the support of Kevin Halpin, the one industrial worker, objected to the composition of the Commission and, in particular, to its domination by full-time salaried Party officials and the derisory representation of the working-class membership. When Mahon had over-ruled these protests, we challenged the programme of work submitted by Betty Reid. We saw our job as being, in accordance with the terms of reference, 'to *examine* and report on problems of inner-party democracy'. This, in its turn, meant that we had not met to discuss abstract principles, but to investigate actual cases and, by examining the files and questioning the people concerned, to determine how Party democracy actually worked.

In a 4,000 word paper which I submitted at the outset I pointed out that it was clear from the 20th Congress that the textbook explanations of democratic centralism bore no relation to the actual way in which the Soviet Party or Soviet society operated. I called for a realistic examination of the workings of inner-Party democracy in the Soviet Union and Eastern Europe. But the majority, while claiming that Soviet democracy was now functioning admirably, could only resist this proposition by pointing to the impossibility of implementing it in the time available and in the conditions that actually existed in the Soviet Union—i.e. where even the text of the Khrushchev speech remained an official secret, and the Soviet Party declined to open itself for investigation.

I then asked, with the support throughout at this stage of Hill, Cadogan and Halpin, for an investigation of three specific cases in our own Party: the handling of the expulsion of Yugoslavia from the Cominform, the handling of the Party press since the 20th Congress, and the operation of the electoral system at national and district Party congresses. The majority did not deny the desirability of questioning witnesses, or at least interviewing those members who had submitted evidence and viewpoints, and said it would have been valuable to discuss 'materials issued by brother

Parties'. But they refused to call for real evidence, or to examine witnesses, or to investigate Party records, on these specific issues or, indeed, on any others. The Commission received no real *evidence* at all. The only 'evidence' we had to go on was a mass of letters and branch resolutions, and only one of these (a letter from the London District Committee) was submitted by a major Party organisation. None of the Party's leading officials or members offered evidence; nor were they asked to give it.

At the outset, the Commission seemed to divide into the ten full-time Party functionaries, briefed and instructed by the leadership in King Street, and the five rank-and file members. It would obviously have been disastrous for the leadership if, after it had packed the Commission, all five of the 'ordinary' members, including the solitary industrial worker, were to reject the line of the officials. In the event, the officials succeeded in detaching Kevin Halpin and Joe Cheek from Christopher Hill, Peter Cadogan and myself, although both attached major reservations to the majority report which they ultimately signed. There were several reasons for the officials' success in splitting the critics. Above all, they were able to apply immense moral and political pressure to both Halpin and Cheek— and to Halpin in particular—playing on the enormously strong tradition of Party loyalty at a time when the Party was under immense strain and intense attack. The remaining three of us were not only outnumbered, but we also lacked the time to engage in any lobbying outside the Commission. We were meeting every Friday for several hours, and on two occasions met at weekends. Christopher Hill was under great strain in his academic and extramural work, and when it came to the crunch had to leave the drafting of the minority report entirely to me. But the single decisive event in splitting the critics was the suspension of Peter Cadogan from the Party in November, for writing a letter to the *News Chronicle* criticizing the Soviet invasion of Hungary. The fact that such a letter could of itself be a formal breach of Party discipline itself shows how tightly the Party leadership controlled dangerous thoughts about the Soviet Party. But tactically, the letter was disastrous. The next meeting of the Commission was suspended because Betty Reid refused to sit down at the same table with a 'traitor'. Peter, Christopher and myself adjourned to a pub to draft a letter to John Gollan, but that occasion finally settled the division in the Commission. We three formed the minority, the remainder the majority, and we proceeded to prepare separate reports. Peter's suspension did not last long, and he signed the minority report, but he took no further part in the Commission.

The procedure the Commission adopted was to divide the job of drafting papers on seven key issues, identified by Betty Reid, among members of the Commission. The issues were democratic centralism; the conduct of Party discussion; elections of Committees and officials; branch life and relations of branches with higher bodies; methods of leadership;

Party unity and discipline, and the Party Congress. Initially, those who came to form the minority were involved in the drafting work although, so far as I can recall, my own contribution was to contribute critical papers in response to the drafts submitted by functionaries, particularly on Democratic Centralism and methods of election. Peter Cadogan drafted a paper with Joe Cheek on the relatively innocuous issue of branch life. Christopher Hill was teamed with James Klugmann (an intellectual official with an extra ordinary rigid mind) to draft a paper on Party discussion. They were only able to produce a joint draft by offering alternative passages on the key points or, in one case, by Hill inserting the word 'not' before a Klugmann verb.

Although we had before us 104 communications from individuals and branches, totalling about 40,000 words, I doubt whether they had a great deal of influence on the outcome. The ten Party functionaries, who dominated the Commission, came to it with their minds made up. Christopher Hill, in a letter apologising for his inability to attend the fifth meeting, offered some comments on the draft paper on 'methods of election':

'It seems to me unexceptionable if its premise is accepted—that basically all is well with the Party, that we need only a little oiling and tinkering. But can we agree on that? The really difficult problem, that we have run up against all the time, is that we have to recreate a democratic spirit and method of working, from above downwards and from below upwards, and that this cannot be done by constitutional changes. But since ours is an interim report, it is even more important for us to state facts and indicate problems than to provide solutions; we should hardly agree on solutions in the short time available anyhow.'

He went on to say that the draft did not take seriously the real objection to the 'panel' system of election—that it makes the leadership at EC and District Committee level self-perpetuating, adding 'the belief that a change is virtually impossible, at any level, has something to do with the sense of frustration and the rapid turnover in party membership that have been such features in the Party's recent history. We should not refuse to face this problem, since it does exercise many members of the Party'. But the functionaries were not ready to face any of these problems. Their over-riding concerns were with ensuring the continuity of leadership, and what they saw as the unity of the Party. The minority did not question the desirability of either of these objectives, but approached the problem from a totally different standpoint. Here are two passages from the Klugmann/Hill paper on Party discussion:

'Normally, discussion should be terminated by Party decisions and the adoption of Party policy which is binding on all members, but in some cases as on problems of art and literature, there is a basis for continued discussion and debate without decision' (Klugmann).

'Our closest friends on the left in the Labour movement are those whom we encourage to fight against bans and proscriptions. Any suppression of discussion in the CP (or appearance of it) will alienate those from whom we must recruit and with whom we must work... There is no reason why on questions of principle (i.e. in the formation of policy itself) the higher organs should allocate to themselves the function of defining these principles, or why free discussion of policy by the membership should have any other limits than those needed to prevent such discussion... from disrupting the unity of the Party.' (Hill)

We tried very hard, initially, to reach an accommodation. The key issue was, of course, democratic centralism, on which Betty Reid had drafted the paper. The debate centred on the wording of Rule 13:

'It is the duty of all members of the Party organisation to carry out to the full the policy of the Party until the final decision is reached. If the individual member does not receive support from his Party organisation, it is his duty to accept the majority decision and carry out to the full the policy of the Party.'

The alternative wording which I suggested (and which was rejected) read:

'The Communist Party has only one policy, that which is adopted by National Congress, or formulated by the Executive Committee in accordance with the decisions of Congress. The effectiveness of the Party in action depends upon the self-discipline and loyalty of the membership in rapidly and fully responding to the leadership of the Executive Committee and other leading bodies.

Members who disagree with decisions by majorities or by higher Party bodies should nevertheless endeavour to the best of their ability to work for the fulfilment of these decisions in a spirit of class solidarity and party loyalty, and refrain from actions which would impede the fulfilment of these decisions. Such members retain all their rights of discussion and criticism under the Party rules.'

I have not made any statistical analysis of the written 'evidence', but, on re-reading it again 20 years later, I am left with the very firm impression that virtually all the submissions were intended to strengthen the Party, not to weaken it, and came from people who even at that date would rather have reformed the Party than abandon it. Some of the submissions, mainly from branches, made criticisms of a minor nature. Most of the individual submissions were more radical, and many of them presented detailed information or case histories that should have been investigated, but were not. The strength of the emotions released by the Khrushchev speech were reflected, for example, in a resolution from the Ashton-under-Lyne Branch which attacked the leadership for its 'blind acceptance' of the words and the crimes of Stalin, and accused it of ignoring the democratic experiences of the British working class.

Perhaps the most striking features of the contribution from the Party intellectuals were their sense of outrage, at the crimes that had been committed in the name of Communism, and their anger at the inability of the Party leadership to perceive that its double standard (talking about democracy while practising or defending ruthless dictatorship) seemed to explain the political failure of the Party in this country. Jack Beeching, for instance, attributed the Party's weakness and isolation, and its inability to discern the reasons, to the self-perpetuation of an authoritarian leadership, and to habits of mind developed by the Party leaders during the Comintern period. This had led, he said, to the 'tragedy' of the CP—the dissipation of the enormous talents it had attracted. The South West Ham Branch observed perceptively that the main weaknesses of Communist Parties had sprung not from lack of control by leading bodies over the rank and file, but from the reverse. Some of the contributions, and some letters in the Party press, had a strong anti-intellectual flavour, but the anti-intellectuals in fact had no answers to the criticisms that the intellectuals advanced. It was obvious from the evidence that if, in the aftermath of Hungary and the 20th Congress, the Commission and the Party were to confine themselves to what Christopher Hill called 'oiling and tinkering', a large body of intellectuals would have no alternative but to leave the Party. This is what happened. The Party retained the bulk of its working class membership, and lost the bulk of its middle-class membership, and so deprived itself of the intellectuals' contribution to its own development.

Although the Commission was confined to an abstract debate about democratic centralism in the British Party, the thoughts of the minority were dominated by the irrefutable facts of the degeneration of democratic centralism in the Parties of the Soviet Union and Eastern Europe. Politics is about power, and although the prospects of power might have seemed remote for the British Communist Party, nobody joins a political party without having the ultimate goal of achieving political power. If, as I had come to believe, the form of democratic centralism operated by Communist Parties throughout the world was largely responsible for the political and moral degeneration of those Parties that had exercised power, the seeds of a similar degeneration must be present in the British Party. It followed that, in the event of the Party ever assuming power, a similar degeneration must follow. These were issues the British CP had never faced, but it was our hope that the events of 1956 would shock the Party leadership into facing them—so making it possible, for the first time, to end the weakness and isolation of the Communist Party in Britain.

As a Party, our blindness to the harsh realities of Communist government in practice had caught us in an impossible dilemma. Our Party claimed descent from those who had struggled for working-class and democratic liberties. It identified with the radical tradition. Our historians— Hill, Hobsbawm, Thompson and several others—had won international reputations in this field. Christopher Hill was the outstanding interpreter of the British revolution of the 17th Century. Yet it was now undeniable that the complete identification of the Party with the state in the Soviet Union and Eastern Europe had destroyed all constitutional safeguards against the abuse of power. And while the new leaders (Khrushchev, Gomulka) had retreated from the worst excesses of the Stalin regime, there was no evidence that they wished to restore democratic rights and liberties that are fundamental both to the development of a healthy Socialist society, and to the development of Marxism. The latter requires the open confrontation of opposing tendencies. The basis of all political development is access to information and to the means of publicity, without which political argument and the resolution of differences is impossible. Mikoyan at the 20th Party Congress reproached Soviet historians for not writing Marxist analyses of Soviet history, and John Gollan has pointed out recently[2] that they have not done so since. But how can they, within the system which Gollan defended so staunchly in 1956?

The gulf on these issues between the majority and the minority could not be bridged. The majority were firmly stuck in the Stalinist mental mould, from which we were trying to escape. As a result, the discussion within the Commission on democratic centralism was circular, and therefore fruitless. The majority argued, as they did in their report, that the crimes and the 'mistakes' arose because Stalin had departed from the principles of democratic centralism by failing to operate a collective leadership, and failing to call the periodical meetings and Congresses at which the abuses could have been stopped, and at which elections could have been held. We argued that, in the absence of any evidence to the contrary, it must be presumed that the enormous power concentrated in the hands of a very small leadership by the rules of democratic centralism facilitated the assumption of dictatorial power. To which the majority replied that this was not democratic centralism, but an abuse of it.

The majority contended that democratic centralism was not a Russian idea imposed on the British CP by the Comintern, but arose out of the experience of the British Labour movement. They pointed to the acceptance by British trade unions of the sovereignty of elected annual conferences as policy-making bodies, the acceptance by the minority and by the lower organisations of the decisions reached between conferences by their central organs and committees. If democratic centralism could be reduced to the normal *modus operandi* of the trade unions, however, there would have been no differences between us. The minority fully accepted the need for minorities to accept majority decisions on practical issues,' such as a decision to hold an election, publish a leaflet or organise or support a strike. But democratic centralism, both in theory and in practice went much further. It resolved the problem of striking a balance between centralism and democracy by placing the major emphasis on centralism. Lenin, in his draft of the conditions of affiliation to the Third International laid the whole emphasis on the need for an 'iron discipline' in the Party, 'bordering on military discipline', to fit it for the tasks of a period of revolution, civil war and imperialist war. According to the majority report:

'Democratic centralism means:

1) The right of all members to take part in the discussion and formation of policy and the duty of all members to fight for that policy when it has been decided.

2) The right of all members to elect and to be elected to the collective leaderships of the Party at all levels, and to be represented at the National Congress, the highest authority of the Party. The duty of all members to fight for the decisions made by those leaderships, and the duty of the lower organisations to accept and to fight for the decisions of the higher organisations.

3) The right of all members to contribute to the democratic life of the Party and the duty of all members to safeguard the unity of the Party, members who disagree with a decision have the right to reserve their opinions and to express their views through the proper channels open to them as laid down in the Party rules.'

The basic issue on which the Bolsheviks, led by Lenin, split from the Mensheviks, led by Martov, at the 1923 Congress of the Russian Social Democratic Party was Lenin's insistence on a small but highly disciplined party of active members, as opposed to Martov's concept of a Party with loosely affiliated members rather similar in concept to the British Labour Party. Stalin unquestionably developed Lenin's concept into a highly authoritarian and centralised one, in which the popular organisations, such as trade unions, simply became the 'transmission belts' through which Party decisions were to be applied. John Gollan, in the article referred to, which is intended as a retrospective view of the 20th Congress, attributes the 'excessive centralisation' of the Party under Stalin to his conception of 'the monolithic party':

'Never, for a single moment, have the 'Bolsheviks conceived of the party as anything but a monolithic organisation hewed from a single block, possessing a single will and in its work uniting all shades of thought into a single current of practical activities.' (Stalin, *Works*, Vol. 6, p. 23).

This concept, which Gollan now criticizes, was, however, the concept to which the British CP, and in particular the majority on the Commission on inner-Party democracy, firmly adhered. The passage quoted was often used in Party education courses, and I myself accepted it when I first joined the Party as the secret of the Party's effectiveness. What I came to realise was that, in fact, it was the secret of the Party's failure.

The majority had some difficulty in reconciling its claim that democratic centralism, as it was practised, arose out of British conditions, with the Communist Party's ceaseless campaign for the end of the 'bans and proscriptions' which excluded Communists from membership of the Labour Party. What was sauce for the goose was not sauce for the gander:

> 'The Labour Party was formed as a co-ordinating body to which many trends of Socialist and Labour opinion, right, left and centre, could affiliate... Surely an organisation to bring all trends together should allow all trends to express their views? But the Communist Party does not admit all views, it is a body of like-minded Marxists and therefore has different rules from the Labour Party.' (Majority report, p. 9).

Heresy hunting, in short, was anathema in the Labour Party, but acceptable in the Communist Party.

One can only resolve the semantic argument about the meaning of 'democratic centralism', where both sides to the argument accept the need for both democracy and central leadership, by turning to the lessons of practical experience. In practice, the insistence on lower bodies submitting to higher bodies, and minorities to majorities, the outlawing of 'factions' in which members group together to support their point of view, and the obligation to fight for majority decisions made it impossible for the membership to change the party's policies or the leadership. All change had to come from the top downwards, and this explains why, even when changes are made in Communist Parties, they tend either to be precipitate (often the result of belatedly recognising previous mistakes) or far too late, or both.

But the problem was not simply one of attempting to convert a minority into a majority; it is only in times of acute crisis that a minority even conceives of such an aim. The attitude taken by the Party leadership towards discussion had the effect, and almost certainly the intention, of requiring unanimity in thought as well as in action. John Mahon, the Commission chairman, never ceased to tell us that the only purpose of discussion was action. But action was itself interpreted narrowly. It usually meant some immediate action by the Party branch: holding a meeting, selling more *Daily Workers,* issuing a leaflet, organising a rent strike, raising more money.

Since all discussion took place on a 'political report', covering 'the situation', and had then to lead to action, no real discussion on political theory or principle was possible, except in education classes or specialist professional or cultural groups.

In the papers submitted to the Commission there were several (notably by John Eaton, Maurice Dobb and Ronald Meek) which argued cogently that all discussion need not lead to action, but could have other aims, such as clarification of ideas, gaining a deeper understanding of a political problem, getting at the facts, changing policy, or even changing the leadership. It was the peculiarly limited concept of discussion leading to action (which is correct to the extent that a political party exists for action and not to provide a debating forum) that led to the peculiarly arid discussions within CP branches with which all former members of the Party must be familiar. These reached their nadir at Party Congresses, where the greater part of the Congress would be devoted to a discussion on the General Secretary's report, which itself would take some hours to deliver.

If one pillar of democratic centralism was the obligation to fight for Party decisions (coupled with restrictions on the right to discuss them), the other was the system of election at national or district Congresses of the Executive and District Committees. Under this system the Congress was presented with a list of recommended candidates. At one time, the Congress was allowed only to vote for or against the list as a whole. Congress would appoint a Panels Commission, which reviewed a list prepared originally by the Political Committee (or inner Party leadership), and then adopted by the Executive (or District) Committee. Delegates who wanted to change the list had to argue the case before the Panels Commission, which would require the member not only to justify any new name he wished to put forward, but also to say who should be knocked off to make room for the newcomer. Latterly, Congress delegates were presented with a complete list of candidates, and were free to vote for those who were not on the recommended list. But this made no practical difference, as the slate was invariably—and inevitably—elected by overwhelming majorities. Professor George Thomson, who had been a member of the EC from 1947 to 1954 submitted evidence to us describing the way in which the recommended list was presented to the EC, so that 'discussion was difficult and amendment almost impossible'. It would have been easy for the Party organisation to have produced the information, for which the minority asked, showing how at successive Congresses the lists had been amended at each stage. This information was denied to us—presumably, because it would have shown that the list finally 'elected' hardly differed from that which Pollitt and the inner group had presented to the Political Committee in the first place.

The minority did not, however, dismiss the Panel system out of hand. We were painfully familiar with the drawbacks of 'democratic' elections, whether for elected authorities or in trade unions and political parties. The principal merit of the panel system was that it made it possible to bring onto the EC able workers from industry whose names had not been made familiar by newspaper headlines. In 1956, nine of the 42 members of the Communist Party EC were industrial workers on the shop floor or in the pit. By contrast, it is almost unknown for active industrial workers to be elected to the EC of the Labour Party, which is monopolised by professional politicians and trade union officials.

Panels Commissions did indeed have prolonged and intense discussion of candidates' merits and demerits, as I know, having once served on one. But my experience convinced me, as his experience on the EC convinced Professor Thomson, that in practice the original list, emanating from Pollitt's office, could only be influenced at the margins, if at all. This was, in all essentials, the system that had operated in the Soviet Union and in Eastern Europe, and it placed limitless powers in the hands of a ruling clique. It gave them virtually complete control of the selection of the EC, and through their henchmen in the Districts, of the District Committees. This, combined with the control by the Political Committee, and of the 'secretariat', its equivalent in the districts, enabled the full-time officials to exercise complete control over the Party organisation and the approved channels of discussion. While, therefore, the EC of the CP could boast of a relatively high proportion of industrial workers, it was dominated by a block of full-time, salaried workers who all owed their jobs to the continued approval of the leading group. In 1956 20 of the 42 members were full-time officials, 10 of them working in the Party centre. These, with Willie Gallacher, the former MP, amounted to half the EC. None of these 20 would have been eligible for election to the Labour Party EC. One has to recognise the problem the CP faced. Having no MPs who are paid out of public funds, it could only sustain a corps of professional politicians by appointing them to jobs in the Party apparatus. I would certainly not take the view that this should disqualify some of the Party's ablest members from election to the EC. But the figures speak for themselves.

The majority of our Commission endorsed democratic centralism without our reservations, but conceded that errors had arisen in its application. Too great an emphasis had been put on centralism, too little on democracy. But the 'serious error' it identified was 'not enough being done to bring the membership into discussion. . . and failure to take sufficient practical measures to build strong Party branches'. To ensure 'a decisive shift in the work of the Executive and the district committees to promote the further growth of Party democracy in the branches' it made a number of recommendations. These amounted, essentially to:

1. the provision of more time and space to pre-Congress discussion, with 'freedom for contending views to be expressed in both the Party branch and the press';

2. the EC 'wherever possible' to consult the membership before deciding on new policy, and to open discussion for this purpose in the Party press;

3. more space to be given for discussion in the Party press, and a theoretical journal (*Marxism Today*) to be published;

4. The electoral system with the recommended list to remain, but delegates to have the right to challenge the recommended list on the floor of Congress, and the number of 'full-time comrades' to be limited to less

than half the EC (i.e. the existing proportion).

The system remained in all essentials unaltered, and the majority re-affirmed specifically the obligation of minorities to fight for decisions and the prohibition of 'factions'—i.e. organising in support of a minority view. The minority's recommendations included:

1. the right of Party members to meet with others before Congress to discuss political questions or prepare political statements, provided notice was given to the district committee;
2. recognition of the rights of individuals or groups to publish matter independently and to circulate it to branches;
3. members to be entitled to speak, if asked, at branches other than their own;
4. opposition spokesmen to be entitled to speak at Congress;
5. the recommended list to be abolished;
6. half the members of the EC to be elected in their own districts by the members who would know them.

The essence of the minority report lay, however, less in its specific recommendations (which were the product of hasty draftsmanship by myself, with little discussion) than in its broad approach to democratic centralism:

'The main question is not the name but the substance. We support the broad principles of democracy and of centralism as the basis of Party organisation, provided that there is a proper balance between the two. . .

If the leadership of the Party is honest and true to principle, if it tells the members the whole truth, or all that it knows, about the situation, if by its record it earns the respect, affection and loyalty of the Party membership, if it refrains from using its control of the Party machine and Press to smack down those who are seeking for information or expressing honest criticism, then in critical situations, where it has to take quick decisions and appeal for a quick response, the response will be given instantly, unanimously and enthusiastically. . . But insistence on the duty automatically to accept and fight for policies in which there is no confidence can only have bad results.'

The majority report was signed by the 10 Party officials, Joe Cheek and Kevin Halpin. Cheek added an addendum, in which he said that the majority report had not been sufficiently critical of the application of democratic centralism. He said the minority report had 'great value' and only disagreed specifically with our view. that 'the aims and ideals of Communism are in process of re-examination'. Halpin endorsed our criticisms of the composition of the Commission, and the lack of time to investigate specific cases. He accepted our view that the electoral system was self-perpetuating, and argued not only for a different method of election, but also for the rights of branches to carry a minority point of view for discussion to any other branch. These were substantial dis-agreements. Essentially, the majority report received the full backing only of the ten officials on the Commission.

The minority report got short shrift at the hands of the Party. It was published with the majority report, and that in itself was a striking innovation, but only the majority report was formally discussed at the Party Congress in May 1957. Of the three signatories of the minority report only Christopher Hill was a delegate to the Congress. I was not elected as a delegate by my own branch in Hampstead, and was in any case in the process of being expelled from the Party for the sin of having participated in launching the *New Reasoner* with John Saville and Edward Thompson. Peter Cadogan had quit, along with many others. Christopher Hill spoke in defence of the minority report, but his speech was not reported in the *Daily Worker*. He resigned immediately afterwards. The majority report was presented to Congress by John Mahon, who referred to the minority report in words that would not have seemed out of place in the mouth of Vyshinsky prosecuting an anti-party group of wreckers:

'The minority report gives some lip service to democratic centralism, and then assembles a number of proposals into a sort of platform from which to wreck democratic centralism.'

As I was not present at the Congress I have no first hand impression of it. But it is clear, both from contemporary reports and from speaking to survivors, that the enormous exodus of members after Hungary, which decimated the Party's intellectual membership, had produced a strong reaction among those who remained, and particularly among the industrial working-class members. The majority report was carried, according to the official report, by a majority of more than 20 to 1, and from that moment onwards the report itself disappeared into limbo. What effect it had on the inner life of the Communist Party I cannot say. But 20 years later Party members tell me that the authoritarian control asserted by the majority report is no longer acceptable and can no longer be enforced.

John Gollan, in the article in *Marxism Today* already referred to, has taken the first opportunity on his retirement from the Party leadership to put to the Soviet Party some of the questions about democracy that we attempted to put 20 years earlier. Yet Gollan, makes but one reference to the Commission on Inner-Party Democracy:

'There was no cult of the individual in our party. . . But in the aftermath of the 20th Congress, we further developed our programme and also developed our democratic life on the basis of a commission appointed to examine it. We had still more open discussion at Congresses and throughout the Party, while preserving the main point of democratic centralism that once a decision on policy has been democratically reached, it is carried out by all.'

This does not suggest, to me at least, that the British Communist Party, even now, is capable of realistically discussing the problems of socialist democracy.

NOTES

1. Although the younger Party members in particular were clamouring for the Party to oppose conscription, the leadership clung to its policy of 'cutting the call-up' to one year. It succeeded in carrying the Congress, but was lagging far behind public opinion.
2. John Gollan, 'Socialist Democracy: Some Problems. . .', *Marxism Today* (January, 1976).

1956 AND THE COMMUNIST PARTY

by Margot Heinemann

I have been asked to give some personal impressions of the immediate impact of the 20th Congress on the British Communist Party and its long-term effects. I shall make no attempt therefore to describe the whole sequence of events in 1956-57, but concentrate on what happened in and to the Party itself.

I should explain that I took part in the discussion and upheaval as a rank-and-file branch member. Although I had earlier done various responsible jobs I had for domestic reasons retired from all these three years before. Thus I was not part of any discussion at higher levels, and can't speak with the authority that would imply. What I have to say must therefore be taken as a personal and in some respects limited view.

To understand the background one must realise the depth of solidarity and admiration for the USSR which had been a cementing force among Communists ever since the Party was founded. The generation of Socialists already politically active in 1917 and the 1920s—many, like Harry Pollitt, Willie Gallacher, Arthur Horner, R. Palme Dutt, still among the foremost leaders of the British Party in 1956—had recognised the revolution led by Lenin as the most decisive break-through in history, the first to get rid of capitalists and begin to construct a Socialist order. The new Soviet state, attacked by capitalist military intervention and economic blockade from its very birth, had to be defended by socialists everywhere as one would defend fellow workers on strike. (Harry Pollitt's work to stop the *Jolly George* was an example.) Its survival and advance, under incredible difficulties, to build up a modern industry and become a world power was an immense achievement which proved that a Socialist economy was not a dream but a practical reality.

Those of us who (like myself) joined the Party later in the anti-Fascist struggles of the 1930s could never forget that the Spanish Republic would have had almost no arms without Russian supplies; that the movement to unite democratic forces against Fascism had been launched by heroic exiles like Dimitrov and Togliatti from the 7th World Congress of the Communist International on Soviet soil (and indeed the illegal revolution-ary opponents of Fascism could have assembled nowhere else). At the League of Nations, we had seen Litvinov's repeated efforts as Soviet delegate to halt fascist aggression through collective security, and the decisive rejection of this by Britain and France at Munich. Even if we argued over Soviet attitudes at the outset of the Second World War (which in any case we understood as resulting from the proven hostility of the Western powers to an anti-Fascist alliance) we knew that the Red Army and the Soviet people, with unimaginable sacrifices and 15 million dead, had broken Hitler's land armies and played a decisive part in his defeat. (Among other things these victories underlined for us the fact that the capitalist press had done nothing but lie about the alleged weakness and incapacity of the young Soviet state for over two decades). And after the war, the immense scale of devastation and Soviet war losses—which might have been ours but for their victories—made the need for solidarity seem as urgent as in the 1920's, especially after the Western threats to use atomic weapons against them. If there were hard times, stern discipline and insistence on the military security of the Soviet state as a guiding principle in foreign policy, this seemed understandable given that background.

The denunciation of Tito, however, and the succession of trials of leading Communists which followed in Eastern Europe, did cause uneasiness and doubts among British Party members. Whether or not one had reservations about Tito's political and economic policies, the argument that these could be attributed to capitalist subversion of leading Communists was not easy to accept. In practice it was the experience of these trials, held in the early 1950's, which helped to convince many of us that the allegations against Stalin at the 20th Congress must be substantially true. They explained so much which at the time had seemed almost inexplicable.

The revelations of mass repression, judicial murder and violation of Socialist and Party democracy under Stalin were not reported to the open Congress of the CPSU in February 1956 but conveyed to a secret session from which fraternal delegates from other countries were excluded. They were later reported orally to CPSU organisations. Thus it was in March when Harry Pollitt and others were already back in Britain reporting the achievements of the Soviet Union in reconstruction, just before the 24th Congress of the British Party,[1] that versions of the Khrushchev report began to leak out in the capitalist press, culminating in the June publication of what was claimed to be a full version as a supplement of the *Observer*. Unofficial and incomplete reports from the Soviet Union were reaching the Party soon after the Reuter report of 15th March, but it was not until the end of June that the Central Committee of the CPSU issued its resolution on overcoming the Cult of the Individual, and that, unlike the Khrushchev report, contained no detailed facts, though it referred to 'serious violations of Soviet law and mass repressions.' Indeed there has still been no full published account from the CPSU itself, though information from official sources has been assembled, for example, by Roy Medvedev in *Let History Judge* and by the French communist historian Jean Elleinstein in *The Stalin Phenomenon* (translation to be published in 1976 by Lawrence and Wishart).

The way in which the British Party got to know about the Khrushchev report (explicible now in view of the divisions in the leadership of the CPSU and the opposition of the Molotov group) increased the shock with which the news was received. The first reaction (of leaders as well as members) was that it must be yet another anti-Soviet lie. When the reports were not repudiated and even confirmed, it appeared that the British Party's own leaders' were almost as much at a loss as the rank and file, defensive and confused (see for example the *Daily Worker's* editorial, 'The Role of Stalin', 18.3.56). Thus the confidence of the Party, which would have been strained in any case, was further undermined by the manner of the disclosure.

It is hard to convey now the degree of shock and horror with which the CPSU critique was received among British Communists. It was soon obvious that support for the CPSU and the Soviet Government could never again be as simple and instinctive as before. Underlying this support had been the conviction that the main forms of oppression and persecution known to us had their roots in the capitalist system and its class and property relations. Once establish a socialist system, it was thought, and such oppression would disappear. This conviction had now been shattered; it left a theoretical vacuum which the CPSU's resolution on the Cult of the Individual failed to fill.

Those who saw the repressions and executions as *unimportant* in comparison with the great advances were few. The *Labour Monthly* in May 1956 commented editorially: 'That there should be spots on the sun would only startle an inveterate Mithra-worshipper': but this drew indignant protests from readers at all levels, and the next issue acknowledged this by withdrawing the phrase and somewhat modifying the original emphasis.

Points from the Party Discussion

From March 1956 to mid-1957 there was intense discussion of the issues raised by the 20th Congress throughout the Party and its press. Short letters in the *Daily Worker,* and longer ones and articles in *World News,* show attempts by hundreds of members to re-examine the fundamental basis of their own thought and actions as Communists, to assess what had been wrong and what was still valid in our attitudes to Socialism, to democracy, to the Party and the state, as well as our own Party's relation to the Soviet Union. 'For or against the E.C.' was not the main issue, at least in the earlier stages, though naturally that came into it. There were some who argued that our leaders must have known it all, and had concealed it from the rest of us. I never shared that view, and neither did the great majority in the Party. But I do think—though of course it's easy to say now, and no-one can prove it—that if our leaders had felt it possible to make at the time the kind of sharply critical statements the *Daily Worker* was already reporting from Togliatti and the Italian CP (see for example *Daily Worker* 16.3.56 and 18.6.56, as well as after the Hungarian events on 13.10.56 and 28.12.56), some though not all of the later divisions, resignations and waste might have been avoided and the way opened for a new advance.

It's impossible to give a full treatment of the discussion here, but a few of the main points round which it centred can be summarised:

Could it, and did it, really happen? The immense prestige of Stalin, as well as the achievements of the Soviet people in the war, made some comrades unwilling to accept the CPSU version of events at all.

How could it have happened? A searching discussion of this was difficult because of the lack of factual information, though Harry Pollitt in his initial statement (*Daily Worker* 24.3.56) and other writers stressed the immense difficulties caused by famine, war threats and war, and the activities of foreign intelligence to subvert the socialist state, all of which tended to give more power to the security forces and seemed to justify secrecy about their actions. But a deeper analysis, going beyond the personal role of Stalin and Beria, was increasingly asked for.

Was our condemnation of the abuses strong enough? Many of us felt that the Party should speak not of 'mistakes' but of 'crimes': that it should admit what Togliatti had called 'certain forms of degeneration' in Soviet society; and that reporting on socialist countries in the Party press should be more frank and objective.

Independence and autonomy of Communist Parties: Was it valid to see the CPSU as having a 'central' or 'hegemonic' role within the world Communist movement? The Communist International had been dissolved in 1943, and the right of Communist Parties to independent determination of their own course of action had thus been established. So far as we were concerned, this independence had already shown itself in our approach to the struggle in Britain, but on international issues, the attitude of the CPSU was still a major determining factor. To many of us this no longer seemed acceptable.

Inner-party democracy: Some comrades thought that part of the trouble was 'democratic centralism', which they believed stifled discussion and made the leadership self-perpetuating. They called for a radical re-organisation of the British Communist Party. Others thought there was no parallel between the situation in the CPSU and the British Party: for one thing, democratic centralism had not been operated for years in the CPSU under Stalin. Many felt that changes of the kind suggested would destroy the unity, democratic organisation and effectiveness of the Party, and could lead in the end to its liquidation.

After the revolts in Eastern Europe later in 1956, and above all after the Hungarian rising, there was a polarising and hardening of attitudes. It became clear that we were not talking simply about the past, about abuses which now that they had been exposed had also been overcome, but about painful changes still in process, about the present and the future.

In October the British Party and its leadership was faced at one and the same moment with the British attack on Suez and the culmination of the Hungarian revolt in armed rising, its suppression by Soviet troops and the establishment of the Kadar government with Soviet support. On the day the E.C. met a crowd of 40,000 was gathered in Trafalgar Square to demand an end to the British attack on Suez. To many of them it seemed that a third world war was imminent.

The EC's immediate statement declared:

'Coming after the murder and lynching of Communists, the open hostility of the Nagy Government to the Soviet Union and the repeated concessions which it made to the reactionary forces. . . the danger of fascism and Western intervention was acute.' It therefore considered that 'the new Hungarian Government and the action of the Soviet forces in Hungary should be supported by Communists and Socialists everywhere.' (*Daily Worker*, 5.11.56.)

The events themselves and the EC statement on them aroused bitter controversy in the Party (as well as in the Labour movement outside it, though there feeling was overwhelmingly hostile to the Soviet action). The dispute at this point centred round these main issues:

a) The sovereignty and independence of other Communist Parties and states, including socialist ones, in relation to the Soviet Union. Could military intervention in the affairs of another State ever be justified, even to support Socialism or prevent a counter-revolution?

b) Was the Hungarian rising really a counter-revolution or a popular movement? And had the events leading up to it and since been truthfully and fairly reported by the Party press?

c) What right of dissent and public criticism did those members have who were not convinced (as in this case) of the rightness of the Executive or Congress stand on a key policy question?

At one extreme there was criticism of the Executive as accomplices of repression: at the other of critics as condoning and aiding counter-revolution. Most comrades held neither of these extreme views, and the *Daily Worker* carried appeals from a number of well-known members to stay in the Party and argue the problems out. Many of us, including some who if put to it would vote for rather than against the EC's statement, agreed with Eric Hobsbawm that while the final Soviet intervention was necessary to prevent counter-revolution and the danger of a Fascist base in

Hungary, the movement against the former Government had been a popular one, however misguided; that the past policy of the USSR as well as the Hungarian Workers' Party was at fault; and that 'the suppression of a popular movement by a foreign army is at best a tragic necessity.' (*Daily Worker*, 9.11.56). Arthur Horner, in an interview headed 'I Stand by Our Party', declared:

> 'The situation in Hungary reminds me of a pit. In a pit you have sparks which need do no damage; but if gas has accumulated an explosion can occur with terrible consequences... I would not be afraid of foreign espionage and subversion—however large the sums of money spent on them—if genuine Socialist democracy is introduced and maintained in any country.' (*Daily Worker*, 19.11.56.)

Among people with differing views about the rising itself, there was a strong demand for the speediest possible withdrawal of Soviet troops. Thus the Marxist scientist J.D. Bernal, who was also President of the World Peace Council, argued that the main aim must be disengagement by the great powers. Foreign troops must be withdrawn from occupation and a serious start made on disarmament. 'Vital questions such as the freedom of Hungary can never be decided as long as small countries are forced to be attached to one side or other in the cold war' (*Daily Worker* feature article 6.12.56).

Discussions among the membership soon after the events showed a majority prepared to endorse the EC's general view of the Hungarian rising and the Soviet intervention, with an appreciable minority against. Roughly three-quarters of the branches discussing the matter supported the Executive statement, just under a fifth opposed and the rest were undecided; two-thirds of the members voting at branches supported the EC. At area and district committee level the proportion in favour of the EC statement was much higher.[2]

In my own branch, Highgate, critics were in the majority. It was a branch with a variety of experienced members determined to discuss the issues fully in a principled way and to avoid 'labelling' and name-calling. I remember vividly a whole series of packed meetings, sometimes with 40-50 present, with arguments going on late into the evening. There were sharp disagreements, but we assumed one another's good faith. In this atmosphere it was possible to face painful realities, to recognise that on many important questions we had been wrong for years, and that a lot still needed sorting out, and yet to feel that we were right to remain in the Party and try to change whatever we disagreed with.

We thought, for one thing, that the British Party had tended to stress central leadership at the expense of informed democracy in its own organisation, and that further democratisation was needed—especially in relation to methods of electing the EC, freer expression of conflicting views by leading members in pre-Congress discussions, and circulation by branches of discussion material for which there was no room in the Party press. We sent amendments on a number of these points to the Commission on Inner Party Democracy set up by the EC. None of our amendments was accepted. The Commission agreed that the Party 'should now correct what we believe to have been a serious error—too great an emphasis on centralism and an insufficient emphasis on democracy', but rejected proposals by a great many branches and individuals for specific changes in rules or organisation to secure this. It did, however, accept the need for more discussion. 'The decision of the EC to produce a regular discussion journal, publishing a number of articles with which the Editorial Board did not necessarily agree, should encourage the publication of contending views' (Report of Commission on Inner-Party Democracy, 1957, p. 13). This new venture was *Marxism Today*, which began to appear later in 1957.

The Special (25th) Congress

Because of the storm over Hungary the Executive decided to hold a Special Congress in April 1957. Meanwhile it instructed dissentients to abide by the rules and refrain from publishing their disagreements in the non-Party press, and suspended the editors of the *Reasoner* for continuing to publish it despite a request not to do so.

It seems now—as it did at the time—that those comrades who continued to issue journals attacking Party policy, still more those who published their condemnation in the *Daily Express,* did not in practice help to advance the discussion, but rather diverted it from the central *political* questions to those of loyalty and splitting. There was already an intense critical discussion taking place within the Party press. Not only was the *Daily Worker* allocating much space to letters, but *World News* was opening its columns to contributions, and added to its limited space with three special pre-Congress discussion supplements so that more comrades could get in. I was one of those who wrote in at this stage, arguing among other things that although we must take account of Soviet experience and policy, 'international working-class solidarity does not imply that we must at all times arrive at the same solution as the CPSU on a given problem. Our solidarity must be based on critical independence of judgment.' (*World News*, 30.3.57.)

At the same time, many of us felt the Executive should have been far more open-minded and flexible in relation to its critics. In this exceptionally confused and difficult situation, if Communists discussed the problems with others outside their own branches, or as individuals signed joint letters of disagreement or protest to the Party press, to condemn this as 'factionalism' was in my opinion entirely wrong. The crisis in Communist thinking and policy went very deep. Unity could not be achieved by enforcing tighter discipline (which increased the divisions it was intended to prevent), but only, if at all, by a patient continuing effort to reach agreement and understanding based on a fresh Marxist analysis of all the available facts.

In preparation for the Special Congress the EC had defined its attitude to the Hungarian events in a draft political resolution. A number of branches which accepted the necessity for the final Soviet intervention nevertheless thought that this resolution did not bring out or criticise sharply enough the Soviet Government's share of responsibility for the whole situation under Rakosi and the events leading up to the rising, including the first Soviet intervention on 3rd October. A composite resolution on these lines was supported by our branch delegate at the Special Congress, but was decisively defeated.

In the event the (25th) Congress, made up of delegates directly elected from branches, by very large majorities endorsed the EC's stand on all the issues under dispute, including Hungary, relations with the Soviet Union and the organisation of the Party itself. Essentially this expressed the feeling of the majority that the CPSU, having boldly initiated the process of restoring socialist democracy, would carry it through, and that criticism, necessarily uninformed, by the British Party would not help it to do so. Further, despite the crimes and errors revealed there and in Eastern Europe, the total achievement of the Soviet Union was seen as over-whelmingly positive and the foundations of socialist economy and state unshaken. While sectarianism was criticised, the greatest danger, nation-ally and internationally, was stated to be 'revisionism'—including a negative and over-critical attitude to the Soviet Union, a weakening of international solidarity and of Party discipline. In general, the analysis accepted was close to that made in the CPSU resolution itself and in Soviet statements on Hungary. But it was clearly stated that this did not represent auto-matic approval of Soviet policy at all times, and that the Party would examine in an independent and critical way all future policies from whatever quarter they came.[3]

Some 7,000 members—around a fifth of the total[4]—had resigned or lapsed before the Congress, and others left soon after it, including some delegates such as Christopher Hill, Michael Barratt Brown, and Hyman Levy, who had argued a case in the discussion there and been defeated. The resignations over this period included a number of the Party's best known intellectual and professional comrades, but also some leading trade unionists, among them Bill Jones (TGWU), Dick Seabrook (USDAW), John Horner (FBU), Bert Wynn and Lawrence Daly (NUM). Many of us who disagreed with the minority on some points were indignant at the irrelevant attacks made on them as 'wavering intellectuals' (mostly, it must be said, by other intellectuals), as if workers were less concerned about freedom of discussion and the rule of law.

The resignations of many sincere and principled comrades were prompted not only by disagreement with the policy adopted, but by a conviction that the Party would never again be a serious force in the British Labour movement, or develop an independent approach and style of work following the lessons of the 20th Congress. I don't think it can be seriously argued that the loss of such members strengthened the unity and effectiveness of the Party; rather it weakened it and slowed down the reassessment of its work. Many of them have continued to make outstanding contributions to Marxist theory and practical politics, and to maintain close relations with friends and comrades still in the Party.

There were many of us, however, who, while very dissatisfied with the positions taken at the Congress, were nevertheless convinced that our right place was still in the Communist Party, and that as a Marxist organisation including some of the finest and most selfless activists in the working class movement it had an essential role to play. Any necessary developments and changes in its work would not be furthered by narrowing the membership. The last twenty years have, I believe, validated this view. For our Party, as for so many others, the 20th Congress was not only an end but a beginning.

Twenty Years On: The Party in 1976

It is hard now, and perhaps unprofitable, to try to separate the effects of the 20th Congress from other factors—such as the long period of cold war and unexampled capitalist boom, the increasing political power exerted by television from which the Party was virtually excluded, and the divisions between Soviet and Chinese Communists—all of which would have made the last twenty years a difficult period for the British Communist Party. But these effects were undoubtedly important.

Not only among its own members, but in the workingclass movement, confidence in the Party and its credibility were undeniably lessened for a time. To that extent it was made less effective in challenging right-wing policies in the Labour movement and in winning support for an alternative, socialist way forward for Britain. Although it neither dissolved itself (as some had suggested it should) nor faded away as its veterans passed out of action, for some years recruitment was low, and when it revived there was still a certain sense of a 'missing generation' that should have been coming into leadership (those who would now be in their forties and early fifties). Nevertheless the Party worked on, above all where it had always been strongest, in the trade unions and in industry.

Communists undoubtedly have greater trade union and industrial support today than they had in, say, the earlier 1950's. Total membership (at 28,500) is slightly lower than in 1956 (though higher than in 1957) but all-round influence is certainly greater—for example in the factories, the unions and the student movement, and in closer relations with a larger and more active left wing in the Labour Party. On the other hand, electoral support (for a variety of reasons) has declined over the period. But contrary to the impression given by the media, the Communist Party today is not an ageing organisation but a relatively young one. The average age of the delegates at the 1957 Congress was 36. Less than half of the present Executive were EC members before 1971. Among the newer EC members are a number in their twenties and thirties, who nevertheless have already years of experience as leaders in the trade union, women's or student movements.

For years the Party's theoretical and cultural work was weakened by the loss of a number of its outstanding intellectuals (particularly historians and writers). The late 60's and 70's brought in many students, who have now grown into a new generation of Communist intellectuals with standing and respect outside the Party. For example, the annual 'Communist University of London' (an outsize summer school organised by the National Student Committee) has grown in size and range till in 1976 it brought together over 1,000 people for 9-day courses in basic Marxism and its application to various fields of knowledge—history, literature, art, science, economics, philosophy and social science—an educational undertaking far larger and more complex than anything attempted in the 1950's, involving both Party and non-Party Marxists.

Divisions on the Left

One of the most obvious results of the 20th Congress has been the increased fragmentation and division of the left. There have always, of course, been alternative Marxist organisations in Britain, but the disillusioned reaction after the Stalin era and the Russian/Chinese divisions helped to encourage their growth, especially though not exclusively among students and teachers. The Communist Party remains by far the largest and strongest organisation on the Marxist left, having both deeper working-class roots and much greater stability in membership and policy; but its members have had to recognise that an interest in Marxism or revolution does not today lead inevitably straight to a card in the Communist Party.

The groups around *New Reasoner* and later *New Left Review*—which included many of those who resigned in 1956-7—have continued active discussions and made valuable theoretical contributions, especially to Marxist history. But they did not provide an alternative organisation to that of the Communist Party (and indeed were not intended to do so).

There is no ban by the Party on political dealings with members of IS, IMG, etc. There is now a good deal of public debate, not all of it sterile, and sometimes practical cooperation with their members. At the same time, in the student, labour and peace movements, the sectarianism and disruptiveness of some ultra-left groups has turned off many of the un-committed and played straight into the hands of the Right. Damage of this kind is part of the price socialists have paid and are still paying for the events that led up to the 20th Congress, and also for our own failure to analyse the facts seriously enough as a Marxist party.

Independent Communist Policy

Some comrades in the 1956-7 discussions complained that the British party would never criticise anything about the Soviet Union unless the CPSU had already done so, for fear of making common cause with the enemies of Socialism. And the readiness of the media to cash in and distort any such criticism still makes this a difficult problem, which cannot be solved by silence or 'sunshine' reporting.

The independence and autonomy of Communist parties have neverthe-less been increasingly stressed in the statements and actions of the British CP over the last twenty years, and especially since the removal of Khrushchev in 1964 (the undemocratic manner in which it criticised). Important aspects of this have been the insistence at international level that all CP's have equal rights, so that agreement between them can be reached only by consensus, not by majority vote or imposed decisions; and the refusal to endorse the exclusion of the Yugoslav or Chinese CP's from discussions between Communist Parties (for details on CP conferences in 1960 and 1969 see Gollan's article in *Marxism Today*, January 1976).

As early as 1951, (in advance, that is, of other parties in Western Europe) the British CP in its programme *The British Road to Socialism* had declared its aim as socialism based on a left parliamentary majority supported by mass action in the country (rather than the earlier concept of a Soviet Britain). Later versions of the programme, amended by successive Congresses, have defined it more precisely to emphasise freedom of speech and publication, freedom of creative work in the arts, and the right of political parties, including those opposed to socialism, to continue legal activity. Moreover the Party has categorically stated that such a Socialist Government would hold regular elections, and if defeated would accept the verdict of the people.

An EC discussion statement on *Questions of Ideology and Culture* (*Marxism Today*, May 1976) spelt out explicitly its view that the Party, during the fight for or under Socialism, should not lay down a 'line' to which scientists or artists should conform. It argued for freedom of debate and experiment among scientists (no more Lysenkos), the widest variety and freedom of subject and style in the arts, and no insistence that all artistic work can or should play a direct political role. It argued also for developing further the dialogue between Marxists and Christians, recognising that religion can be a support for reaction but may also inspire progressive actions, and laid down a present and future policy of 'complete freedom of religious worship, for the right of all faiths to worship in their own churches with their own sacred books, and for making available the resources necessary for ritual articles'. 'Both under capitalism and socialism, religious and non-religious views should freely contest' and religious beliefs are no bar to CP membership. This remains the fullest statement of the Party's attitude on questions of art, science and religion, in accordance with which it later made public criticisms of the trial and sentence of certain writers in the Soviet Union (Sinyavsky, Daniel and others) and the treatment of dissent generally.

Czechoslovakia

The British Communist Party's commitment to the autonomy of each Party and sovereign state, and its determination to examine events critically and independently, were clearly demonstrated in its reaction to the Czechoslovak events in 1968. The Soviet invasion was immediately condemned by the Political Committee ('intervention' was the actual term used) and solidarity expressed with the Czech Communist Party, which had attempted to move towards a different and as it considered a more democratic version of Socialism. This was a quick but not an unconsidered decision, since the Executive of the British Party had been in touch with both Czech and Soviet comrades over a considerable period, and its press had been closely following the course of events. Its attitude (later endorsed by, among others, the Italian, Spanish and French Communist Parties) was steadily maintained when it repeatedly protested against the treatment of Dubcek and other leaders of the Czech party, and gave Marian Sling the opportunity to write in the Party press on her own experiences of Stalinist repression and imprisonment and the trials of old Communists in the early 50's. Successive Congresses of the Party, after considerable debate, have upheld the critical attitude taken by the Executive on this issue.

In the resolution on the international situation passed at its 34th Congress in November 1975, the Party, after paying tribute to the steady advance in living standards and quality of life in the Soviet Union in contrast to the deepening economic crisis in the capitalist world, went on to say:

> This does not mean there are no problems, including those involved in the further development of socialist democracy and the handling of dissent. We believe that socialism must provide for the expression and publication of dissenting views, and that political dissent and the combatting of anti-Marxist ideas should be handled by political debate and not by administrative measures.

Ever since 1968 successive Congresses have shown that there is a substantial minority opposed to this whole political trend in the British Party and in particular to any criticism of the Soviet Union. Although the vote has consistently upheld the Executive's stand the minority have at each Congress been given the opportunity to re-raise and re-debate the issues involved, often repeating previous discussions. The leadership and Congress have relied on the Marxist method of settling policy by full and free discussion of opposing ideas, rather than limiting controversy by administrative methods, even on the grounds (often true enough) that other important questions are being robbed of time.

Resolutions and speeches by this minority have often urged the British Party to 'get back into the mainstream of the world Communist movement', and stop criticising the policies of the Soviet Union. But it is a strange kind of 'mainstream' that would exclude, for example, the great Italian, French and Spanish Communist parties, all strong enough to have great influence on the transition to socialism in countries with a long history of popular struggle for democratic rights. In many points their approach to these questions, decided independently by each Party, is similar to ours.

Anyone who thinks there is now little rank and file participation in policy-making in the British Party, or little political controversy, need only listen to debates like those at the 1975 Congress (largely centred round over 1200 amendments to the draft resolutions submitted by the Executive, and over 200 resolutions from the branches) or read the discussions in *Marxism Today*. It is true, though, that despite illuminating articles by individual comrades like Maurice Dobb and Monty Johnstone, there has been an unwillingness by the Party leadership to examine fundamentally what *caused* the disastrous turn of events in the Soviet Union exposed in 1956, on the grounds that we have not sufficient facts on which to base an analysis and that it is the reponsibility of the Soviet comrades themselves to provide it. At present, however, this seems unlikely to happen.

Now, with the publication of John Gollan's important article *Socialist Democracy—Some Problems: The 20th Congress in Retrospect (Marxism Today,* January 1976) these hesitations have been set aside. I myself think this should have been done much sooner. Our Party is now in a position to make what contribution it can, along with other Communist Parties, to a serious Marxist examination of these events which will help to plan its future course.

Gollan's article does not advance any new facts, though some of the horrifying ones he quotes from Khrushchev, Medvedev and Elleinstein (all derived from official Soviet sources) will be new to many comrades. It does offer a serious treatment of developments in the Soviet Union and open the whole question of socialist democracy (which must include the trade unions and industrial democracy) for discussion in the Party. This should help many who were not around in 1956, including some who have argued for a 'firmer', less 'liberal' attitude by the Communist Parties in Western Europe, to understand exactly what the rejection of Stalinism was about. On the other hand, any socialist Government will have to face hostility and economic sabotage by the old capitalist class, and new forms of active democracy will have to be evolved, especially in industry, so that the power of the organised workers can counter them.

Why it still matters

In reacting defensively to attacks as they hit the working-class the Party has been at its strongest. It has had less success in winning support for socialist and Marxist ideas in the wider labour movement, and its programme is not as yet widely supported by workers who readily look to the Communists they know to provide effective shop stewards or trade union officers. Reservations (in the Party and outside it) about freedom, human rights and democracy in Socialist countries have reinforced the 'economist' tendencies which have always been strong anyway among British workers, to see trade union action on wages as sufficient and shy away from involvement in socialist politics, which are left to the 'political wing'—and often in practice, to the Right.

With the deepening crisis and unemployment in which the British capitalist economy is now trapped, it is becoming obvious that the standards and quality of life of the people cannot be maintained or advanced without *political* changes. And there is a pressing danger that if the left doesn't offer a clear alternative policy and leadership, right-wing Tory and Fascist trends could gain ground.

In this situation, where socialist alternatives seem so necessary and urgent, socialist democracy is more than ever a crucial question. This cannot be resolved merely by programmes. Because the Soviet Union is seen as the outstanding socialist state, any deformation or degeneration of democracy there is not a matter of private worry or guilt for the Communist Party, but affects the perspective and support for the whole socialist left. The fear that socialism or any move towards it must entail repression or foreign domination is still a powerful argument with millions now suffering the effects of capitalist crisis. (This, and not his literary skill, is why the media give so much publicity to Solzhenitsyn.)

It would be useless for us to try to forget that the bad things ever happened: we still need to explain *how* they happened, to show that they are a perversion of socialism and not its inevitable outcome. This is vital for the fight against reaction, the unity of the Left, and the removal of the bans and proscriptions which still prevent Communists from playing their full part within the political as well as the industrial movement.

Postscript (July 1976)

At the recent conference of European Communist Parties in July 1976—long-delayed because of differences on the relations that should exist between them—it was publicly agreed that no Communist Party has a leading or directing role, though the struggle against war and reaction is of common concern to them all. Each Party works out its own path to socialism in accordance with the conditions in its own country. All have the right to differ and where necessary, publicly to criticise one another's policies: for example, criticism of Soviet attitudes to democracy and dissent was expressed in the discussion by, among others, the Italian and British leaders, and the conference was addressed by Marshal Tito as well as by Communist leaders from the Soviet Union and Eastern Europe. A full treatment of the conference cannot be attempted here, with this article already in proof: but the changes it indicates have been long maturing, and will clear the way for new advances towards socialism, especially in Western Europe.

NOTES

1. It was immediately after this Congress that Harry Pollitt resigned the secretaryship. He was 66 and had been in poor health for some time, but on 25th April he suffered a haemorrhage behind the eyes which made him unable to read at all for three months. He was ordered to rest and did not return to work until August. Pollitt had been an exceptionally loved and trusted leader: his illness and incapacity could hardly have come at a more difficult time for the Party. He was well enough to chair the controversial Special Congress in March 1957 with what most of his critics agreed was admirable fairness. From that time, though he went on working, he suffered a series of strokes from the last of which he died in 1960.

2. Detailed figures were given in *Daily Worker*, 17.12.56. Reports from 322 branches showed that 240 supported the EC statement, 69 were against and 23 undecided. Of these, 188 reported voting figures—2,095 for, 745 against and 301 abstentions. Area membership meetings showed 1,029 for, 295 against and 89 abstentions. On area committees voting was 167—8—7 and on district committees 291—32—17.

3. One practical example of criticism going beyond the official attitude of the CPSU was in the report of the British Communist delegation which went to the Soviet Union in November 1956 to examine progress in carrying out the decisions of the 20th Congress. The section on anti-Semitism and treatment of the Jews in particular was highly critical not only of the past, but of continued restrictions of cultural rights and current policy generally. On the Stalin period the report stated: 'Crimes and distortions of this type cannot be the work of one man. It must have been the case that sectors of the administrative personnel must have been aware of what was taking place and must have taken the steps necessary to implement it. This argues a certain level of degeneration in this sector.' (*World News and Views*, 12th January 1957). The report was signed by J.R. Campbell (Chairman), W. Alexander, I. Hackett, J. Law, H. Levy, W. Moore, A.L. Morton and W. Warman.

4. The membership reported at the 1956 Congress was 33,960.

THE KHRUSHCHEV SPEECH, THE PCG AND THE PCI

The two following interviews were first published in *Politique Hebdo* in the Spring of 1976 and are reproduced here with the kind permission of its Editors. The translation is by A. and F. Strugnell.

1. *The PCF*

(Jean Pronteau and Maurice Kriegel-Valrimont, who were members of the Central Committee of the French Communist Party in 1956, were interviewed by Paul Noirot of *Politique Hebdo*.)

P.N.: What happened at the famous meeting of the Central Committee that followed the 20th Congress?

J.P.: Duclos summarised the Congress without revealing anything more than we could have read in *L'Humanité*.

M.K-V.: Thorez wasn't there. He let Duclos carry the can.

J.P.: So Duclos vaunted Stalin's talents and proposed a resolution praising him to the skies. About a dozen of us spoke in favour of destalinisation. Others were in agreement, but would say nothing. We didn't constitute a faction, we were still bound by the Stalinist conception of democratic centralism which forbade organic links among militants. We were scattered and isolated, and so incapable of forcing a change in direction.

M.K-V.: There were a relatively high number of speeches for a debate in the CC. They didn't add up to an organised movement. Waldeck-Rochet and Benoît Frachon were among those who demanded that the problems raised by the 20th Congress should be widely debated within the Party.

J.P.: On the other hand Servin and Casanova defended Thorez' position.

M.K-V.: The fullest speech was made by Florimond Bonte who was still editor-in-chief of *France Nouvelle*.

J.P.: Yes. He had a good grasp of German and he had got to know about a pamphlet published by the East Germans which contained a watered-down version of the K. report. He was able to speak knowing what it was all about.

M.K-V.: Bonte's speech touched on most of the problems raised by the 20th Congress. Apart from a small group centred round Duclos, he was well received by the CC. The same day a full-scale campaign to denigrate Bonte was launched, but what had started it off was never mentioned.

P.N.: Did Thorez in fact let the Moscow delegation have the text of the K. report?

J.P.: It is impossible to believe that Duclos and the others didn't find out about the contents of the report while they were in Moscow.

P.N.: But did Duclos mention the secret report to that meeting of the Central Committee?

M.K-V.: No, not at all.

J.P.: None of those who spoke on the resolution knew anything. After our speeches the Political Bureau decided to adjourn the meeting and nominated a commission to redraft the text. In this way a second resolution was passed, a little less outrageous and a little more honourable. But the members of the CC continued to be ignorant of the report, as was the rest of the Party.

In this connexion, I should like to tell you of a personal recollection. Just after the meeting of the CC we have been talking about, I went to Poland to attend a congress of economists. There I met a leader of the Polish party, who asked me: 'Well, comrade Pronteau, how did the discussion of the K. report go in your CC?' I told him about the discussion on the official report. He interrupted: 'Don't let's beat about the bush. What did you think of the secret report?' I looked at him, astounded: 'A secret report? What secret report?' Suspicious, he asked me: 'You are a member of the Central Committee, aren't you?' 'Yes, of course.' 'Well then, it's very important, you really must know.' He gave me a copy of the secret report in Polish and called in a secretary who spoke French. Through the night she translated the report for me, and I took notes feverishly.

Immediately on my return to Paris, I asked Maurice Thorez if I could see him. It was natural to report to the secretary general after a mission abroad. I was convinced that the report was going to appear in the bourgeois press and that we had to prepare our militants for the possibility. Thorez received me in his office. Straight away, I said to him: 'I've just got back from Poland, I've seen the report.' He looked at me, expressionless: 'The report? What report?' I replied: 'The report K. made in closed session, the secret report.' Without turning a hair, Thorez said: 'There is no secret report.' I started to get worked up, and took out of my briefcase the notes I had taken in Poland. At that point Thorez said to me: 'Oh! so you've got it. You should have said so straight away.' And he added in a pontifical manner: 'Anyway, just remember one thing. This report doesn't exist. Besides, soon it will never have existed. We must pay no attention to it.'

Thorez' cynicism was no longer a surprise to me, and later I understood the quiet pleasure he showed, when the 'anti-Party group' almost managed to seize power and overthrow K. It was a near thing. Molotov, Malenkov and Kaganovitch had a majority in the Praesidium. If it hadn't been for Zhukov's tanks, K. would have been beaten. They had put together a resolution, which I saw, in which they made out K. to be *an enemy of the people*, particularly on account of his report to the 20th Congress, which was described as a *'tissue of lies and infamy'*. Well, Thorez had links with the 'anti-Party group'. They held splinter meetings, and Thorez was banking on their winning.

M.K-V.: One day Courtade, who had also been sent to Moscow, came back to Paris instructed by Molotov to tell the 'French comrades' that there were still some in Moscow who remained real bolsheviks. It was the opposition to the line taken at the 20th Congress, which Thorez upheld in France. In this fight against K. Thorez and the Chinese Communist Party took up parallel positions. It's a little known fact. This parallelism lasted until K. emerged the victor from the confrontation with the 'anti-Party group'.

When the victory of K. was confirmed, Duclos recognised with deep regret that he had had the masses on his side.

J.P.: That's right, I remember it clearly. I came back from Moscow where I had been sent into 'exile', for 'retraining', just after the defeat of the 'anti-Party group'. I went straight from the airport to the National Assembly, where I met Duclos who asked me what had been happening in Moscow. Delighted, I told him: 'A right old clear-out, it was.' And I told him all about the battle. It was then that he said to me, with an air of consternation, 'He had the masses on his side.' Let me add that, coming from him, it was almost a major accusation. Because the Stalinist apparatus is characterised by contempt for and fear of the masses.

M.K-V.: We're getting to the nub of the matter. The main subject of debate in 1956 was the manner in which the Party should link itself with the masses and promote their movement. In France this debate vanished into thin air. When K. turned out to be the winner, the about-face was total. Thorez even went as far as to bestow upon him the title of an exceptional Marxist theoretician for his discovery of the importance of political facts in class confrontations. This clean sweep of old grievances was a way of avoiding any criticism. There was no debate. All prospect of change was blocked. History was held back by twenty years.

II. *The PCI*
(An interview with Rossana Rossanda, one of the founders of *Il Manifesto* and a member of the Political Bureau of the Party of Proletarian Unity (PDUP). P.H. stands for *Politique Hebdo*.)

P.H.: What impact did the Khrushchev report have within the Italian Communist Party? When and in what form was it known to the cadres and militants?

R.R.: We got to know about the 'secret report' at the beginning of June 1956 when *Espresso,* a left-wing weekly, reprinted it from the *New York Times.* I remember it was a Thursday and on the Saturday the federal committee of the party met, as usual, in Milan. Questions poured out from all sides, particularly as *Unita* had decided to ignore the document, refusing either to confirm or deny its authenticity. The replies of the party leaders were evasive: 'We don't yet know whether this document is authentic; we didn't know about Stalin's errors, mistakes or crimes (the choice of term defined the attitude); but we know from the public speeches at the 20th Congress that there have been violations of socialist legality in the Soviet Union.' These replies, which were both flexible and reductive, had the effect of softening the shock. What is more, we were right in the middle of an election campaign—it was for local elections but they were being held nationwide—and we had to return our opponents' attacks.

To understand the debate that took place between June and October, you have to remember that the CPI had received the arguments propounded at the 20th Congress with considerable enthusiasm, including the criticisms made of Stalin's simplified version of history and violation of legality. The Soviet Union had thereby demonstrated, in the eyes of the CPI, that it had at last made the move essential to the advent of a 'mature socialism.' Broadly speaking, it was the view which Isaac Deutscher had been defending for a long time, and which the Italian communist press had treated with caution. Consequently, when Pietro Nenni immediately after the 20th Congress had started, in an editorial in *Mondo Operaio (In the light and the shadow of the 20th Congress)*, that we were facing a 'degenerescence of the system', he was roundly criticised by the PCI. But Khrushchev's 'secret report' changed the nature of the problem. For it was one thing to talk about violations of legality, but quite another to portray Stalin as a bloodthirsty old man, whose misdeeds could be placed in the category of genocide. Such accusations were both outrageous and over-simple: one man could not be held accountable for actions of that kind.

So Togliatti intervened by giving his now famous interview to *Nuovi Argumenti*, a non-communist journal, without giving prior warning to the Party secretariat. In it he initiated an attack on the inadequacies of the 'secret report' and on the concept of the 'personality cult'.

Togliatti's interview wasn't well received in the Soviet Union, nor by the French CP, nor even by all the leaders of the PCI. But it helped the Polish October and the Hungarian uprising. It was then that the debate became dramatic, confronted with photographs of party workers hanged in Budapest by angry workers, and with Soviet tanks entering Hungary, despite the solemn declaration of 30th October on the total independence of popular democracies. Once more Togliatti decided to ride the tiger: in a long communiqué he defended Soviet intervention, but at the same time he denounced the errors of the Hungarian Party which had led to the insurrection. The leadership urged the Party at all levels not to take action against any one who, even outside the Party, had adopted a different attitude towards the Hungarian affair. In fact, the main concern of the leadership was on the one hand to prevent the debate calling into question the PCI itself and Togliatti in particular (hence the tough reaction to those who were claiming that the Party had hidden the truth about the Soviet Union from its militants), and on the other to try for the first time to disengage itself from too close a link with the Soviet Union by presenting at the 8th Congress a 'Programme for an Italian path to socialism.'

On the whole the operation succeeded for a number of reasons: a) the PCI didn't try to stifle the debate, even if today it may seem to have been inadequate; b) it kept to a minimum recourse to disciplinary methods; c) the Socialist party started to move in the direction of social democracy, which had the effect of arousing the Communists' loyalty; d) the employers tried to take advantage of Budapest in order to intensify their offensive in the factories against Communist organisations, which had already been sorely tried over the past five years. The Communist rank and file responded by mobilising in desperation and as a consequence a few months later in Italy (in June 1957) a new impulse was given to the workers' movement which has continued to grow ever since.

P.H.: How do you explain after the event the decision of the leadership of the PCI to authenticate the report and engage in a process of 'destalinisation'?

R.R.: Togliatti had long been of the opinion that Stalin's methods were not correct; but that didn't prevent him from considering as irresponsible—and he hardly hid the fact—Khrushchev's manoeuvre which had placed the popular democracies and the communist parties in a difficult position. However, given a 'fait accompli', he saw no point in denying the obvious, preferring to 'historicise' the past and face up to the present, and making the most out of the 20th Congress that he could.

And that wasn't negligible. Most of all, he strengthened his own position within the Party. In 1951 Stalin had asked him to give up the post of secretary of the PCI to take on that of the Cominform: but, while he answered Moscow in the negative, the leadership of the PCI, on the contrary, gave Stalin to understand that it accepted and could do without him. Togliatti refused to give in and came back to Rome determined to change the power structure of the leadership. In fact, he only managed to do this with the help of the 20th Congress of the Soviet CP and the 9th Congress of the Italian CP: the debate which had been touched off led to the revamping of the cadres along the lines of 'the Italian path'.

To what extent had Togliatti always set his sights on this way? It's impossible to answer a question like that in a few words. Certainly, right from the beginning, he had made the CPI into a party 'with a difference'; more flexible in its internal organisation, more closely linked with the masses, and strongly unitary in its structure. It shouldn't be forgotten that it was a party that had been more or less reborn out of the resistance to the German occupation, and that it had escaped the destructive disputes of the Thirties.

The struggle against fascism gave it a strongly democratic flavour. In the last analysis, if you consult *Rinascita*—which more closely expresses Togliatti's ideological line than any other organ—and if you think about the publication of Gramsci's works, you realise why after the 20th Congress the section of the leadership behind Togliatti adopted the belief (at least formally) in autonomy and an end to the idea of a 'guiding state'.

Basically, this arose out of the idea that Italian society was much more complex than Russian society in 1917, that the modern State was something other than an autocracy, and that democracy could not be conceived of simply in tactical terms. It was in this context and as early as this that the CPI called into question the 'dictatorship of the proletariat', although in an ambiguous manner; at the same time it gave pride of place to the concept of the *hegemony* of the new revolutionary social block, in as far as it had the ability to maintain a radically new leadership, and enjoy the specific consensus of a wide variety in an advanced Western society. Under Togliatti the formulas remained vague: it was only after his death that the ambiguity resolved itself in the direction of explicit parliamentarianism.

P.H.: Didn't the liberalisation that then set in in the CPI strengthen the drift to reformism? Wasn't the fascination with the CPI which quickly spread among other European Communist parties ambiguous?

R.R.: The CPI was never 'liberal'. The flexibility of its line has no effect on the very firm conception it has of the Party. The Party is the 'new prince' of Gramsci's Machiavelli—it implies a great deal of dexterity and tractability, but very little 'liberalism'. It is a party which goes in for discussion, because it knows that discussion can be a factor of powerful cohesion. It is a party which seeks to incorporate within itself the reasons for every divergence, in order to retain overall control. This method requires a real capacity for synthesis, and it functions, naturally, as long as that synthesis is possible.

That was proved in the last years of Togliatti's life, between 1958 and 1964, when the Communist Youth, followed by the workers' federations, in keeping with the new pattern of struggle emerging, opened up a left-wing front within the Party. Togliatti tried to mediate from his 'advanced position', either by recognising the novel features of the situation, or by skirting round them: he rarely tried to deny their existence. After his death, when synthesis became both subjectively and objectively more difficult, the leadership refrained from mediation. At the 11th Congress in 1966 Ingrao was badly defeated and at the 12th Congress in 1969, it was to be our turn; defeat was followed by exclusion.

Having said that, why should 'liberalism' strengthen the drift to reformism? It appears to have legitimised a left-wing current in the CPI as it did in the unions. Reformism has never been much a feature of the Party's style: the French CP has always had a more rigid internal structure, but it has often taken a more right-wing line than the CPI (Algeria, May

1968, worker and student struggles, its attitude towards leftist groups). The fascination exerted by the CPI surely lies in the fact that it has always projected, if not a democratic image of itself, at least one which is more 'democratic' than that of other CPs; but it mainly lies in the fact that it represents far and away the largest Communist power group in Europe.

The reason for this is because it had posed the question of the specific nature of a revolution in the West, both through Gramsci and through the more ambiguous Togliatti; because too of its indisputable ability to maintain and feed a movement which has no equal in Europe. To the extent that it has undermined the ruling class and its State, so that it will probably become, with the next elections, the largest Italian party—three times larger than the Socialist party—and be in a position to take on the responsibility of a government in a position of strength.

From this arise a number of problems that are of equal concern to us. 1) Why is it that the most widely spread and best sustained workers' and socialist movement, and also the one that has developed the most advanced anti-capitalist line in Europe, should express itself mainly, either directly or indirectly, through a reformist party? Even if it is true that it also feeds an extreme left which is stronger than anywhere else? Well, the answer to this question may possibly be found in the 'destabilising' nature of the CPI's position. For the Party has always been successful in maintaining a real link with the masses, offering them even on the level of power politics a line that they can follow, even if only to go beyond it afterwards. The answer is also to be found in the political complexity of the CPI's reformism, in the sense that one has the impression that it is offering concrete answers, albeit practical ones to the global problem of an advanced society, a problem which part of the extreme left has often underestimated. 2) Although Berlinguer's reformism has succeeded in modifying the power structure of Italian society to the point where the Party finds itself on the threshold of governmental power, doesn't it, by its very nature, risk being rendered incapable of controlling the processes that its accession to power will set in motion? In fact, it is then that a number of things will become apparent: the poverty of a democracy conceived along parliamentary lines; the illusory character of a programme which aims at overall political control of economic affairs, instead of preparing the ground for a transition to another system; and above all the limitations of a conception of consensus and alliances which instead of enriching the class front, blur it, and, as a consequence, risk leaving the masses defenceless in the face of a new right-wing coalition.

P.H.: Now, twenty years later, are we not witnessing a breach between the interests of the Soviet bloc and those of the Communist parties of Europe (particularly Southern Europe), so that the polycentrism advocated by Togliatti has become an objective reality? Are we not seeing the consolidation of a 'Southern Communism', characterised by an 'electoralist' conception of alliances and transition, and a 'national conception' of socialism? And if so, what are the consequences?

R.R.: The Soviet Union has no interest in seeing any change take place in Europe, as much because of a desire not to upset the dialogue/confrontation taking place elsewhere with the United States, as because the CPI in government would constitute a danger. For a defeat, as in the case of Chile, would amount to a setback for the whole Communist movement. On the other hand, a victory would constitute a challenge which would provide uncontrollable movements in the popular democracies. This is the first bone of contention affecting relationships between Western Communist parties and the Communist Party of the Soviet Union. The second is the fact that the Soviet Union is becoming more and more a military society and that she is tending to militarise as a compensation for her internal failures. This represents a serious danger for the Communist parties: indeed, they fear that Brezhnev, after Angola, might play the same card elsewhere, particularly as they have every reason for thinking that it wouldn't be the cause of internationalism, but because of the need to increase his bargaining power in opposition to the United States.

P.H.: What is your analysis of the open attitude adopted by the CPI towards the extreme left, in particular the PDUP (Party of Proletarian Unity)?

R.R.: Because the CPI is a highly realistic party; because the Party of Proletarian Unity (of which the *Manifesto* is a part) exists, as do Avanguardia Operaia and Lotta Continua; because a left-wing majority can also be achieved with our organisation, as has already happened in some regions and localities. That is what counts in politics. The CPI has not managed to crush us and acts accordingly.

P.H.: Six and a half years after the creation of the 'Manifesto' how effective do you think it has been, and in particular how far does it offer an alternative form of revolutionary politics? From this point of view can you comment on the debates at the Bologna conference of the PDUP and define the direction taken by the party?

R.R.: This will have to be dealt with at greater length another time. I would like to remind you of one fact, which brings us back to the theme of the 20th Congress: namely that in Italy a coherent left-wing criticism of Stalinism has led to the formation of a party with a real worker, student and union base. Admittedly, it is a small party, but it is firmly established, on the left of the vast river of the CPI. It has succeeded in forcing the CPI into a confrontation, on the level of struggles and strategy. Tomorrow, if the country has a government made up of left-wing parties, I do not think it will be possible to avoid the fate of Chile or Portugal, unless a position like ours is adopted. It will be achieved by blocking the dual temptation of a reformist government sliding further and further to the right, and of a movement torn between vanguard groups who rush headlong forward leaving the masses disorientated.

It is against that situation that we are working; looking to Gramsci and the struggles of the sixties for the formulation of a riposte which can already be discerned in our action. Tomorrow, we hope it will be re-integrated with the movement as a whole.

DAYS OF TRAGEDY AND FARCE

by Mervyn Jones

On Tuesday, 30th October, 1956, after a week of street-fighting in Budapest between Hungarian insurgents and Soviet troops, Imre Nagy announced the formation of a multi-party government. Its Communist members—Nagy himself as Prime Minister, Géza Lozonczy, and János Kádár—represented a repudiation of the detested regime of the former Party boss, Mátyás Rákosi; Kádár, indeed, had been imprisoned and tortured under Rákosi's rule. The other Ministers were drawn from the Social-Democratic Party, the Smallholders' Party, and the National Peasant Party (just renamed the Petöfi Party in honour of the democratic revolutionary hero of 1848). The people were promised that elections would be held, but the four parties envisaged a period of 'democratic collaboration'.

This was the culmination of a growing crisis, opening with the death of Stalin in March 1953 and the realisation by his successors that his nominees—such as Rákosi—had reduced their respective countries to a condition of instability. In Hungary, Moscow's policy was initially to find a new Communist leadership which would regain a degree of popularity. Accordingly, Nagy was made Prime Minister in July 1953 and did something to lighten the burdens loaded by Rákosi on to the working-class and the peasants. But Rákosi still had friends in Moscow, remained Secretary-General of the Party, worked to limit or nullify Nagy's policies, and eventually regained full power with the dismissal of Nagy in March 1955. In June 1956 Rákosi was removed as a political liability, but his replacement by the equally contaminated Ernö Gerö meant that the crisis was merely accentuated. In October there was an upheaval in Poland; the Russians appeared to be on the verge of crushing unrest by force, but at the last moment accepted the replacement of the Stalinist team by an apparently 'patriotic' Communist, Wladyslaw Gomulka, who promised democratisation and free elections. In the event, this promise was kept in a pretty dubious way; independent candidates did appear on the ballot, but heavy pressure was put on the voters to approve the official list and no non-Communist parties were legalised. Gomulka proved in time to be as bad as his predecessors and had to be jettisoned in the course of a still more violent upheaval in 1970. However, this was not to be foreseen in October 1956, and the Hungarians—inspired by the Polish example and the

67

Soviet concession, and having burned their boats after fighting began on the night of 23rd October—were in a mood to settle for nothing less than full political freedom. On 24th October Nagy returned as Prime Minister, while Kádár replaced Gerö as Party Secretary-General. The broadening of the government and the promise of elections followed logically.

Also on 30th October, the Soviet Government issued a statement making some remarkable admissions:

> There have come to light several difficulties, several unsolved problems, and several downright mistakes, including mistakes in the relations among socialist states. These violations and these mistakes have demeaned the principle of equal rights in socialist inter-state relationships... The workers of Hungary have... justifiably raised the questions of the need for eliminating the serious inadequacies of the economic system, of the need for further improving the material well-being of the people, and of the need for furthering the battle against bureaucratic excesses in the state apparatus.

Crucially, the statement recognised that the stationing of Soviet troops in Hungary was legitimate only with Hungarian consent; remarked that 'the continued presence of Soviet units in Hungary could be used as a pretext for further aggravating the situation'; announced that the troops were to be withdrawn from Budapest at once, and from the country by means of negotiations; and wound up by saying that 'the defence of socialist gains' was the task of the working people of Hungary.

While these events were greeted by rejoicing in Budapest, the situation on that Tuesday was still rather unstable. During the morning, insurgents attacked the Budapest Party headquarters, which had been occupied by men of the AVH, the hated security police. The building was stormed, and forty-five AVH men were lynched. It turned out later that these particular men were not torturers but young conscripts who had, by no choice of their own, been drafted into the AVH instead of the Army. Still worse, the Party secretary for the city, who was lynched too, was a man of recognised integrity, a veteran of the Spanish Civil War and the French Resistance, and an opponent of Rákosi.

It was on 30th October, too, that the Political Bureau of the Soviet Communist Party held a hastily summoned meeting in Moscow. To all appearances, the policy of withdrawal and concession had been established. The statement quoted above had been issued; Radio Moscow had been allowed to say: 'Reports pouring in from all over Hungary show that the workers support the new Government and approve its programme'; and Marshal Zhukov, the Minister of Defence, had told journalists: 'In Hungary the situation has improved. A Government has been formed in which we have confidence.' It may have been at this meeting, nevertheless, that the decision was taken to crush the Nagy Government and subdue the Hungarian revolt. At all events, on the following day railway workers in eastern Hungary began to inform Budapest that Soviet troops were not moving out of the country, but into it.

*   *   *

On 30th October, 1956, Israeli forces advanced across the frontier with Egypt and reached the vital road junction of Nakhl, in the middle of the Sinai desert. It was revealed later that they were covered, and supplied by means of parachute drops, by French Air Force units, some based in Cyprus—then still under British rule—and some in Israel itself. Two French squadrons had arrived in Israel the day before.

In the afternoon, the British House of Commons heard a statement from the Prime Minister, Sir Anthony Eden. He said that the Israelis were 'not far from the banks of the Suez canal' and that unless hostilities were stopped 'free passage through the canal will be jeopardised'. Accordingly, both Israel and Egypt had been told to stop fighting within twelve hours. Egypt had been asked to agree to the occupation of three towns on the canal by British and French forces. Failing compliance with this ultimatum, the British and French troops would 'intervene in whatever strength may be necessary'.

The same afternoon, the Security Council of the United Nations met in emergency session. The British delegate said that he had not received Eden's statement, but the Soviet delegate read it from a news agency tape. The American delegate moved a resolution calling on Israel to withdraw and on all nations to 'refrain from the use of force or threat of force'. Supported by the USSR, the resolutuion was vetoed by Britain and France.

The next day, British planes began bombing Egyptian airfields.

*   *   *

The double crisis was to last only one more week. At dawn on 4th November, Soviet troops attacked Budapest in overwhelming strength. Resistance here and there continued almost until the end of the month, but on the very first day the outcome was beyond doubt. Nagy took refuge in the Yugoslav Embassy. On 22nd November he emerged to go home, having been given a promise of safety, but he was arrested by Soviet security men and taken to Rumania. In 1958 he was tried in secret and executed.

Nagy had not been surprised by the Russian attack, although most of the citizens of Budapest were. What had been presaged by the troop move-ments in the wrong direction was made certain when Kádár, supposedly a key member of the Nagy Government, did not return from a visit to the Soviet Embassy. In due course Kádár turned up as the head of a new Government which claimed to have invited the Russians to restore order.

Meanwhile, British and French troops were invading Egypt. Paratroops landed on 5th November, seaborne forces the following day. By this time, however, the operation was already doomed to failure, chiefly because the United States refused to tolerate it. Eden is said to have told Mollet, the French Prime Minister, on 16th October: 'The USA will show displeasure, but won't stop us.'[1] He was completely wrong. Not only did the Americans organise effective UN action by using the General Assembly to nullify the Security Council veto; they also exerted financial pressure which threatened a disastrous run on the pound. On 6th November Britain and France had to agree to a cease-fire, effective at midnight. The commander of the invasion force, General Stockwell, remarked later: 'There are many who say: why didn't we take Cairo? It would have been bloody good fun and we would have enjoyed it.' But his troops were stopped by the gong even before they took Ismailia, their objective in the canal zone. In December the British and French troops were compelled to withdraw, and in March 1957 the Israelis had to give up the conquered territory of Sinai and Gaza.

It was difficult, at the time, to establish an intellectual and psychological scale for one's reactions to the double crisis. The Hungarian uprising— whether the Russians tolerated it or crushed it—was clearly an event of tremendous importance. The essence and meaning of the conflict seemed to dwarf the day-to-day happenings and to assume an air of Tolstoyan inevitability. For anyone aware of the historical processes that dominate this century, and particularly for a socialist, it illuminated all the political and moral questions that had presented themselves unavoidably since the death of Stalin, and whose resolution is still being pursued. It was in 1956 that Togliatti first declared that the Soviet Union must not be taken as the 'obligatory model' for socialism, opening a development that leads to Berlinguer's Moscow speech of 1976.

By contrast, the Suez adventure (many commentators were led almost automatically to speak of 'the Suez adventure' but of 'the Hungarian tragedy') had an air of pettiness and absurdity, reflected in the half-nauseating and half-pitiable levity of General Stockwell's words. Never, I think, has history so ironically worn the faces of tragedy and farce at the same time. Suez was a throwback to a vanished age of imperial posturing, a diversion from reality. It was the outcome of a string of silly miscalculations (about everything, even the real importance of the Suez canal when super-tankers were round the corner); it need never have happened, it was as near to being accidental as any actual event can be. One could scarcely help—I was working on *Tribune* at the time—adopting a tone of derisive satire when writing about Suez, while trying to rise to the dignity and gravity of the issue when one turned to Hungary. I well remember the Sunday afternoon of 4th November, when we demonstrated for a Suez cease-fire. While we were pressing toward Downing Street (resisted by the police, whose routine hustling and shoving evoked yells of 'Fascists!' and 'Brutality!', in itself a sign of how far we were from the fatal realities) someone said to me: 'Do you know that the Russians have sent the tanks into Budapest?' I was filled with rage against Eden, not so much for what he had done as for forcing me to waste my time on him.

Now that I return to these disparate themes twenty years later, I still feel as though I were required to review productions of *King Lear* and *Rookery Nook,* and asked by the editor to introduce a link. There are indeed links, to which I shall return in considering the effects of the double crisis on the social and political atmosphere, particularly in Britain. But I want—not merely because I am writing for *The Socialist Register,* but chiefly because time has confirmed the balance of significance which we felt intuitively in 1956—to concentrate on the Hungarian tragedy. The tragedy is precisely that it had to happen; that so many people had to suffer and die in order to reveal the distortions that had been imposed on the socialist ideal.

*   *   *

The antecedents of the Hungarian crisis lie in the imposition of the Soviet system, more or less disguised under the label of 'people's democracy', on eight countries of central and eastern Europe (counting what was at first the Soviet-occupied zone of Germany) following the second world war. The realities which made this a difficult enterprise, in which any schematic timetable was bound to bring more problems than achievements, may be thus summarised:

1. These were economically backward countries in which modern industry either did not exist or had been badly damaged in the war. To create a solid industrial base was necessarily a long undertaking, bringing no rewards for years. To be done at all it required mutual co-operation, not the attempted development of eight self-sufficient economies, with no outside links except bilateral deals with the USSR. External aid was lacking; the deals with the USSR were indeed exploitative, designed to repair that country's war losses, rather than helpful. The rejection of American aid, available to the capitalist nations of western Europe, was bound to be a political handicap.

2. Above all these were peasant countries, and the peasants were hoping for a distribution of land to replace feudal estates by family farms. Considering the low level of equipment, and the number of able-bodied men from the peasant class killed in the war, the nurturing of family farms demanded the maximum both of encouragement by authority and confidence among the peasants. Moreover it was the peasants, denied virtually all human rights in the past, to whom 'liberation' had the most concrete meaning.

3. Politically these countries had lived under open or thinly veiled dictatorships, now discredited thanks to their alliance with Hitler. Habits of popular initiative could be developed only by degrees. Yet there was a considerable demand for a free political life, understood in simple terms of diversity of opinion. There were more people wanting this kind of freedom than ready for socialist objectives. Thus, for a Communist Party to champion such yearnings could only yield political advantages, while to crush other trends of thought and enforce a monopoly of power could attract only distrust. Wisdom suggested isolating fascists and reactionaries, not isolating the Communists from social-democrats or liberals. Imre Nagy had learned this by 1956, but by 1974 it had still not penetrated to Alvaro Cunhal in Portugal.

4. The Communist Parties themselves were small and attenuated by persecution, as well as by losses in the resistance to Hitler. Years of imprisonment or exile had isolated the leaders from popular experience, so that they stood in need of learning as well as teaching. They were by no means automatically accepted as the future guardians. It was simply not possible to run the country on the principle that only a Communist could be trusted. Yet this was done; it was as though, by virtue of having once been secretary of the Chalk Farm branch of the CP, a comrade should be appointed to control the ICI chemical complex, or the port of Liverpool, or Charing Cross hospital. Some comrades were devoted and capable, but of course some were unequal to their tasks and some were corrupted by power and privilege. When things went wrong, they falsified the production figures for fear of punishment, while demanding harder work from the workers in place of effective planning. Meanwhile, even the thin ranks of the Communists were depleted by arrests and purges of the supposedly unreliable, and only the totally subservient—who in many cases had never become Communists through conviction at all—were trusted. Before long, Communists became simply the new masters, hated and despised by the people.

5. Each of these countries cherished its national independence with a sensitivity that had been sharpened by subjection to German overlords. However, the war-weary peoples (especially the peasants) did not necessarily hail the Russian armies as liberators, but sometimes saw them as another invading horde, bringing destruction and prone to looting and raping (of which there was a good deal). Moreover, patriotic and democratic traditions were to a great extent anti-Russian because the Czarist power had appeared as an oppressor. If 'friendship with the Soviet Union' were to be made a reality, it could only be through tactful handling and genuine equality. Instead of this, as soon as Communist governments took control it was apparent that the real authority rested with the Soviet ambassador and the commander of the

Soviet troops. Adulation of all things Russian—Russian, not specifically Soviet—became compulsory; Russian models were enforced in every sphere of economic, cultural and educational life; criticism of the USSR became the worst of crimes. The worship of Stalin intensified the evil, for in Russia he was at least a national ruler and a successful war leader, while in other countries he was simply an alien potentate.

This general picture requires substantial modifications, simply because we are speaking of eight different countries. Czechoslovakia possessed a substantial amount of modern industry, which moreover was largely un-damaged in the war. Czechoslovakia, too, had been a political democracy between 1918 and 1939; a large Communist Party enjoyed so much support that it won 38% of the votes in contested post-war elections. In Yugoslavia, patriotic feelings strengthened the hand of the Communist leaders of the partisan armies; this made Yugoslavia the staunchest champion of the whole bloc until 1948, though it naturally had the reverse effect after the break between Tito and Stalin. In Bulgaria, the ancient enemies were the Turks and the national traditions were pro-Russian. The two countries that conform most accurately to my overall sketch are Poland and Hungary, so it is by no means accidental that the threads snapped in just these countries in 1956.

What the upheavals of that year did was to confront deception with reality. Several Western Communists, who had been to Poland or Hungary as honoured guests to attend peace conferences or youth festivals, or as members of carefully shepherded delegations, went again when the facade had crumbled and found themselves in an utterly different land-scape. The fact is that, as well as the mere ruthless enforcement of the Soviet model, there had been an element of visionary utopianism in the way eastern Europe was managed in the heyday of 'people's democracy'. Huge new industries—for instance, a steel industry in Hungary which had never had one before—were created and at once proclaimed to be a triumphant success.[2] Peasants, having been given land with the break-up of the feudal estates, saw it taken away after a couple of harvests and grouped into collective farms; these were supposed to be an instant success too, though in reality livestock were slaughtered and crop yields declined just as in the USSR in 1929-31. The 'transformers of society' pressed on in a kind of death-or-glory spirit, as though the splendour of the ambition were a talisman promising at least some results. The controlled press and controlled litterateurs fostered the illusion, sometimes cynically and some-times in the grip of auto-intoxication. A poet said to me in Bratislava in 1953 (after several drinks): 'If we had as many tractors as we have poems about tractors we wouldn't know where to put them.' Not only society, but also human nature, was allegedly transformed. There was a great deal of talk about 'the new man', who was said to conduct himself in every respect in a fashion undreamed of before. (This 'new man' went into limbo after 1956, but I was fascinated to meet him again when I went to Cuba in 1968.) Social and psychological changes that would actually have taken decades even if all the material projects had been successful, even if everything had been done by genuine popular initiative and not under orders, and even if there had been no resentment against the privileged class of Party bosses and against the USSR—these changes were imagined to have been completed from one year to the next. I say 'imagined'... I don't know to this day how much was deception and how much was self-deception.

Nagy, in a document submitted to the Central Committee in December 1955, made an eloquent protest that was also a warning:

> Power is increasingly being torn away from the people and turned sharply against them... The leaders have made virtues of self-abasement, of cowardice, of hypocrisy, of lack of principle, and of lies... At atmosphere of suspicion and revenge is banishing the fundamental feature of socialist morality.

Thus the Communist elite, by isolating themselves, produced just the situation that endangered them. They trusted no one, they listened to no one, no one was allowed to tell them the truth, and so they could not know what was going on outside their doors or the curtained windows of their limousines; could not know what the people thought and felt. But the people knew the truth, because that truth was their own experience. The result could only be an intense bitterness, and though it could be deflected by humour (both Poles and Hungarians are proud of their jokes, some of which are indeed very funny) it also built up into a growing anger. At least on the level of consciousness—and it is consciousness, after all, that makes men and women act—outraged impatience with the diet of lies was the fuel for the explosions of 1956.

It was in Poland that the truth was first openly spoken. After the serious disorders at Poznan, which led to many arrests, trials were held at which defendants and witnesses insisted on speaking freely. A young girl shouted: 'My father died for Poland in 1939 and now we are more oppressed than ever.' A young man related that his father had been falsely imprisoned and his mother forced to beg for free soup from a Catholic charity, and went on: 'Poverty made me steal. Can you imagine what this meant to me? My father brought me up in the socialist tradition.' A defence lawyer said: 'People now speak of violations of legality. That is easy to say, but how much suffering, how much unhappiness, lies in those words! The sentence against the defendants will be a sentence against all of us.'

When the lid was really off, it was seen that all the institutions and even the terminology of Communism had been discredited by their perversion under Stalinist regimes. A Hungarian writer, himself a disillusioned

Communist, records what happened when Nagy began his first speech to a
huge crowd on the night of 23rd October:

> 'Comrades', he began—and there were protests and boos from all parts of the
> square. The demonstrators shouted back: 'We are not comrades!' ... At this
> moment all who had eyes must have understood that Hungary was rejecting not
> only Stalin and Rákosi, but all the dictates of the Party, whatever their
> manifestation. The Communist Party had encountered failure, and in an
> irrevocable way.[3]

Similarly, soldiers tore the red star from their cap badges and the
hammer-and-sickle emblem was cut out of the Hungarian flag. Naturally,
this aspect of events was the most painful and disturbing for honest
Communists, whether in Hungary or abroad, and the most gratifying for the
capitalist press. And yet, what was being repudiated was not socialism
itself, as an ideal or as a social system, but the Party's monopoly of power,
its 'dictates'. Within a week, the multi-party government and the promise
of elections became necessities.

Indeed, by 30th October the Communist Party had fallen apart.
Typically, one member pasted his card on a wall with a note reading: 'A
testimony to my stupidity'. The official newspaper, *Szabad Nép*, ceased
publication after hailing the revolution in its last issue. (But new papers
were appearing every day, and by that time there were twenty-five in
Budapest). On 3rd November, Kádár announced on the radio the formation
of a new party, to be called the Hungarian Socialist Workers' Party and
based on 'Communists who fought against the despotism of Rákosi.' Its
role would be 'to defend the cause of democracy and of socialism, the
realisation of which should be achieved not by servile imitation of foreign
examples but in compliance with the economic and historical peculiarities
of our own country.'

The new Party organ told its readers:

> We will no longer be a Party of a million members. We will operate in a more
> modest framework, with limited resources. Those who wish to join the Party must
> understand that their membership will bring them neither an important post nor
> an elevated position. . . Daily tasks, arduous and devoid of any gratitude, will be
> their lot. We face a harsh and laborious future, inconspicuous, without honour,
> without any false supremacy guaranteed by bayonets.

Given this dramatic repudiation of Communist rule, the question that
arose—and was to be furiously debated throughout the European Left—
was whether the Hungarian revolution was actually a counter-revolution.
There are really two questions: (1) was it a genuine popular movement or,
as orthodox Communism later claimed, a plot fomented by American
agents? (2) what was its political content, and hence its probable outcome
had it not been crushed? The first question is much the easier to answer.

Kádár himself is the best witness. In his broadcast of 3rd November, he said:

> In their glorious uprising, the people have shaken off the Rákosi regime... Thousands and thousands of workers and peasants, and veteran fighters who had been imprisoned on false charges—all fought in the front line... You were filled with true patriotism and with loyalty to socialism.

Even if the speech was hypocritical (which on that date it obviously was) the necessity for speaking in such terms proves the point. On 13th November, though Kádár was by now a puppet ruler whose authority was guaranteed by fifteen Soviet armoured divisions, the necessity had not entirely ceased to operate. Speaking to delegates from the Budapest Central Workers' Council—his aim was to persuade them to call off the general strike which was their means of protest—he referred to 'the great popular movement of these last weeks' and said:

> The recent events in Hungary cannot be looked upon as a counter-revolution. But the fact cannot be ignored that, quite apart from the deep indignation of the workers... there were also counter-revolutionary manifestations in the rebellion.

On the same occasion, Kádár repeated his belief in free elections and, making a realistic estimate of the popularity of the reconstituted Communist Party, remarked: 'We must envisage the possibility of total defeat in the elections.' It may be that he really intended to hold elections; if so, the Soviet ambassador told him not to be silly. At all events, whatever was said in *Pravda* or in the *Daily Worker,* no one in Hungary tried to deny that there had been a 'great popular movement' until many months later, when order had been fully restored and the process of myth-making could begin. There is not much myth-making, however, in the official *History of Hungary* prepared by the Academy of Sciences and published in 1973. It tells the reader disarmingly that 'serious and detailed historical research' into the recent period has not yet been undertaken, and it makes the obligatory allusion to 'counter-revolutionary groups'. But it is firm about the evils of the Rákosi regime; it says that in 1956 'the leadership was held in such low esteem and the strength of the opposing forces was so great... that the avalanche of events could no longer be stopped'; and in the context of the uprising it speaks of 'nationalist sentiments supported by a significant percentage of the workers.'

The striking fact is that the Hungarian conflict was in no sense a civil war—unlike, for example, the Spanish civil war in which, though it was right to speak of the Republican cause as 'the cause of the Spanish people', thousands of Spaniards did voluntarily fight for Franco. No Hungarians at all fought alongside the Soviet troops, except the men of the AVH, and they were fighting for their lives. Thousands of Hungarians fought on the side of the uprising, and its strongholds were the working-class quarters of Budapest and industrial towns throughout the country. No Army or police units, let alone workers and peasants, obeyed Gerö's call on 23rd October to 'defend the achievements of our people's democracy.' Soldiers and policemen either joined the insurgents, handed out weapons to them, or merely stood aside. A satirical poster, no doubt composed by someone who listened to Radio Moscow, declared:

> Ten million counter-revolutionaries are at large in the country. Former aristocrats, cardinals, generals and other supporters of the old regime, disguised as factory workers and peasants, are making propaganda against the patriotic government and against our Russian friends.

The second question is more open to argument. There is certainly solid evidence for the view that Hungary would have remained a socialist country. Power 'on the ground'—and guns—were in the hands of workers' councils. All manifestoes by insurgent groups stressed determination to maintain the social gains of the post-war period. Nagy, of course committed to socialism, was by 30th October a highly popular and generally accepted figure. His coalition partners made statements like these:

> No one, I believe, wants to re-establish the world of the aristocrats, the bankers and the capitalists. That world is definitely gone. (Bela Kovács for the Smallholders' Party).
> We shall retain the gains and conquests of socialism to the fullest extent that they can be useful in a free, democratic and socialist country, following the will of the people. (Ferenc Farkas for the National Peasant Party).

Even Cardinal Mindszenty, the most obvious reactionary in Hungary, made a broadcast which was at worst ambiguous and was certainly not, as John Gollan called it, 'the virtual signal for the counter-revolutionary coup.'

On the other hand, most Hungarians were not socialists. In the 1945 election the Social-Democrats had won 71 seats and the Communists 67, while the Smallholders with 246 had a clear majority. The inspiration of the uprising was to a great extent the demand for national independence, with social objectives taking second place, and in Hungary it has never been easy to discern what is patriotism and what is chauvinism. I have noted the presence of indiscriminate anti-Communism. There was no real 'white terror', as Communist organs later claimed,[4] but incidents like the one I described earlier show that any Communist functionary was suspect. Self-styled leaders here and there, and some councils in the provinces, were demanding a government with no Communist members of any stripe. George Mikes, a writer of Hungarian origin who was in Budapest during the uprising as a BBC correspondent, has told us:

> Some people dragged out their hidden Horthyite uniforms and paraded in them. . .
> Reactionary parties smelling strongly of a disreputable past were also re-formed
> in the short period of the victorious revolution. . . I accept that there were
> reactionaries, even Fascists among the revolutionaries. There are such elements in
> all nations and as the Hungarian revolution embraced the whole nation, there
> must have been Fascists among the rebels too.[5]

This is a fair view, I think; and of course the point of principle is that
the task of dealing with reactionaries or Fascists belonged to the Hungarian
people, not to the Soviet Army. But as to what kind of socialism would have
endured in Hungary, one can only speculate. It is pretty certain that the
collective farms would have been dissolved (in Poland, Gomulka allowed
the peasants to revert to individual ownership and they were virtually
unanimous in doing so). Nagy had been pushed by 2nd November into not
merely securing the withdrawal of Soviet troops, but also announcing that
Hungary would leave the Warsaw Pact and follow a policy of neutrality.
In the circumstances this was likely to mean a more or less pro-Western
policy, beginning no doubt with the acceptance of large-scale American
aid to restore the economic situation. Dependence on western markets and
investment by American or other capitalist interests could easily have
followed, as both have followed in non-aligned Yugoslavia. But in
Yugoslavia the national Communists hold undisputed power, whereas in
Hungary this would not have been the case. Even in the revolutionary days
there were voices in Hungary forecasting the country's future as 'a sort of
Sweden' or 'a sort of Austria', and this might well have been the reality.
An important point is that—in contrast to Czechoslovakia during the Dubcek
period in 1968—there had been very little thinking about the lines on which
a democratic form of socialism could be built. In this sense, the Hungarian
revolution happened too soon.

*   *   *

Why did the Soviet Government decide that the Hungarian revolution had
to be crushed? Was the departure of Soviet troops a mere trick, or was
there a rapid change of mind in Moscow—and if so, why? Unluckily, the
secrets of the Political Bureau are well guarded and historians are unlikely
to be given access to the papers even after thirty years. It is also true that
the period from the death of Stalin to the assumption of complete power
by Khrushchev in June 1957 was one of exceptional flux. Decisions like
the rebuff to Rákosi in 1953 (attributed to Beria, interestingly enough)[6]
and his restoration in 1955 show that there was a large element of
vacillation in external as well as internal policy, while Malenkov,
Khrushchev, Molotov and others struggled for the levers of command.

Among the reasons advanced for Soviet action, the following seem significant:

1. On the military level, no General Staff likes to lose a position. Moreover, while the proposition up to 30th October was that Hungary would not be garrisoned (as indeed Czechoslovakia was not) but would remain an ally, the slide toward secession from the Warsaw Pact and neutrality was another matter and might well have been too much for Marshal Zhukov to swallow.

2. Again on the military level, the promise of withdrawal may have been a necessity. The local commander may not have consulted Moscow, and may have blundered, when he instantly responded to Gerö's request for intervention on 23rd October. (A similar request by Gomulka in 1970, when rioters overwhelmed the police at Gdansk, was rejected.) While no rational person would suggest that the Hungarian rebels could have defeated even the Soviet occupation force, that force may well have found itself in difficulties. A single rebel group in Buda is said to have knocked out thirty Soviet tanks, of which there were probably only a few hundred in the country. In several provincial centres the Russian officers came to terms with the rebels and agreed to remain passive unless they were fired on. The main Soviet base was in western Hungary, surrounded by liberated territory and not far from the Austrian frontier, which was soon open and unguarded. It is also suggested, though without much evidence, that Soviet soldiers who had been living in Hungary showed themselves to be unreliable. Altogether, to continue fighting during the last days of October presented problems, whereas to concentrate fresh forces for the 4th November operation was easy.

3. It was widely suggested in Britain that the news of the Suez adventure was a deciding factor. Actually, when the Political Bureau met on 30th October, reports of the Israeli advance were only a few hours old and Eden's ultimatum (prepared in great secrecy, and a surprise to the Americans too) can have come on the tapes only during the meeting. This suggests either quick thinking or panic. The Russian leaders would not have known yet that the Americans had been deceived by Eden, nor that they would take strong measures to check him. A natural suspicion would have been an aggressive move planned jointly by the imperialist powers (it was only a year since the USSR had begun to supply Egypt with arms and think seriously of winning a position in the Middle East)—possibly the danger of world war, in which a retreat from a forward position would have been a distinctly poor start.

Whatever weight one may attach to this theory, I was never much impressed by the related argument that Suez left the Russians free to use force in Hungary without being the only targets of moral odium. Naturally, this argument appealed to Labour leaders like Hugh Gaitskell and anti-Suez Tories who would have liked to see the West—

with Britain and the US in happy amity—concentrating on denouncing the Soviet Union. But (notwithstanding the vain hopes of many Hungarians and the criminally deceptive propaganda of Radio Free Europe) Khrushchev and Zhukov certainly knew that no Western power intended to take effective action to halt the Soviet action; and when the chips are down Moscow has never been greatly bothered by moral condemnations and the cancellation of ballet tours. There was no Suez in August 1968, but that didn't prevent the Russians from sending the tanks into Prague.

But although the balance of moral guilt may not have influenced the decision, Suez did prove very useful to the USSR—especially, of course, in the third world. An *Observer* report from Karachi was typical enough: 'The war in Egypt—a sister Islamic country—killed interest in the Hungarian story... All Hungarian news was relegated to short paragraphs on inside pages of newspapers.' Nehru, who almost took India out of the Commonwealth in revulsion against the Suez aggression, uttered only formal disapproval of Russian behaviour. I can recall an evening at Doris Lessing's flat in which, after hours of agnoized discussion about Hungary, one of her African friends was asked for his opinion; he said that, if we really wanted to know, he thought it was rather nice to see white people shooting other white people for a change.

4. Those who believed that Moscow's withdrawal statement had been sincere argued later that the situation in Hungary changed for the worse as the Soviet evacuation was beginning. Apologists for the Soviet action divided into those who upheld the pristine theory of the counter-revolutionary plot, and those who said that Nagy would have been all right but was being pushed off the stage by more sinister elements. This was the version first advanced by Kádár, who alleged in a radio speech of 11th November that the 'total impotence' of the Nagy Government had 'opened the door to counter-revolutionary forces.' Of course, if this was true it could not also be true that Nagy was the master-mind of the 'armed revolt launched with the active collaboration of imperialists on 23rd October, 1956'—the version 'established' at his trial. But by that time plausibility had ceased to matter.[7]

In reality, any impotence attaching to the Nagy Government was being quickly overcome in the final days. Its authority was recognised by councils in provincial towns who had reserved their attitude before 30th October. Combatant groups accepted subordination to Colonel Paul Maléter, the hero of the defence of the Killian barracks in Budapest, as Minister of Defence at the head of a recognised national army. The morning of the 30th saw the last of the lynchings; after that, AVH men were taken into custody to have their individual records investigated. The workers' councils agreed to call off their strikes, trains and city transport began to run again, shops re-opened and food supplies became normal. Jószef Dudás, who was trying to set himself up as a rival of Nagy and had a band of armed adherents, was arrested—'the order was executed promptly, providing a convincing demonstration of the Government's strength.'[8] Altogether, the most charitable thing one can say is that these hopeful signs appeared too late, since the juggernaut of re-occupation was already rolling. (This would excuse Khrushchev but not Kádár, who was pretending to be loyal to Nagy until late on 3rd November.) One could also say, however, that what Moscow found intolerable was not the impotence of the Nagy regime but its consolidation.

5. Mikes, among others, urges that the turning-point was the formation of the multi-party Government and the promise of free elections:

'The Soviet Union might have tolerated an independent, Communist Hungary; but the decision to hold free elections was an altogether different matter... It was all right for Hungary to become a second Poland; but for her to become a second Finland, or even Austria, was not on the Russian agenda.[9]

This seemed convincing at the time, especially in view of the Soviet decision to tolerate Gomulka, who appeared to be as much of a 'national Communist' as Nagy. (Of course, Poles would say now that the Russians knew more about Gomulka than the rest of us did.) But the explanation loses much of its force when one thinks of Moscow's 1968 decision to put paid to dissidence in Czechoslovakia, where there was no question of a multi-party government, the Communist Party had not collapsed but was functioning vigorously, and the perspective was certainly that of an 'independent, Communist' regime.

So one is driven to the conclusion that the Soviet rulers will not tolerate, in any of the countries subject to their power, the existence of a Government free to take its own decisions and to remould society in response to popular aspirations; that this was as true in 1968 as in 1956, and is doubtless just as true in 1976.

One further question remains. How is that the Kádár regime contrived, from about 1960 onward, to become reasonably viable and—so most reports indicate—to gain a degree of popularity among the Hungarian people? This has been quite a surprise to all the people who wrote in 1956 (including Mervyn Jones in *Tribune*) that Hungarians would never be reconciled to this traitor and quisling. Many Hungarians who fought in the uprising and were passionate followers of Nagy have since accepted posts of responsibility and are doing their best to make the system work. The contrast with Czechoslovakia is striking. There, eight years after the installation of Husak as the Kádár of Prague, few if any adherents of Dubcek have been lured into working for the regime, and the moral and political gulf between Government and people remains as wide as ever.

Kádár, in fact, made serious efforts to avoid any restoration of the Rákosi system. He benefited from the gentler winds blowing in Moscow, where anti-Stalinism reached its peak in the early 1960's, and (it's said) from good personal relations with Khrushchev. People imprisoned for their part in the uprising were released long before the expiry of their sentences and the AVH, with its apparatus of persecution and torture, was not rebuilt. Hungary to this day is in advance of the rest of the Communist bloc in terms of intellectual tolerance and of decision-making based on taking intelligent soundings of opinion. And in the economic sphere it was not too difficult, through rational management and a cautious version of Yugoslav methods, to produce a marked improvement in living standards. Real wages, which had sunk from a 1949 index figure of 100 to 87 in 1953, were up to 159 in 1962.

Most important, perhaps, is the most developed and confident ideology of democratic socialism that took the field in the Prague of 1968—over a period of months, too, rather than ten hectic days—compared to the Budapest of 1956. And the reforming Communists of Czechoslovakia need not feel themselves to be alone; their ideas and hopes are echoed, notably in Italy and throughout the international Communist movement. Despite the dead weight of Moscow, despite all the heartbreaks of the last twenty years and the heartbreaks doubtless yet to come, there is a real sense in which we are entitled to say: *Eppur si muove.*

* * *

The double shock of Hungary and Suez awoke many people, and especially young people, from a kind of political trance. In Britain (I speak of Britain through experience, but in most respects the judgement applies elsewhere) politics had largely ceased to be a real concern. There was a Left in the Labour Party, represented by the figure of Aneurin Bevan, but the dominance of right-wing leaders in the trade unions forced it to batter in vain against the impregnable fortress of the party machine. On the industrial front, union bosses like Arthur Deakin sent in their metaphorical tanks against unofficial strikes and openly declared that they were happy to deal amicably with Tory ministers. Left of Bevan, there was nothing but an impeccably Stalinist CP and a handful of Trotskyist ascetics. What one felt most miserably was an absence of genuine belief or genuine protest. 'There aren't any good, brave causes left'—Jimmy Porter in *Look Back in Anger* seemed to speak for a generation. The phrase was widely quoted, with a kind of melancholy guilt; and yet the play, produced in May 1956, was also one of the signals of still inchoate stirrings.

The first impact of the shock, after a period in which events were generally heard through mufflings of cotton-wool, derived from its brutality. Guns were actually firing and killing people; Tories like Eden were not gentlemen after all, nor was Khrushchev a fumbling but amiable reformer.

According to the chief surgeon, Dr. Esseldine Hoseny, more than 500 Egyptians died in his hospital during the two days of fighting in Port Said. At one point corpses were piled nearly as high as a man's head in three sheds and covered the entire back lawn of the hospital. (Report in *Time*.)

British and French tanks went into the Arab quarter. If a sniper was sighted, a shell was fired at the window where he had been seen. . . Many people were killed in this way. Many more were burned to death. (Report in the *Daily Herald*.)

The Russians behaved with a savagery which surpassed their outrages in 1945 and even those of 1849. On innumerable occasions they opened fire on bread queues. It only took a single shot to be fired from a building for the huge tanks to stop in front of it and fire at it until it was razed to the ground. Ulloi Road. . . practically all the university hospitals stood along this street, one beside the other. Most of them were bombarded, shelled with phosphorous or ordinary shells, many were burnt out, and hundreds of patients, nurses and doctors were killed and wounded. (Mikes, *The Hungarian Revolution*.)

The second impact came from the stench of hypocrisy, transparently false excuses, and plain lies that accompanied both aggressions. The Suez ultimatum was intrinsically dishonest, since the Israelis were told to keep away from the objective—the canal—which they were far from reaching, while the Egyptians were being told to keep clear of a vital artery well within their national territory and behind the bulk of their army. It was soon obvious that the aim of Anglo-French intervention was really to bring down Nasser, the 'military dictator' seen by Eden as a personal enemy. A 'black' radio station in Cyprus was putting out false news in Arabic and urging the Egyptians to rise against Nasser (of course, they rallied round him). Suspicions quickly arose, too, that Eden and Mollet had not been surprised by the Israeli attack, as they claimed, but had been in collusion to take advantage of it. This word 'collusion' became the big issue of succeeding weeks. It is now known that the whole operation had been concerted at a secret meeting near Paris on 16th October.[10]

As for Hungary, the contradiction between the Moscow statement of 30th October and the onslaught of 4th November spoke for itself. The reoccupation was supposed to have been requested by Kádár's new Government, which could not have existed when the dawn attack was launched and was never constituted even under the most rudimentary procedures applied in 'people's democracies'. The Soviet ambassador made repeated denials when questioned by Nagy about reports of Soviet troop movements. Maléter was kidnapped by a trick, when visiting Soviet military headquarters on 3rd November to discuss details of the supposed evacuation (it is said that the Soviet general was not informed and was offended by the irruption of KGB men): Nagy was later kidnapped by another trick. And so on, and so forth.

Stomachs were turned, too, by the outpourings of ideological deception and self-deception—if one may use the word 'ideology' to describe the death-flush of British imperialism. The boasts of the period make pathetic reading today. 'I see Suez as a challenge to our greatness', declared General Glubb, lately bundled out of Jordan where he had commanded the Arab Legion. A now defunct paper, the *Daily Sketch,* assured its readers: 'We do not believe that Nasser would face force even for a day.' (It identified him helpfully as 'the curly-haired mountebank of Cairo'.) In the House of Commons, Tory MPs were moved to utter phrases like this: 'I find myself proud to be living upon this day' (Lord Hinchingbrooke)... 'There are millions of people in every continent who are now thanking God that British leadership in the world has revived' (Mr. John Biggs-Davison)... 'We have accepted the risks. I believe we shall soon see the prizes.' (Mr. Nigel Fisher).

Meanwhile, the Communist press was justifying intervention in Hungary with phrases about 'proletarian internationalism', 'aid to the fraternal Hungarian people', and 'defence of socialist achievements'. The Rákosi regime in all its ugliness was not being restored, although at the time one could not be sure of that. But what was certainly being restored was the contrast between reality and deception.

Out of anger at the killing and disgust at the lies, there came about a rebirth of the moral sense in relation to politics. Good, brave causes—and resistance to fraudulent, evil causes—began to matter again. Not much more than a year after Suez and Hungary, we saw the astonishing response to the Campaign for Nuclear Disarmament. In the early 1960's young English men and women were willing to sit down on missile sites and incur jail sentences of eighteen months—serious sentences for us, if not by the yard-sticks of eastern Europe. Before 1956 that would not have happened, or would have been a disregarded instance of individual quixotry. After the period of the Aldermaston marches came the period of protest against the Vietnam war. I have a sad feeling that this capaicty for strong feeling, for alertness and response, has waned in the 1970's; but it is still stronger than in the dull years before 1956.

Moral conviction, we know, has to go hand in hand with political understanding. This too showed itself in new forms. Three of the side-effects are worth mentioning: (1) Israeli complicity in the Suez aggression sowed the first doubts about whether the cause of Israel was necessarily the cause of the Left. (2) In France, the guilty men of Suez—outstandingly, Guy Mollet—were leaders of the Socialist Party. Their own brand of pseudo-ideology (*'ces hommes de la Résistance incarnaient dans la gauche de l'Assemblée une tradition jacobine de lutte ouverte contre les tyrans aggressifs'*)[11] soon fell apart, the more so as their guilt extended to the horrors of the Algerian war. Across the interlude of Gaullism, one can trace the collapse of this rotten old party and its present revival in a considerably more respectable form. (3) Suez was the last flicker of the authentic old British jingoism. The way in which Britain was brought to heel by the US settled once and for all the relations between the declining and the dominant capitalist power; but there was also, despite a skilful rearguard action by Harold Macmillan, a crucial loss of heart in the Tory Party, and one of the consequences was the concession of independence to most of Britain's African colonies in the ensuing years.

However, one must repeat that if Suez was the end of an era (or the irrelevant postscript to it) Hungary was an early landmark in a still un-folding process. In 1956 we called it de-Stalinisation; now we can see it as a laborious and complex turn toward new perspectives of socialism. It is no denigration of the Hungarian rebels to say, as I think one must, that the lesson they gave us was more negative than positive. They showed conclusively that the old model of despotic Communism was barren and useless. Their repudiation automatically raised the question of what should be put in its place.

Among Marxists, and within Communist Parties such as the British, there had been attempts at new thinking for a number of years. In 1945-48 the idea of 'people's democracy' in eastern Europe—as a form of society that was emphatically socialist but was not the dictatorship of the proletariat—had been seen as innovative and fertile, until the theory was buried under the reality of Soviet tutelage. The debate revived with the 'thaw' following Stalin's death and was greatly stimulated by the revelations of the Twentieth Congress. Then came the Polish October. . . and then came Hungary.

The Communist Party, naturally enough, reeled under the shock. About 7,000 out of 33,000 members left. The *Daily Worker* (which had refused to print the reports of its own correspondent in Hungary, and in various ways covered itself with shame and ridicule) lost prominent and irreplaceable members of its staff. The Party leaders floundered about, un-certain whether to resist all criticisms or to make concessions. Their most obvious difficulty was that they had no sanctions against frank discussion, which often took place on what had been secure territory. For instance, Unity Theatre presented a 'living newspaper' on Hungary and Suez, and the cast and audiences stayed for discussions that went on half the night, in which some speakers roundly condemned both Khrushchev and Gollan. Neither 'loyalty to the Party' nor 'loyalty to the Soviet Union' could be relied on to bring the old Pavlovian reactions.

Fruitful developments were handicapped by the cheap paeans of the press to Hungary's 'freedom fighters'—it was easier for the *Daily Worker* to claim that they had fought to bring Hungary over to the 'western way of life', if the *Daily Express* said so too—and by the general wave of anti-Communism. In Paris the Party headquarters was attacked by a crowd of

Fascists (or they were naturally so described in *l'Humanité*) which was quite a windfall. It was also regrettable, though inevitable, that to the individual Communist the issue presented itself as one of whether to stay in the Party or not. Some people who thoroughly disagreed with the line considered that they ought nevertheless to keep their cards, and quarrelled with friends who were leaving.

Now that one looks back, the encouraging thing is that so many of those who left the CP—in a mood of understandable bitterness and disillusion—retained their socialist convictions. (In saying this, I don't mean to imply that those who stayed have no such convictions.) They joined with socialists who had never been in the CP, or had left it earlier, to set up Socialist Forums and similar bodies all over the place, opening a period of lively discussion which was greatly aided by journals such as the *New Reasoner* and, a little later, the *New Left Review*. Some joined the Labour Party, some found their way in time into groups such as International Socialism, some remained unattached and simply talked and wrote. When CND started, one often found an ex-Communist running the local group. As a whole, what may be called the 'generation of 1956' has made a noteworthy contribution to the politics of the Left and of the Labour movement. It certainly has been a factor in loosening the grip of the heirs of Gaitskell on the Labour Party and carrying on a fight for socialist policies.

In France and Italy, not so many people were inclined to leave Communist Parties that possessed massive working-class support. But there was, none the less, a widespread and insistent pursuit of all the questions raised in 1956. It had been assumed hitherto that a socialist France (or Italy) would be another recruit to the ranks of 'people's democracies', whose alleged successes had been so ritualistically lauded. But ought this to be so, now that at least two of these countries had witnessed a violent repudiation of the system by their own people? Must there be the same subservience to the USSR and alienation of national feelings, the same copying of Soviet methods and institutions, the same rigid discipline and police power, the same outlawing of independent thought, the same single-list elections, the same monopoly of power by the Communist Party? The Italian Communists under Togliatti made a flexible and thoughtful response to these questions, and benefited accordingly. The French Communist leaders set their faces against new thinking and paid the price in May 1968, when the younger generation preferred to follow the independent *groupuscules* and a great popular movement got under way against the will and outside the control of the CP.

It is beyond the scope of this article to trace the steps whereby the international Communist movement has freed itself from the dogmatic control of a single orthodoxy. In the course of the 1960's, however—with China presenting a radically different model of socialist society, with heretical Yugoslavia readmitted to the discussion table, with fresh ideas coming from the third world—Togliatti's dictum that there could be 'no single centre' of socialist development became a plain statement of fact. The demand for national independence was no longer a mere concession to traditional patriotism, but the hopeful pre-condition for variety and initiative. Clearer conceptions of a genuinely democratic form of socialism had been worked out—among western Communists, in the third world, in eastern Europe, and even in the Soviet Union. In 1956 it was axiomatic that the Soviet use of force in Hungary would be endorsed by all official Communist Parties, not to mention 'reliable' fellow-travellers. In 1968 the invasion of Czechoslovakia was condemned by most of these parties—even, with some gritting of the teeth, by the French. This indeed was the start of a change in the French CP, which by degrees has pretty well aligned itself with the Italian. Both stand openly for national independence, rejection of the Soviet model as an infallible guide, diversity of opinion, and a multi-party system under socialism.

When the people of Budapest took to the streets in 1956, they expressed a simple repudiation of the travesty of socialism to which they had been subjected. Yet their action made this travesty unacceptable, for the future, to the intellects and consciences of honest socialists and Communists anywhere; and so it was bound to lead to a refashioning of all our hopes and purposes. Twenty years after the confusion and the tragedy, that ought not to be forgotten.

NOTES

1. *Les Secrets de l'Expédition d'Egypte*, by Merry and Serge Bromberger (Editions des Quatre Fils Aymon, 1957). This curious book, which gives a completely frank account of the aims and planning of the Suez operation, seems to have been fundamentally the work of Guy Mollet. Its main thesis is that Mollet's plan was bound to lead to success, but was stymied by fatal changes on which Eden insisted.
2. The steel complex (named after Stalin, naturally) worked at half-cock because the plan was based on the use of Yugoslav iron ore, which did not arrive after the 1948 break. This might have been admitted without undue loss of face, one would imagine, but it never was.
3. *Thirteen Days that Shook the Kremlin*, by Tibor Meray (Thames & Hudson, 1958), p. 80.
4. The 'White Book' later published by the Kádár regime to sustain the thesis of counter-revolution found 143 'Communists' killed by the rebels; it is certain that the great majority were AVH men. By comparison, over 200 people were killed—before the lynchings—when the AVH fired on unarmed crowds in Budapest and at Magyaróvár. A detailed account of the latter indicent is in *Hungarian Tragedy*, by Peter Fryer, the *Daily Worker* correspondent (Dennis Dobson, 1956). A report by the Indian Embassy stated that 7,000 Hungarians were killed by the Soviet troops, but this can only be an estimate.
5. Mikes, *The Hungarian Revolution* (Deutsch, 1957), p. 161.
6. Meray, p. 7.

7. Fragments of the trial of Nagy and his associates were published in the 'White Book'; the 'evidence' is as poorly concocted as in the Moscow trials of the 1930's. Nagy's nefarious plans were said to be found in a 'secret document', which was in fact the statement he had submitted to the Central Committee in 1955. He was said to have given orders for the 'forcible overthrow of the legal Hungarian Government' at a meeting of conspirators in Budapest at a time when he had actually been seen by hundreds of people at a wine-harvest festival in the countryside.
8. Meray, p. 228. Dudás was executed in January 1957.
9. Mikes, p. 139.
10. The details of collusion are now of purely academic interest, but they may be pursued in *Guilty Men 1957,* by Michael Foot and Mervyn Jones (Gollancz, 1957) and in the Brombergers' book.
11. Bromberger, p. 11. It was this sentence that convinced me that the book was written by Mollet, at least in the sense that the famous *Short History of the CPSU* was written by Stalin.

THE WORKERS' COUNCILS OF GREATER BUDAPEST*

by Bill Lomax

'We may not be able to hold out for long, so let us do such things during our brief tenure of power that the working classes of the world will remember them for ever.'

V.I. Lenin, October 1917

With the second Soviet intervention of 4th November the first phase of the Hungarian revolution was brought to a sudden and violent end. The Government of Imre Nagy collapsed, and he and his leading supporters sought refuge in the Yugoslav Embassy. The leaders and spokesmen of the various political parties disappeared from the scene even more quickly than they had arrived upon it. The armed forces of the revolution put up a last ditch defence in both the towns and the countryside, but soon they were either defeated or forced to flee to the West. The revolution, however, was yet far from over. Instead it was to develop into a new phase, a phase in which the leading role was to be taken by the Hungarian working class.

Unable to keep up armed resistance in the face of overwhelming military supremacy, the workers of Hungary now turned to the most basic and traditional weapon of the working class—to a general strike which was to become one of the most total and united in the whole history of the world working class movement. Their strike was even to lead one Western academic to remark that:

'This was the first time in history that the syndicalist myth of the revolutionary general strike. . . actually became the basis of sustained political action by the entire industrial population of a country.'[1]

The strike, lasting for well over a month, was in its very essence a political strike, employed as a weapon against both the Soviet military occupation and the new Kádár regime. It demonstrated that despite the paper existence of the Kádár Government, despite the very concrete existence of the Soviet armed forces, power in Hungary remained where it

---

*This essay is a chapter from Bill Lomax's forthcoming book *Hungary 1956*, to be published in the autumn of 1976 by Allison and Busby.

had been ever since the 23rd of October—in the hands of the ordinary people, and first and foremost in the hands of the workers.

In the following weeks, the power of the working class was to achieve an even greater strengthening and consolidation. In its beginnings, the strike had been an instinctive reaction of the working class, completely spontaneous and neither centrally directed nor organised. Having realised their power, however, the workers were to proceed to consolidate and organise it in a revolutionary structure of workers' councils set up at the level of the factory, the district, the city and eventually the country itself.

Thus while the Soviet military intervention had crushed overnight the purely political achievements of the revolution, it led at the same time to the consolidation and strengthening of the real social base of the revolution. In the weeks which followed 4th November, the Hungarian workers were to seize the opportunity and to establish a revolutionary structure of workers' councils which would ensure that power remained in the hands of the working people themselves.

The workers' resistance

When Janos Kádár announced the formation of his Revolutionary Worker-Peasant Government on 4th November at the same time as the Russians launched their second armed invasion of Hungary, it was the committed Hungarian socialists, and the Hungarian working class, who turned most strongly against him. And it was in the working class districts of Budapest, and in the industrial centres of the countryside, that the Soviet forces were to meet with the strongest resistance.

On the 5th of November, Radio Rajk issued an appeal to resistance, declaring: 'Comrades! The place of every true Hungarian Communist today is on the barricades!' On the 7th of November, the huge iron and steel complex of the workers' council of Dunapentele, formerly Stalin-varos, the great new industrial city built under the Communist regime, announced that it was being attacked from all sides by Soviet forces:

'Dunapentele is the leading socialist town in Hungary. In this town all the inhabitants are working and they hold the power in their hands.

... The population of the town is under arms... they will not give in because they have erected the factories and homes of the town with their own hands.

... The workers will defend the town against fascism—but also against the Soviet troops.'[2]

A week later it was the turn of the workers' council of Ozd, an industrial centre in North-East Hungary, to defiantly reject the appeal of Kádár's Government for the support of the Hungarian workers:

'No! The working class let Kádár and his colleagues know, that they will never under any circumstances work together with traitors.

The workers from Ozd, Diosgyor, Kazinbarcika, Borsodnadas and Salgotarjan, the miners of the coalfields of Borsod and Ozd stand firm and united against Kádár and Co'.[3]

Similar rebuttals were received by the Kádár regime from all the leading working class centres of the country. The greatest armed resistance of the Soviet forces also occurred in the large iron and steel centres of Dunapentele, Ozd and Miskolo, and in the mining regions of Borsod, Dorog, Tatabanya and Pecs.

In Budapest itself, the Soviet military authorities had to concentrate their heaviest armoured units on the workers' suburbs of Kobanya and Csepel, where the workers had occupied their factories and continued to defend them for several days against the Soviet tanks. One writer claims that hospital figures show that 80-90% of the wounded were young workers, while the Kádár regime's own reports show that the greatest damage to buildings and the greatest number of deaths occurred in the predominantly working class districts of the city. The stately villas and gardened houses of the fashionable middle class districts on the slopes of the Buda hills were hardly touched by the fighting.[4]

The major organised centres of resistance in Budapest—the Kilian barracks and the Corvin cinema, the citadel on the Gellert hill and the Buda castle, as well as such prominent intersections as the Moricz Zsigmond, Szena and Marx Squares—were the first targets of the Soviet assault, but even so they were not put out of action until the 6th or 7th of November after three days and nights of heavy fighting. In the outlying districts of Ujpest and Kobanya fighting continued for a few days more. 'Red Csepel' was the last workers' district to fall but then only when, having put down resistance in the rest of the city, the Soviets could move all their major units against Csepel on the 10th and 11th of November.

The military defeat of the workers, however, by no means assured the immediate victory of the new authorities for the workers still held the trump card—their control over production. Following the Soviet occupation, the workers were to refuse to return to work, and in the course of the ensuing general strike, to organise themselves in workers' councils at factory, district, city, and eventually national level. Through the strike and the workers' councils, they were to carry on the struggle of the revolution and to withstand for several weeks the counter-revolutionary assault of both the Kádár regime and the Soviet authorities.

The development of district workers' councils

Those workers' councils which had been in an active stage of development prior to the 4th of November were also the first to reorganise as the fighting died down. They were also the first to realise that to defend the achievements of the revolution they would have to cooperate with one another and coordinate their activities. With this aim in view, the workers' councils of the larger factories took the lead in setting up district workers' councils in their local neighbourhoods. The first of these was probably that in the Kellenfold district of Budapest, where the lead was taken by the workers of the Beloiannis electrical equipment factory. As early as the 8th of November, a delegation from this district workers' council was even received by General Grebennik, the Commander-in-Chief of the occupying Soviet forces.

The Ganz electrical works in Csepel took a similar lead in the creation of a Csepel Workers' Council, which also sent delegations both to the Soviet Commander and to Kádár. Between the 8th and 12th of November, further local workers' councils were established in the districts of Kispest, Zuglo, Obuda, Angyalfold and Ujpest.

In slight contrast to the factory workers' councils, whose major task had been to take over the management of their enterprises, these district workers' councils were from the start essentially political organs. They saw their role as to defend what they could of the achievements of the revolution, and to represent the interests of the workers vis-a-vis the Kádár Government and the Soviet military authorities. Uniting their common stand, however, was the demand that the factories should be the common property of those who worked in them, that production should be managed by the democratically elected organs of the workers themselves, by the workers' councils.

The first statement of the political demands of the workers to be made after the 4th of November was put forward in a resolution of delegates from workers' councils of the Kellenfold district at a meeting on the 12th of November. This resolution declared the readiness of the workers to return to work and to negotiate with the Kádár regime, on condition that certain of their political demands were met. In the forefront of these demands stood the immediate release of Imre Nagy and his supporters, an immediate cease-fire, and a commitment to the withdrawal of the Soviet troops and the holding of free and democratic elections. At the same time, the workers emphasised that the factories and the land must remain in the hands of the working people, and called for the enlargement and strengthening of the power and authority of the workers' councils.[5]

The creation of the Central Workers' Council

It was also on the 12th of November, at a meeting of the Revolutionary Workers' Council of Ujpest, that the first move was made towards the creation of a central body to coordinate the activities of workers' councils throughout the whole of Budapest. The meeting was also attended by workers' delegates from the neighbouring district of Angyalfold, and by a few students and young intellectuals.

It was a young Budapest intellectual, Miklos Krasso, who called upon the Ujpest workers' council to take the lead in issuing an appeal for the formation of a central workers' council which would represent the workers of the whole of Budapest, and be able to negotiate in their name directly with the Kádár regime and the Soviet authorities. The suggestion received support from the older workers present, and the workers' council agreed to call upon other workers' councils throughout the city to send delegates to a meeting in the town hall of Ujpest the following afternoon in order to set up a central workers' council.[6]

The students attending the meeting agreed to arrange for the duplication of the appeal, and its distribution throughout the city. Indeed, two of those present left the Ujpest meeting to proceed directly to the district workers' councils in Csepel and Kellenfold.

However, on the morning of the 13th of November, several members of the Ujpest workers' council were arrested, and delegates arriving for the meeting to set up a central council found the town hall of Ujpest surrounded by Soviet tanks. Many of them, nevertheless, were directed to the nearby United Lamp Factory, *Egyesult Izzo,* but since many of the districts and large factories were not represented there, it was decided to put off the founding meeting of the central council until the following day.

This is how it came about that on the afternoon of 14th November, the founding meeting of the Central Workers' Council of Greater Budapest finally took place in the *Egysult Izzo* factory in Ujpest. Some fifty delegates were present, representing all the major factories and districts of Budapest. Delegates also attended from the provincial centres of Miskolc and Gyor.

Some confusion now arose from the fact that the proceedings were not presided over by the members of the Ujpest workers' council who had originally convened the meeting, but by the leaders of the workers' council of the *Egyesult Izzo* factory in their capacity as hosts. Consequently, when the young intellectual who had originally proposed the creation of a central workers' council two days earlier arose to expand on his ideas, he was pulled up short by those now present who argued that they had not come to be lectured to, least of all by someone who was neither a worker nor a representative of any workers' organisation. Then, while a lively debate ensued in which the workers' delegates were quite clear and united in their political demands and in their will to create a central organisation, they were vague and unsure as to the form of organisation they required, and the strategy to adopt for the realisation of their demands.

It was Sandor Bali, a delegate of the Beloiannis electrical equipment factory, who was the first to impose any real direction on the meeting. Bali argued that the workers' councils should not recognise the Kádár

Government, but that they should be prepared to parley and negotiate with it. With this aim in view, he proposed the creation of a central workers' council which, at the same time as giving overall direction to the general strike, would be able to represent the demands of the workers and win concessions from the Kádár Government.

Bali's proposal was accepted by the meeting, which declared the establishment of the Central Workers' Council of Greater Budapest with the authority to negotiate in the name of the workers of all the factories of Budapest. The meeting also called for the election of district workers' councils throughout the city, and for new elections to the factory workers' councils as soon as possible. Finally, the meeting passed a resolution which declared the workers' loyalty to the principles of socialism and their determination to defend the collective ownership of the means of production. The resolution went on to outline the workers' political demands which included a general amnesty, a Government under Imre Nagy, the withdrawal of the Soviet troops and the abolition of the one-party system. Until these demands were met, they declared, the general strike would continue.[7]

The Composition and Organisation of the Central Workers' Council

The delegates to the founding meeting of the Central Workers' Council made up an interesting selection of workers from the major local districts and the larger factories of Budapest. Many of them were long-standing members of the working class movement, with past political experience in either the Social Democratic or the Communist Party, and often both. Several of the older workers had also been active in the militant pre-war Metalworkers' Union. At the same time, the meeting was remarkable for the strong representation of young workers, almost a half of the delegates belonging to the age group 23 to 28. These younger workers added enthusiasm and dynamism to the experience and responsibility of the older delegates. There was also, within both age groups, a very strong representation of skilled workers—engineers, metalworkers, toolmakers and electricians. A number of students and young intellectuals also attended the meeting as observers.

Following the debate and the decision to set up the Central Workers' Council, it became increasingly clear that some more formal structure was necessary to give order and direction to the proceedings. Consequently, the meeting elected a provisional committee of some twenty-odd members, whom it authorised to draw up a more orderly and precise programme of action. Amongst the members of this provisional committee were to be found most of those who were subsequently to become the effective leaders of the Central Workers' Council. Though the exact composition of this committee has never actually been documented, we do know the identity of a good half of its members, who may not be unrepresentative of the body as a whole. They included:

Istvan Babay:	Delegate of the Municipal Company of Tramways.
Arpad Balazs:	Delegate from Ujpest, and a worker in the mining machinery factory.
Jozsef Balazs:	Delegate from Angyalfold, and a turner in the steel works *Magyar Aczel*. Veteran of the Metalworkers' Union, and Communist Party member since 1945.
Sandor Balazs:	Delegate of *Egyesult Izzo*, toolmaker and veteran of the Metalworkers' Union.
Sandor Bali:	Delegate of the Beloiannis factory and the Kellenfold district. A 40-year old toolmaker, veteran of the Metalworkers' Union, member of the Social Democratic Party before the war and of the Communist Party since 1945.
Jozsef Devenyi:	Delegate of the workers' council of the Csepel iron and steel works.
Gyorgy Kalocsai:	Delegate from Csepel, and a 32-year old chemical engineer in the Vegetable Oil Factory.
Sandor Karsai:	Delegate from Kobanya, and a 26-year old metal engineer in a factory producing radiators.
Miklos Sebestyen:	Delegate of the Hungarian Optical Works, and a 26-year old metallurgist.
Ferenc Toke:	Delegate from Zuglo, and of the workers' council of the Telephone Apparatus Factory. A 26-year old toolmaker, and former member of the Social Democratic Party.

From the very start, the most prominent of these individuals was Sandor Bali who had given both drive and direction to the creation of the Central Workers' Council. It was also he who was to provide the larger political conceptions within the framework of which the Central Workers' Council was to develop and organise. Characteristic of his personal honesty and socialist spirit, despite being an active member of the Communist Party since 1945 and a more than able toolmaker, he had remained amongst the workers on the shopfloor when many others were seeking positions of management and privilege. Now too, though the undisputed driving spirit of the Central Council and frequently its most prominent spokesman, he was content to remain in the position of a simple member.

Shortly to achieve an equal prominence to that of Sandor Bali was Sandor Racz, another toolmaker at the Beloiannis factory and the president of its workers' council. Only twenty three years old, Sandor Racz was the most active representative of the younger workers, and a man whose character combined profound sincerity with both dynamism and determination. Somewhat more militant than Sandor Bali, he was a vocal advocate of the creation of a national workers' council, and was later to be elected president of the Central Workers' Council.

Elected secretary of the Central Workers' Council was Istvan Babay, a delegate of the Company of Tramways. The Council's headquarters were shortly to be moved to the city centre offices of the Company of Tramways, and Istvan Babay was to perform the day to day administrative tasks involved in running the Council.

Sandor Karsai, a young fitter who had worked his way up to become a metal engineer at a factory producing radiators in Kobanya, was very popular with the workers and became head of the political commission of the Central Council. He had insisted from the start on the importance of formualting a long-term perspective for the workers' councils, and of clarifying their proper role within the economic and political system.

Two other members of the provisional committee, Miklos Sebestyen and Ferenc Toke, are also worthy of special note since they have both subsequently provided accounts of the activities of the Central Workers' Council. Miklos Sebestyen, a young engineer who had learned a number of Western languages, became head of the Council's press commission and assumed responsibility both for holding press conferences for foreign journalists, and for producing the Council's information bulletin. Ferenc Toke, a young worker who had attended evening classes at the Technological University where he had come into contact with the students' movement, was made responsible for organisational matters.

Besides those already mentioned, amongst others who joined later in the work of the Central Council was Lajos Varga, a worker from the workers' council of the Zuglo district who could speak Russian, and who took charge of the Council's relations with the Soviet military command.

The plenary meeting of the Central Workers' Council, however, was not a permanent body but a delegate assembly, made up of two representatives from each of the district workers' councils of Greater Budapest. Consequently, the delegates attending its different meetings were not necessarily always the same people. At first the only appointed official was the secretary, Istvan Babay, and members of the Council took it in turn to preside over its meetings. This arrangement, however, proved to present a number of problems, and eventually Sandor Racz was to be appointed as a permanent president, with Gyorgy Kalocsai as vice-president.

The Central Workers' Council also set up a secretariat with seven commissions for the supervision of particular fields of its activities. Their heads were Sandor Racz, Sandor Bali, Gyorgy Kalocsai, Sandor Karsai, Istvan Babay, Miklos Sebestyen and Ferenc Toke. Since they included the three permanent officials of the Central Council, it is obvious that these seven constituted the effective leadership or working executive of the Central Workers' Council of Greater Budapest.[8]

The Strike Issue

Having created a working executive and prepared a platform of political demands, the Central Workers' Council appointed a 19-man delegation under the leadership of a Csepel delegate, Jozsef Devenyi, to present the demands of the workers of Budapest to the Kádár Government. This delegation met with Kádár in the parliament building on the evening of 14th November.

Kádár, in a most remarkable speech, declared his agreement in principle with most of the demands of the delegation, namely in regard to Imre Nagy's participation in the Government, to democratic elections with several political parties, and to the eventual withdrawal of the Soviet troops. In the same breath, however, he argued that these demands could not be met immediately under the prevailing circumstances, and while calling upon the workers to first return to work, he offered no guarantee that their demands would be implemented. Thus, while appearing conciliatory, Kádár did not in fact give way on a single point. Consequently, the Central Council delegates felt that they could not make any concessions either, and the meeting broke up with no obvious results or achievements.[9]

Meanwhile, the initial informality of both the structure and proceedings of the Central Workers' Council was giving rise to a number of problems. At first the Council had no permanent chairman or president, or even officially appointed spokesman. Rather, the first meeting had been chaired by an Ujpest delegate, Arpad Balazs, and he was then mandated to act as spokesman to make known the Central Council's standpoint to the public. Arpad Balazs, however, used the opportunity to issue a radio appeal that same evening, 14th November, calling for an unconditional return to work in the name of the Central Workers' Council. Learning of his action, other members of the Council concluded that he was a Government agent who had infiltrated the Council, and he was removed from its membership.

Arpad Balazs was then replaced by Jozsef Devenyi, who had led the delegation to Kádár on 14th November, but in subsequent days he too took up an almost equally equivocal attitude towards the strike, and generally acted in a rather indecisive manner. Consequently he soon came to be regarded as an opportunist who was inclined to compromise with the Kádár regime, and he too was removed from the Central Council. The situation was eventually resolved by the election of the more militant and combative Sandor Racz as a permanent president of the Central Council.

Meanwhile, the debate continued within the Central Council over the attitude to adopt towards the Kádár Government and towards the continuation of the strike. The Central Workers' Council had now moved its headquarters to the offices of the Municipal Company of Tramways in central Budapest, and a second meeting was held there on the 15th of November which was considerably more representative of the workers of the whole of Budapest. More district workers' councils had sent their delegates to this meeting, while a meeting of delegates from the workers' councils of another twenty-five large factories had also voted to join forces with the Central Workers' Council. Several delegates from workers' councils in the provinces also took part in this session.

The main issue before the meeting arose from the failure of the meeting with Kádár. While some delegates called for outright opposition to the new authorities—'We have no need of the Government! We are and shall remain the leaders here in Hungary!' declared Sandor Racz—the majority of delegates favoured seeking a compromise settlement with the Government. It was Sandor Bali who proposed that while refusing to grant *de jure* recognition to the Kádár Government, they should not hold back from establishing a *de facto* relationship with it.

The central question, however, remained that of the strike. A number of delegations, most notably those from Csepel and Gyor, favoured an unconditional return to work designed to give the Government time to prove the sincerity of its intentions. Others, in contrast, argued for a total and resolute strike, refusing all offers of compromise and holding out for the full implementation of their demands. Once again, Sandor Bali won support for a policy of moderation. The country, he declared, was in a condition of severe devastation, and the workers' councils had no reserves to draw on for a long strike. In this situation, he suggested, the workers should offer to return to work in return for substantial concessions from the Kádár Government. Moreover, by such action they could demonstrate that the strike was not just a spontaneous and unorganised reaction of the workers, but an organised and formidable weapon consciously directed for the implementation of the workers' demands.

A new delegation was formed and sent again to Kádár in a deliberate spirit of conciliation. However, this delegation met with just the same rebuttal as the earlier one. While Kádár appealed to the Central Workers' Council to call off the strike, he would not, or could not, offer any guarantees for the satisfaction of their demands.

Nevertheless, pressures for a return to work were building up throughout the city. As the bitter Hungarian winter approached, the general strike came to be seen as a lethal weapon to those who used it as well as to those against whom it was directed. On the 15th of November, the Central Workers' Council of Csepel had called for a return to work. The next day, the Central Workers' Council of Greater Budapest followed suit, and agreed to call for the resumption of work throughout the city on Monday, 19th November. At the same time, they insisted that they were not abandoning any of the popular demands of the revolution.

Not everyone, however, was happy with the decision to call off the strike. Far from having been pressganged into going on strike by the Central Workers' Council, as the Kádár regime tried to make out, many of the workers were bitterly opposed to the return to work, and felt that the

Central Council had betrayed the strikers. Indeed, some members of the Central Council were almost beaten up by angry crowds of workers protesting outside the Council's headquarters. When other delegates arrived later from the countryside, several of them turned angrily on the leaders of the Central Council, 'calling us all possible names: scoundrels, traitors, etc.'[10]

Relations with the Soviet Military Command

Besides attempting to negotiate with the Kádár Government, the Central Workers' Council also entered into direct contact with the Soviet military authorities under the command of General Grebennik. The first contacts were made in an effort to prevent deportations, and to secure the release of Hungarians arrested by the Russians. An agreement was reached whereby the Central Workers' Council presented the Soviet military command each day with a list of missing workers' council members, and the Russians then saw to their release from prison. The workers' councils also acted as intermediaries in the distribution of provisions and medical supplies to the population.

In these arrangements, the Soviet command dealt directly with the Central Workers' Council, completely over the heads of the Kádár Government, and in so doing effectively recognised the Central Council as the representative organ of the Hungarian workers. Indeed, each member of the Central Council was even issued with a special Soviet pass authorising the bearer to travel freely after curfew, as well as a permit to carry arms.

At first, representatives of the Central Council would go to the Soviet military headquarters for talks, but later on Soviet officers were sent to attend the sessions of the Central Council. Eventually the Russians actually delegated a Soviet colonel with an interpreter as a permanent representative to the Central Workers' Council, and on one occasion a group of Soviet officers accepted an invitation to visit a local factory and hear the Hungarian workers express their views.

On the whole, the Soviet representatives acted very correctly and with apparent sympathy for the workers' councils. Most reports, however, suggest that they were somewhat confused as to just what role the workers' councils were seeking to perform, and it is very probable that their conciliatory attitude had been ordered from above. Certainly their attitude was quick to change at the beginning of December when General Grebennik was recalled to Moscow and replaced by the Russian secret police chief, General Ivan Serov.

The National Workers' Council

Proposals to create a National Workers' Council had been put forward at several meetings of the Central Workers' Council ever since its foundation, but the action had been put off until a meeting could be held of democratically elected delegates from the workers' councils of the whole country.

A detailed plan for the constitution of a National Council which would serve as a 'Parliament of Workers' Councils' was put before the Central Workers' Council on the 18th of November. The plan proposed the creation of a 156-member assembly of delegates from the workers' councils of the districts of Budapest, and of the counties, as well as from a number of the largest factories. This assembly would elect a 30-member presidium which would have the right to co-opt up to 20 further representatives of the universities, the army, the police, the intellectuals' organisations and the political parties. The Central Workers' Council approved the plan and on the 19th of November issued an appeal to all workers' councils in Hungary to send delegates to a conference in the Budapest sports stadium on 21st November to set up a National Workers' Council. 'The principal task of this national conference', states one of the signatories of the appeal, 'was to create a power under the direction of the workers, and in opposition to the Government.' Invitations to attend the meeting were also issued to both the Kádár Government and the Soviet military authorities.[11]

At 8 a.m. on the morning of the 21st of November it almost looked as though General Grebennik had accepted the invitation to the conference—some four hundred Soviet tanks had appeared on the streets, surrounding the sports stadium, and blocking off all the roads leading to it. Delegates arriving for the conference, however, were quietly redirected to the headquarters of the Central Workers' Council in the city centre, where the national conference was able to take place after all, despite the Soviet display of force. Besides the representatives of Budapest, delegates arrived from workers' councils in Gyor and Veszprem, Tatabanya, Pecs and Komlo, Ozd and Salgotarjan. There were also a number of peasants' delegations from smaller villages.

Many of these delegates, however, had arrived in an angry mood, believing that the leaders in Budapest had betrayed them by calling off the strike. The miners' delegates from Tatabanya, Pecs and Salgotarjan were the most angry and uncompromising. 'You can work if you want,' they declared, 'but we shall provide neither coal nor electricity, we shall flood all the mines!' The sending of Soviet tanks to prevent the meeting of the national conference showed what one could expect from negotiations with Kádár. The only answer to such people, they declared, was to maintain the general strike.

With some difficulty, the leaders of the Central Workers' Council managed to convince the delegates from the provinces that they were not collaborating with the Government, and that a continuation of the strike in Budapest would only cause misery to the population and disorganise the workers' forces. At the same time, the meeting decided not to officially constitute a National Workers' Council for fear that this might serve as a pretext for the Kádár regime to ban the Central Workers' Council too and clamp down on the workers' councils elsewhere. Nevertheless, the meeting had in fact established the basis for a permanent liaison between the Central Workers' Council and the workers' councils in the provinces, and in this way a National Council had in effect been brought into being. Finally, the meeting issued a proclamation restating the workers' demands and declaring that their full cooperation with the Government could not be assured until their demands were met.

Meanwhile, the news that the sports stadium had been surrounded by Russian tanks had given birth to rumours throughout the city that the national conference had been prevented from meeting and the delegates arrested. Before the national conference had completed its deliberations, the workers had launched a protest strike, and by the time the Central Workers' Council learned about it, the strike was almost total throughout the city. Faced with the reality of the strike, the leaders of the Central Council agreed to give their backing to it, in protest against the attempt to prevent the national conference from meeting. Acting partly in solidarity with the strikers, partly under the pressure of the delegates from the provinces, they declared an official 48-hour protest strike.

From the sports stadium to the parliamentary conference

From the very beginning, the Central Workers' Council of Csepel had acted in a somewhat independent fashion. They had from the first been opposed to the strike, and in favour of a more trusting attitude towards the Government. At the same time, though, they were just as adamant as the Central Council in Budapest in demanding the withdrawal of Soviet troops and free elections with a plurality of political parties. Equally resolutely, they condemned the attempt to prevent the meeting of the national conference on the 21st of November and the continuing arrests of members of workers' councils.

However, on the 22nd of November, the workers' council of the Csepel iron and steel works went a good step further out of line in condemning the call of the Central Workers' Council of Greater Budapest for a 48-hour protest strike. The time for such head-on collisions with the Government had, they delcared, passed. Nevertheless, the Csepel workers themselves proved as ready as those in the rest of Budapest to answer the strike call. In view of this situation, the Central Workers' Council decided to send a special three-man commission to Csepel to investigate the local workers' councils' opposition to the strike and to the Central Council. In the following days, however, the workers of Csepel themselves set matters right in new elections to their workers' councils. In these elections those leaders who had opposed the strike, including the former president of the Central Workers' Council of Csepel, lost their positions and were replaced by more militant workers prepared to work in greater solidarity with the Central

Workers' Council of Greater Budapest.

Following the over-reaction of the Soviet authorities in sending tanks to prevent the meeting of the national conference on the 21st of November, the Central Workers' Council went out of its way to avoid any action that might be taken as a provocation and prejudice the attempt to reach a compromise settlement with the Kádár Government. With such considerations foremost, the Central Council's activity turned increasingly to the organisation of passive resistance. One of the first instances of this was the silent demonstration on the 23rd of November in commemoration of the revolution. The suggestion that noone should go out onto the streets of Budapest between 2 and 3 p.m. in the afternoon was put forward by the Revolutionary Council of Intellectuals and taken over by the Central Workers' Council. The call to the people of Budapest was followed unanimously, perhaps particularly so because on this very day came the news of the abduction of Imre Nagy and his companions from the Yugoslav Embassy. The occasion is recalled by an eye-witness:

> 'Budapest, in a matter of one second, became a haunted city. Haunted only by the Russian armoured cars driving from one place to the other, but to no avail. The silence was more eloquent than any shot which might have been fired at them.'

The most significant attempt to reach some form of agreement between the Central Workers' Council and the Kádár Government occurred on the 25th of November, when a conference between the two sides was held in the parliament building. In speeches to the workers' leaders, Janos Kádár, Gyorgy Marosan and Antal Apro appealed to the workers' councils to help the Government in the estbalishment of order and the resumption of production. The workers, Kádár argued, were confused and did not know which road to follow. It was the duty of the workers' councils, he continued, to support the Government in leading the workers away from the counter-revolution. To this, Sandor Bali replied: 'There is no confusion in the spirit of the workers, but rather in yours!'

'You ruffians!' exclaimed Marosan in return, 'To think you can give us a lecture! You are prolos indeed! But what have you in common with the workers?'[12].

In such an atmosphere, it is hardly surprising that the conference ended without any agreement being achieved, and if anything the two sides moved further apart. Having failed to win the cooperation of the workers' leaders, the Government was increasingly to charge the workers' councils with being unrepresentative of the working class as a whole, and to use force and coercion against them. At the same time, the confrontation hardened the views of the workers' leaders, and strengthened the arguments of those calling upon the Central Workers' Council to act as an independent political force. This standpoint was made clear in a speech to the conference by Sandor Bali who asserted:

> 'It is the Hungarian working class which has set on foot the workers' councils, which for the moment are the economic and political organisations that have behind them the working class.'

In similar tones, in an appeal to all workers' councils throughout Hungary issued on the 27th of November, the Central Workers' Council proclaimed:

> 'We reaffirm that we have received our mission from the working class. . . and we shall work with all our might for the strengthening of the workers' power.'

'The time has now come,' recalls Miklos Sebestyen, 'to strengthen the activity of the Central Workers' Council and to assert ourselves as a political force recognised as such by the people.'[13]

A Workers' Journal

The last week of November saw increasing efforts by the authorities to misrepresent and undermine the workers' councils. For instance, at the parliamentary conference Gyorgy Kalocsai had denounced provocative actions by stalinist elements in the factories, but his speech was reported on the radio as an attack on 'provocative fascist elements'. The Central Workers' Council took even greater exception to the overall picture of the parliamentary conference given by Kádár in a radio broadcast on the 26th of November, in which he attacked the workers' councils as counter-revolutionary forces, and said they would either have to support the Government or shut up shop.

The re-formed secret police also set to work to undermine the workers' councils, and forged leaflets in the name of the Central Workers' Council calling both for a continuation of the strike and for armed action against the Soviet authorities. These provocations were obviously aimed both at disrupting the unity of the workers' councils, and lending support to allegations that they were instigating counter-revolutionary actions.

In view of these incidents, the Central Workers' Council came to the conclusion that it would have to issue a journal to keep the factories and the country truly informed of its activities. Most of the printing shops, however, were occupied by the Soviet forces, and the Government was adamant in refusing the Central Council any authority to publish its own journal. Despite this, the Central Council set up a press commission under Miklos Sebestyen who got together with a number of young journalists, intellectuals and students to bring out a paper under the simple title of *Munkasujsag* or *Workers' News*. They even arranged with the workers' council of a small printing shop to print the paper without official authorisation.

The first numbers of the *Workers' News* were already coming off the press, when leading members of the Central Council arrived to announce that the Government had made it known that it would regard such activities as a provocation, and so the Central Council had decided not to go ahead with publication. Instead, they agreed to continue with the duplicated *Information Bulletin* which was already being produced and distributed through the workers' councils.

Despite the step-down by the Central Council, the Hungarian authorities still raided the printing works, seizing the few copies of the *Workers' News* that had been printed, and trying unsuccessfully to arrest Sebestyen. At the same time, the Soviet authorities seized the duplicating machines in a number of large factories, in an attempt to prevent the propagation of the Central Council's bulletin. These actions, however, served only to increase the workers' interest in the *Information Bulletin,* typed copies of which were now passed from hand to hand in the factories, read out to workers' meetings, and relayed to provincial towns over the telephone. At the same time, the Central Workers' Council called upon the workers to boycott the Communist Party daily *Nepszabadsag,* and all other official papers with the exception of the *Sports News.*

Battle for control in the factories

Meetings between the Central Workers' Council and the Kádár Government continued almost daily but while Kádár continued to express his agreement in principle with the workers' demands, he insisted that in the existing situation the first task had to be the restoration of order, i.e. the strengthening of his Government's power. In practice, however, the more the authority of the Government was increased, and the more it sought to restrict the activities and competence of the workers' councils. In this spirit, a decree on the workers' councils was issued on the 22nd of November which sought to restrict their activity to purely economic and not political functions.

At other times Kádár seems to have been on the verge of reaching some compromise with the Central Workers' Council, but to have been over-ruled by the hardliners in the Government and Party leadership. For instance, at one point Kádár offered to recognise the Central Workers' Council as a national council of producers which would have a leading role in the administration of the economy, but the decree effecting this proposal was vetoed by the stalinist members of his Government.

For a time the Government sought to persuade the workers' councils to function within the framework of the official trade unions, but the Central Workers' Council categorically refused even to negotiate with the official trade unions which they regarded as bureaucratic organs of Party control in no way representative of the workers. As Sandor Bali explained:

'We mustn't, indeed we cannot, talk about trade unions until the Hungarian workers have themselves built up their organisations from the base up, and have won back the right to strike.'

The Central Workers' Council, its leaders explained, was ready and willing to cooperate with independent and democratic trade unions which represented the interests of the workers. To make the unions into such organisations, the Central Council demanded new democratic elections within the trade unions. Such elections had been agreed to before the second Soviet intervention, but after the 4th of November the official union leadership continually postponed the elections, contending that, 'the atmosphere in the factories. . . was not conducive to the holding of democratic and secret elections.'[14]

The end of November also saw the intensification of conflict at the level of production itself, as the Communist Party attempted to rebuild its organs of control within the factories, to deny the workers' councils the right to appoint and dismiss factory directors, and to reorganise the trade unions and the secret police.

The workers' councils had been unanimous that they would allow no party organisations within the factories, and when Communist Party officials sought to return and re-establish the organisations that had existed before the revolution, many were banned or even physically prevented from entering the factories. With regard to the trade unions, the workers' attitude varied from place to place. Where the unions had remained under the control of former stalinist functionaries, they too were banned from the factories, and the workers demanded that they be represented either by the workers' councils themselves, or by unions independent of party control. In other cases, where local union leaders had supported the revolution and now refused to join Kádár's Communist Party, the unions were able to retain the confidence and support of the workers.

During the revolution or shortly afterwards, a large number of workers' councils had dismissed and replaced their Communist factory directors. Now, however, the Kádár regime declared that it alone, not the workers' councils, had the right to appoint or dismiss leading executives, and sought to re-instal those factory directors who had been replaced.[15]

Finally, Kádár had repeatedly asserted that the hated secret police would not be re-formed, and that the workers themselves would be incorporated into the new organs of public security. From the first days of his regime, numerous workers' councils had offered to assist Kádár in his proposal to arm the workers—offering to provide the workers to be armed— but they had been totally ignored, and as the new security force was established it was not units of factory workers' guards but members of the former secret police who provided its mainstay.

In this battle for control of the factories, a battle which was fought for no less than direct control of the means of production, and fought out at the very point of production itself, the workers succeeded for a considerable time in resisting the onslaught of the Party bureaucracy. In the terminology of the latter, 'for several days at the end of November the counter-revolution ruled over a significant proportion of the factories.' But, aware of their structural weaknesses, and their total lack of any base amongst the workers themselves, the Communist authorities came increasingly to use intimidatory and coercive measures against the workers' councils. Verbal attacks on the councils' 'anti-Government policy and anti-Party campaign' were stepped up, and in the first days of December some two hundred members of various workers' councils were arrested.

In this atmosphere of growing repression, calls were increasingly raised for more determined and open resistance to the Kádár regime, and for a new general strike. This placed the Central Workers' Council in a somewhat awkward position. While its power was being undermined by the coercive actions of the Government, it was coming under increasing pressure from below to take firmer and more energetic action. While fearing it might lose the confidence of the workers if it did not act strongly enough, it was also aware that almost any action might be considered by the Government as a provocation and an excuse for even more coercive measures.

Meanwhile, proposals were being aired for some action to commemorate the victims of the second Soviet intervention of the 4th of November. One plan which had been drawn up was for a great workers' demonstration through the streets of Budapest on the 4th of December. The Central Workers' Council firmly rejected this idea for fear of bloodshed and further repression, and decided instead on a silent procession of women, dressed in black and carrying flowers, who would march to the Tomb of the Unknown Soldier in Hero's Square. The Central Workers' Council also called upon the rest of the population to demonstrate their solidarity by placing lighted candles in their windows at midnight.

The women's procession took place despite the presence of Soviet tanks and armed troops trying to disperse them, and although the Government had withdrawn all candles from the shops, almost every window of Budapest was lit up that night.

Kádár and his Government were evidently outraged by this open flouting of their authority. The Central Workers' Council, they declared, was now 'in the tow of the counter-revolution.' The Central Council's leaders gained the impression that the Government was now preparing for a final blow against them, and in view of their good relationship up till now with the Soviet authorities, they decided to appeal for help to none other than the Soviet Government. A delegation from the Central Workers' Council went to the Soviet military command and asked them to inform the Soviet ambassador that the Central Council would like the opportunity to present its case before representatives of the Soviet Government. They also sent a letter to the Soviet Premier, Bulganin, with a similar request in which they declared that:

> 'the various measures of the Government... against the revolutionary elements serve only to splinter the best and most progressive forces of socialism in Hungary.'[16]

Last Engagements

In the first weeks of December, faced with increasing attacks from the Government, with many members of workers' councils disappearing daily, and increasing demands from the provinces for action, the Central Workers' Council recognised the necessity, come what may, of calling a further national conference of workers' councils.

A secret and extraordinary session of the Central Workers' Council was held on the 6th of December, at which plans were discussed to create a National Workers' Council with a definite political programme. The proposals envisioned the extension of the Central Workers' Council of Greater Budapest into a National Workers' Council with a permanent presidium, secretariat and committee structure. In addition, a provisional Workers' Parliament would be set up, composed of representatives of workers' councils throughout the country, which would replace the National Assembly until the 23rd of October 1957, on which date free national elections would be held between the democratic political parties.

The Central Council also adopted a Memorandum addressed to the Government, in which it protested that while it has been prepared to negotiate with the regime and work for the resumption of production, it had met with only force and intimidation from the authorities. Repeating once again the fundamental demands of the workers' councils, the Central Council demanded a public reply from the Government saying what steps it would take to meet the workers' demands.[17]

Finally, the Central Workers' Council arranged to secretly convene a meeting to create the National Workers' Council on the 9th of December. However, the Kádár regime learned of these plans from secret police agents who had infiltrated the Central Council, and in the early hours of the 9th of December the Government arrested a majority of the Central Council's members and issued a decree declaring its dissolution.

Nevertheless, several members of the Central Council as well as a number of delegates from provincial towns had already arrived at the headquarters of the Central Council on the evening of the 8th of December. Learning that their plans were about to be forestalled, they went into immediate session. In fact, a member of the Central Council was called to the telephone by a representative of the Government who demanded to know if they really were planning to create a National Council. 'Yes,' he replied, 'We are already in session. . . We shall continue.'

A few moments later, news came that Soviet troops had opened fire on demonstrating miners in Salgotarjan. The atmosphere, related Ferenc Toke, became 'a tempest of indignation.' Without hesitation, the delegates declared a 48-hour protest strike against the terroristic and intimidatory actions of the Government. 'Let the lights go out, let there be no gas, let there be nothing!' declared one delegate. 'Strike till the Spring, or even till our lives end!' called another.[18]

Finally, the meeting issued a proclamation in support of the strike in which it declared that the Kádár Government was no longer capable of resolving the country's troubles, and called upon trade unions throughout the world to hold strikes in solidarity with that of the Hungarian workers.

As already planned, the Government replied to the strike call by outlawing the Central Workers' Council and arresting the majority of its members. Two of its most prominent leaders, Sandor Racz and Sandor Bali, spent the 9th and 10th of December in the Beloiannis factory under the protection of the workers, who refused to permit the police to enter and arrest their leaders, even when the factory was menacingly encircled by Soviet tanks. On the morning of the 11th of December, Janos Kádár offered a personal invitation to Racz and Bali to meet with him in the parliament for discussions. Racz and Bali accepted Kádár's invitation and presented themselves at the parliament, whereupon they were immediately arrested and imprisoned.

The banning of the Central Workers' Council and the imprisonment of its leaders gave an added impetus to the strike of the 11th and 12th of December. As work came to a halt both in Budapest and throughout the country, even the Communist Party's own paper *Nepszabadsag* was to describe the strike as one 'the like of which has never before been seen in the history of the Hungarian workers' movement.' In the course of the two-day protest, demonstrations, disturbances and even armed clashes with the authorities occurred in a number of provincial towns, at Eger, Miskolc, Ozd and Kecskemet.

In reply to the strike, the Government declared a state of emergency and banned all meetings and demonstrations called without official permission. At the same time all territorial workers' councils, at district, town, and county level, were declared disbanded. On the 13th of December, the Government issued a further decree establishing detention without trial for up to six months, and setting up special courts of summary jurisdiction throughout the country.

These actions, however, only further increased the antagonism of the working class towards the Government. Straight on the heels of the 48-hour strike, the workers of the Csepel iron and steel works occupied their factory with a sit-in strike, demanding the release of Sandor Racz and Sandor Bali. Their action was immediately joined by the workers of the

Beloiannis factory, and followed by those in at least a dozen more large factories. In counter-action, many of these factories were now occupied by Soviet troops.

The following month saw the last-ditch stand of the workers' councils, operating in semi-legality, to prevent the control of the factories being wrested out of their hands by the Communist Party bureaucracy backed up by the Soviet armed forces. Spasmodic strikes and demonstrations continued to occur throughout the country, and further armed clashes took place between workers and both secret police and Soviet soldiers in the industrial centre of Csepel and in a number of provincial towns. In the face of terror and intimidation, and overwhelming military might, the workers' resistance was courageous but doomed to eventual defeat.

On the 5th of January a new decree reduced even further the legal competence of the workers' councils, and Kádár's Revolutionary Worker-Peasant Government extended the death penalty to striking or inciting to strike. Faced with daily increasing intimidation, on the 8th of January the workers' council of the Csepel iron and steel works announced its resignation, declaring that:

> 'Under the presently prevailing circumstances, we are no longer able to carry out our obligations. . . and for this reason, we are returning our mandate into the hands of the workers.'

Many of the remaining workers' councils followed the lead given by Csepel and announced their own disbandment. The Government responded to what it considered 'the provocative dissolutions of the workers' councils' by increasing the scope of the death penalty to almost any act of criticism. In Csepel itself, Soviet troops sent in to disperse demonstrating workers were again involved in heavy fighting.

On the 15th of January, the Central Workers' Council, still functioning in illegality, issued its final appeal to the workers to keep up their resistance:

> 'Because of the terror, however, and the death penalty even for distributing leaflets, the Council exhorts the workers to spread all news concerning the underground by word of mouth. Sabotage and passive resistance are the order of the day.'[19]

Sabotage and passive resistance, and even the occasional strike and demonstration, continued throughout 1957, but the organised power of the Hungarian workers' councils had now been broken. Finally, on the 17th of November 1957, a Government decree declared the dissolution of all remaining workers' councils.

NOTES

1. P. Kecskemeti, *The Unexpected Revolution: Social Forces in the Hungarian Uprising* (1961), p. 115.
2. J.J. Marie and B. Nagy, eds. *Pologne-Hongrie 1956* (1966), p. 222.
3. E. Kiraly, *Die Arbeitereselbstverwaltung in Ungarn* (1961), p. 35.
4. B. Nagy, *La Formation du Conseil Central Ouvrier de Budapest en 1956* (1961), p. 9.
5. Marie and Nagy, op. cit., pp. 223-224.
6. Ibid., p. 224.
7. Ibid., pp. 225-226.
8. Information about the foundation of the Central Workers' Council and its leading members can be found in B. Nagy, op. cit., pp. 41-45 and 54-58, and in Ferenc Toke, 'Ce que Furent les Conseils Ouvriers Hongrois' in Marie and Nagy, op. cit., p. 252, and M. Sebestyen, 'Mes Expériences dans le Conseil Central Ouvrier du Grand Budapest', also in Marie and Nagy, p. 300.
9. For Kádár's speech, see M.J. Lasky ed., *The Hungarian Revolution: A white Book* (1957), pp. 262-263.
10. Toke, op. cit., p. 258.
11. J. Molnar, *A Nagybudapesti Kozponti Munkastanacs* (The Central Workers' Council of Greater Budapest) (1969), pp. 63-64 and Sebestyen, op. cit., p. 301.
12. Quoted in Toke, op. cit., p. 260.
13. Sebestyen, op. cit., p. 303.
14. Relations between the workers' councils and the trade unions are discussed in Kiraly, op. cit., pp. 41-52.
15. Considerable information relating to the conflicts between the workers' councils and the Party organisations, trade unions and factory directors is provided in Molnar, op. cit,, pp. 73-82.
16. Marie and Nagy, op. cit., pp. 317-318.
17. Details of the Central Council's memorandum, and of its plans for a National Workers' Council and a Workers' Parliament can be found in Molnar, op. cit., pp. 118-119 and 129-130.
18. The meeting is described in some detail in Toke, op. cit., pp. 267-268.
19. Marie and Nagy, op. cit., p. 326.

HOW NOT TO REAPPRAISE THE NEW LEFT

by Ken Coates

'In Hungary in 1956 Stalin's tanks blew apart the Left in the rest of the world. Old complacencies were shattered. . .' So opens the half-title page introduction to David Widgery's compendium on *The Left in Britain*,[1] providing the first words one meets in a labour of 549 pages. Discriminating readers soon discover how appropriate it is that even the blurb is wrong. Stalin was safely dead, and the tanks were Khrushchev's. Khrushchev himself had already 'blown apart the left' six months earlier, with his liberating speech to the closed session of the 20th Congress of the Communist Party of the Soviet Union, which had, according to the brothers Medvedev, been the result of a purely personal initiative, launched at the end of the Congress, while the General Secretary temporarily held isolated power, before the new Central Committee had been convened to elect the other members of the leadership.[2] It is hardly accidental that this book opens with such a mistake: not only is the whole compilation slipshod to a remarkable degree, but this particular error is not the only one which arises from a desire to establish a special reading of the events in question. It is mainly for this reason that it is worthwhile to pay some attention to the work.

On the surface, David Widgery is concerned in a modest, if nonetheless brash, act of cultural imperialism, attempting to incorporate all of the post-1956 British New Left under the hegemony of the International Socialists, a rather shrill, if also intellectually infertile, sectarian grouping, which did in fact play a largely recalcitrant role in stimulating the argument which is inadequately treated in his pages. Widgery is a whimsical fellow, and he annexes his mental territories with a certain good humour, so that his innumerable offences against the facts may not seem so important as they might have done if they had been the work of a serious historian.

The crudest of his aggressions are structural to his account: he never misses an opportunity to offer the final word to the International Socialist grouping, or to their energetic, if commonly shallow, guru, Tony Cliff. Accordingly, the first section, on the 'double exposure' of Suze and Hungary, culminates in an oration of Cliff's delivered in 1967, ten years after the events recorded and statements anthologised in the rest of the chapter. The summation on the Campaign for Nuclear Disarmament is made over to a much cleverer spokesman of the same faction, Michael

111

Kidron. Kidron's thoughts on the anti-nuclear movement culminate with the notion that 'Education in socialism has to become a first priority for the Campaign against the Bomb'. So ended that Campaign.

The third chapter, less inaccurate than the rest, is the sole property of Peter Sedgwick, perhaps the most interesting of the genuine New Left converts to the ranks of the grouping. Four more groups of articles follow, each liberally peppered with unrepresentative selections from the writings of the faithful. Then we are in 1968, where we wind up once again with a long and irrelevant interview with Tony Cliff, reprinted from an aptly named journal called *Idiot International*.[3]

Yet it is worthwhile to examine such a one-sided advocacy, even one so lamentably devoid of systematic thought as this, if only to point up some of its inadvertent lessons. But first, because this work will undoubtedly have a modest circulation, it is necessary to establish exactly how unreliable it is from a factual standpoint.

In Chapter One we instantly meet the editor's obsessions. We are told at once that in 1956 'The Trotskyist Left was operating within the Labour Party to little visible effect' although they and other leftists 'possessed a formidable organized working class base'. Small though they were, 'their membership was overwhelmingly of industrial workers'. The fact is that there were at that time, three Trotskyist groups noticed by David Widgery: the forerunners of the Socialist Labour League, the 'Socialist Review Group', which subsequently became International Socialism, and the Revolutionary Socialist League. The first of these was always extremely secretive about its membership, but it is quite certain that at the beginning of 1956 this numbered less than fifty on the most generous possible count: the second grouping had not many more than twenty members, while the last grouping could not yet count a dozen. By 1956, not only British, but European Trotskyism, was fatigued: an aging, beleaguered and faction-ridden force. It is doubtful if the English sections of the movement could have survived even a few years longer, had Khrushchev not helped them with his denunciation of Stalin. Widgery goes on to say that the theorists of these currents, 'Cliff from Palestine, Healy from Ireland, James from the West Indies' gave them 'an unorthodoxy which was to give... great strength'. James, of course, had long since repudiated orthodox trotskyism, but had no organised following. He was, however, a genuine and imaginative thinker of considerable interest.[4] The others were never in any real sense theorists: while Cliff had produced a number of books, they contain little matter of originality and that is commonly trite as well as wong-headed.[5] Healy has never written anything worthy of note in his life. He is simply a brilliant, if somewhat brutal organiser.[6] Having falsified the micro-history, Widgery then blunders into the world of major events.

A little further on, he tells us that Kardelj, the Yugoslav foreign secretary, was imprisoned in the 'series of trials of many real or imagined Titoites' which set in from 1949. Presumably we are expected to believe that President Tito put this Titoist in jail. Once he has garbled this large matter, our historian goes on to announce that Khrushchev's secret speech reached England via the *Manchester Guardian*. It did not. It was first published in the *Observer*, and only subsequently reprinted by the Guardian as a booklet. In the same spirit, he returns to the small world of leftwing personalia. These are no more accurately rendered. Len Wincott, the Invergordon mutineer, who was imprisoned by Stalin's officials, becomes, for no good reason, Winnicott. *The Reasoner* was on public sale, and could not be, as Widgery claims, an 'internal discussion bulletin' because the British Communists possessed no constitutional mechanism for distributing oppositional materials. Peter Fryer, a young man, could only be described as a 'lifelong communist' if one were prepared to limit his span to thirteen years. Saville taught at the University of Hull, not the WEA. Thompson was an extramural lecturer. Professor Brian Simon taught at Leicester, not Leeds. Don Renton did not lead a strong dissident focus in Nottingham, because he was an Edinburgh party official. The 1958 Kessingland Summer Camp was organized by NALSO, the Labour Party Student body, not the *New Left Review*, and it was not held under canvas. Michael Stewart was anything but a 'leftist' when he visited this gathering as opposition spokesman on education. No new translation of Trotsky's *Revolution Betrayed* appeared at the time in question, because there was no need for any such thing. The English Trotskyists took over the American edition from Pioneer Publishers. They did not have the resources to reprint a book of this length until a year after the maturing of the crisis in the communist party. Even then they published it under the original New York imprint. Mercifully, soon after this catalogue of errors, chapter one breaks into cannibalized excerpts, and these offer less scope for creative reporting.

But then we get Chapter Two. This reports the first Aldermaston March with 'the glares of the Trots marshalling well-drilled Young Socialist squaddies on the final day': but the Young Socialist organisation was not created until after that demonstration (and indeed, I remember representing NALSO, the Labour Student Organisation of which I became the secretary, at a subcommittee of the Party's National Executive, and arguing that it would be quite impossible to develop a youth organisation if it were not allowed sufficient autonomy to be able to support the Campaign for Nuclear Disarmament. Sarah Barker, the Party's arch-disciplinarian, took due note of our insistent nagging on this score).

When it comes to describing the struggle for unilateralism inside the Labour Party, Widgery's account is a total confusion. He has the leaders of the National Union of General and Municipal Workers recall their Conference in order to reverse their unilateralist vote before the unilateralist victory at the Party Conference, when what really happened was that this folkloric bureaucratic adjustment took place during the following summer, in the year of Gaitskell's fight back, which also reversed the overall Party decision.

In describing, in travesty, the ideas of 'positive neutralism' put forward by the New Left, he mockingly cites the examples of 'Yugoslavia and Ghana, India and Algeria'. Leaving aside his earlier deference to C.L.R. James, who had the highest opinion of Nkrumah, Algeria at the time was a French colony, engaged in bitter war against colonialism, in which the International Socialists, for a long time, took the side of Messali Hadj, a one-time fellow-traveller of some Trotskyist currents in France, who played no active part whatever in the actual liberation. While many advocates of 'positive neutralism' gave active support to the efforts of the National Liberation Front of Algeria, which finally won the war against French colonialism, they do not escape reproach for their alleged support of 'politics of a religious water colour'. Peter Sedgwick subsequently echoes this somewhat chauvinist outburst by denouncing positive neutralism in another tirade in which he blithely speaks of 'the Chinese invasion of India' as 'undermining its viability'. What really undermined this viability was the persistent intrigue of the Central Intelligence Agency, the massacre of the Indonesian left,[7] the fall of Nkrumah,[8] and a whole succession of similarly disastrous reverses for the radical 'neutralist' forces. The Sino-Indian border conflict has been the subject of a major scholarly study,[9] which throws a very different light upon it from that in which it was portrayed by the Western press, and which Sedgwick uncritically accepts.

A similar random list of mistakes about those matters with which I am familiar could be continued for many pages. Others would surely augment it. The Centre for Socialist Education was founded in 1965, not 1967. *Clarion*, the Labour Student journal, was not founded by me, but by the Oxford University Labour Club. Before I edited it, my predecessors had included Kenith Trodd, Dennis Potter, Stephen Hugh-Jones, and, if my memory serves me fairly, Brian Lapping. Tony Smith, subsequently of *24 Hours* on BBC television, also had a hand in it. The Institute for Workers' Control never abandoned the seminar structure of its conferences, and indeed, had to defend it against various 'leftist' groupings, including the International Socialists, who were bored by practical discussions and preferred to talk about 'consciousness' and other luminous abstractions. The *International Socialist Journal* was never 'influenced by the Unified Secretariat of the Fourth International', since it was always effectively controlled by Lelio Basso. While it is true that the journal published various articles by Ernest Mandel, it was in no fundamental sense responsive to his ideas, and he regarded it, somewhat impatiently, as a 'centrist' organ. John Daniels, the first editor of *Labour Review*, never taught in an extramural department. NALSO was not 'periodically disaffiliated'[10] from the Labour Party, but survived unscathed until it was finally broken up after a take-over by the Socialist Labour League. 'Walden, Price and Hattersley' had all left the organisation before the 'early sixties', and in fact it was dominated by the New Left from 1958 onwards. Michel Pablo was not arrested in Holland for 'running documents, money and weapons to Algeria', but on charges concerning alleged forgery.[11]

If circumstantial detail is offered, it ought to be accurate. David Widgery is blessed with sublime over-confidence in a shockingly bad memory, and that is a handicap in a historian. Because its errors of fact, large and small, must be numbered in hundreds, this book is absolutely useless as a source of detailed information. That is why it is not only more interesting, but also infinitely more chariable, to concentrate upon the main themes, which he appears to think should dominate our consideration of his chosen period. This would be easier if such themes were more explicitly focused in the reprints he has chosen: but he never misses a chance to republish something flippant or amusing, so that even this task is more difficult to unravel than it should be.

Nonetheless, there is one fairly clear thesis which emerges with the choice of the events which bound the work. A book which begins in 1956 and ends in 1968, and concerns the development of socialist and communist ideas, might have arched between the Twentieth Congress and the Prague Spring. But this one does not: it moves from the Hungarian revolution to the 'events' in France. Czechoslovakia *is* just mentioned: 'A liberalising leader's need to weaken the artistic intellectual bureaucracy was turned to advantage by the working class', we are told. In the same absurd paragraph, we discover: 'The Prague Spring. . . was, far more than the Hungarian Revolution, due to impetus from above. . . Although some of the impetus for the foundation of workers' councils was actually provided by Dubcek's own need to create a counterweight to the very rapid growth of organizations among the white-collared working-class, "anti-Soviet soviets" were once again pungently in the air'. Later on, in the chronology, we learn that: 'Dubcek spends a week in Moscow accused of right-wing revisionism before returning looking pale'. Under the heading 'reaction of the British left', the index points us to an untitled page of diary reminiscence of how London members of the International Socialists occupied themselves in demonstrations and leafletting during the day after the Soviet and Warsaw Pact invasion. And that is all we learn from David Widgery about Czechoslovakia.

Of course, in this reportage, we can see a clear application of the same standards of factual accuracy as are to be discovered elsewhere in the book. The 'artistic intellectual bureaucracy' was never more firmly linked to the Czechoslovak workers than during the Spring and Summer of 1968.[12] The growth of workers' councils began in response to the economic agitation, based on solid technocratic motives, which accompanied the strategy of Ota Sik, who might have been a bureaucrat, but could scarcely be described as an artist.

The Hungarian Revolution, very like the later Czech upsurge, was rather much a result of 'impetus from above', involving key party leaders like Imre Nagy, the agitation of Laso Rajk's widow, and the growth of the Petofi circle among communist youth, students (and later, intellectuals). Until the Party hierarchy had divided, political criticism of any kind was quite impossible in either case. Almost the only perception of these un-flattering lines which is very likely on target, is that Dubcek returned from Moscow 'looking pale', and well he might. Equally well might he expect the concession of a degree of solidarity from David Widgery and his snide battalions, if only they were capable of nourishing, even for a moment, a non-factional thought.

But the silences of a book are often as important as its utterance. The truth is that Widgery does not really convince even himself that 'anti-Soviet soviets' were anywhere near the offing in Dubcek's Prague, and that is why Czechoslovakia scarcely figures in his story. His primary concern is the rehabilitation of what he understands by council communism, moving from the workers' councils of Budapest across to the student rebellion and factory occupations of those celebrated French 'events'.[13] And it is this concern which is one-sided to the point of travesty, and therefore bound to bring its proponents to stalemate unless they enrich their social vision.

It was, of course, natural that the original soviet idea should re-emerge after the fall of Stalin, who amputated all remnants of direct democracy from the Russian political structure, substituting a fraudulent semi-parliamentary system based upon absurdly rigged 'elections' involving unanimous rates of mythical turn-out for lists of approved nominees who moved in a degree of unison only equalled in our country by the Tiller Girls, to an Assembly which had hardly greater political authority than the Windmill Theatre, and remained considerably less amusing. For all that, once Stalin was displaced as the impresario of this remarkable show, it was completely plain that there remained a vast body of scriptural justification for a return to pristine Soviet forms. Yet the soviet model, which had been embraced by communists all over the world, was never successfully repeated in any subsequent revolution. Eastern Europe achieved the changes in its social structure largely as a result of conquest, except in Yugoslavia and Albania, where it resulted from guerrilla struggle in a war of national independence from the German occupation. In postwar Czecho-slovakia, the change could be held to have issued in part from a parliamentary victory, not unaffected by the results of conquest and liberation.

In the East and the 'third world', China's communists fought their way into the cities on the basis of their strength among armed peasants. Cuban communism grew out of the initiative of a handful of fearless adventurers.

Mozambique, Angola and Guinea-Bissau have probably by now definitively escaped from imperialism, and there is no disagreement about the fact that they emerged from an anticolonial war which broke up the integrated power of the oldest metropolis of empire in the modern world. As for Vietnam, it is fairly clear that its revolution was by no means patterned on St. Petersburg in 1917. For the International Socialists, all these various regimes taken together, constitute the species 'state capitalism', so the social transformation which they have initiated invites no markedly curious efforts of enquiry. Nigel Harris, the main theorist of the IS group to address the problems of the Third World, describes them as 'backward economic autarkies'... none of which he says, 'has yet been able to demonstrate the superiority of its mode of economic development.'

In this way, we find ourselves confronting a model which offers the experience of the 1917 October Revolution, in a somewhat markedly idealised form, together with odd incidents such as the outburst of the German *Rate,* the Hungarian Soviet Republic of 1919, the Catalonian upheaval during the Spanish Civil War, and possibly, less clear examples from Bolivia: none of which has been formally or explicitly stated, but all of which is invoked by hint and analogy.[14] The Socialist revolution is workers' councils plus the Bolshevik Party, and that is that.

It would assuredly be wrong to dismiss this model. In a number of industrial countries, it remains possible, if not actively or immediately likely. Even the fall of fascist Portugal, and the unravelling of authority in Spain, have not yet produced any unambiguous support for it. Whilst the most radical section of the Portuguese Armed Forces, together with the parties of the New Left, have given a new currency to a modified form of 'popular power', the majority of Portuguese workers have also given support to the socialist and communist parties, which in the main eschew such a programme.[15] That the revolutionary upsurge in the Iberian peninsula is still very much alive does offer a prospect that there might yet be important new developments. But the strength of Council Communism outside Russia has up to now everywhere been divorced from the kind of centralised political apparatus which existed there in the shape of the Communist Party.

Probably communist orthodoxy is justified in claiming that decentralised 'soviets' are doomed to failure, since the seizure of power is a highly centralised business. The extent to which power must be 'seized' in late capitalism, is, however, a complex and difficult issue. Were the working class to become a genuinely hegemonic force, 'seizure' would become a rather misleading metaphor. The key question remains, how far can working-class organisations strive, from within a capitalist structure, to become the dominant social power? The 'revisionist' theses which have produced such programmes as the British Communists' 'Road to Socialism' or the different strategies of Italian and French communism, are nowhere explicitly discussed, leave alone refuted, in Widgery's arguments. Naturally, such theses have unleashed a process of political evolution which has already seen the rise of a variety of more or less explicit tendencies in 'official' west European communism, ranging from simple Parliamentarism on the social-democratic model across to an adaptation of Gramscian grand strategy. All of this is important as well as interesting, but it cannot be discussed sensibly in a pastiche such as that we are considering.

But, it may be argued, Widgery is documenting the affairs of the *British* far left. Yet, to do British socialists justice, most of the controversies of European socialism nowadays quickly cross the channel. Indeed, an assiduous reader of the press from which David Widgery has culled his book might be forgiven for wondering whether poor England had not long since been dissolved in a corrosive fog of dialectics from foreign parts, so vigorously have our own factions responded to the quarrels of their opposite numbers in every imaginable European language. Certainly British communism has reflected all the tendencies which have emerged in its brother parties, from Italy down to Portugal. To regard all this with a blind eye cannot possibly rehabilitate the call for workers' councils, since what remains valid in that call must come to life in a world of labour which is alive with other ideas and stratagems, some plausible, some far-fetched, but all very conspicuously present.

The obvious point about Soviets is that they will not emerge in any society which maintains an apparently satisfactory framework of bourgeois democracy,[16] within which the corporate interests of working people can conceivably achieve representation and a degree of satisfaction. Parallel organs can be mooted, but no-one would consent to repose power in them unless they appeared to offer greater scope for democratic action than the established machinery. Should such parallel organs gather modest strength within a still living established framework, they would commonly be assimilated once it becomes obvious that they could not be annulled in any other way. This is what has happened to trade unions, and is happening to shop stewards' organisations.[17] It is quite pointless to argue that it should not happen, because the established power cannot succeed in the attempt to incorporate rebellion within its own structures without paying a real price, and if the price is real, a majority of working people will wish to accept it. At the same time, we have no reason to suspect that the political appetites of a modern working class movement are satiable. An expanding capitalism might be able to sublimate political aspirations into neat economic demands: but a moribund or contracting capitalism has no such capacity. For this reason, even a short downturn is dangerous to the stability of the balance of power, while a long one might well prove fatal. In such a case, parallel powers might well be one of the ingredients of a decisive shift in power relationships. But even while that was evolving, traditional democratic politics would be bound to reflect the shift of class forces, and rather directly at that. In any case, while Parliament and the County Council are not easy to bypass, neither is the Labour Party in England, or German Social Democracy, or Italian Communism. Would-be revolutionists who turn their backs on the reforming institutions thrown up in the struggles of established labour movements do so at their peril. Of course, it is possible that these institutions could collide with capital, and it is possible that they might be defeated. If bourgeois democracy were rolled back in Western Europe, the scene would become radically different. No-one should be sanguine about this prospect, which would be cataclysmic in its impact. The battle to maintain and advance the conquests of bourgeois democracy remains a key priority of Labour in every advanced country, and will be neglected only at the direst imaginable risk.

This leads us to consider another major flaw in the Widgery/International Socialist perspective. Let us imagine, for a moment, for the sake of argument, that the Soviets erupted in one or more major West European nations, and established their power. The only thought that would pre-occupy Widgery on that day would be how they might extend their example and influence. But the lessons which come to us from Russian experience do not allow us to regress to 1917, and work only for a rebirth of innocence. The discussions of the New Left involved an extensive revaluation of this experience, and this book does no service whatever in glossing over it.

In 1919 Bukharin and Preobrazhensky published a primer for communists which was quickly translated into all the major European languages. *The ABC of Communism* reflects their expectations about the immediate future of soviet power. On the question of 'proletarian justice', for instance, they write:

As far as the revolutionary tribunals are concerned, this form of proletarian justice has no significance for future days, any more than the Red Army will have any significance for the future after it has conquered the White Guards, or any more than the Extraordinary Commissions have any significance for the future. In a word, all the instruments created by the proletariat for the critical period of the civil war are transient. When the counter-revolution has been successfully crushed, these instruments will no longer be needed, and they will disappear.

On the other hand, proletarian justice in the form of the elective popular courts will unquestionably survive the end of the civil war, and will for a long period have to continue the use of measures to deal with the vestiges of bourgeois society in its manifold manifestations. The abolition of classes will not result in the immediate abolition of class ideology, which is more long-lived than are the social conditions which have produced it, more enduring than the class instincts and class customs which have brought it into being. Besides, the abolition of class may prove a lengthy process. The transformation of the bourgeoisie into working folk and that of the peasants into the workers of a socialist society will be a tardy affair. The change in peasant ideology is likely to be very slow, and will give plenty of work to the law-courts. Moreover, during the period which must precede the full development of communist distribution, the period during which the articles of consumption are still privately owned, there will be ample occasion for delinquencies and crimes. Finally, anti-social offences arising out of personal egoism, and all sorts of offences against the common weal, will long continue to provide work for the courts. It is true that these courts will gradually change in character. As the State dies out, they will tend to become simply organs for the expression of public opinion. They will assume the character of courts of arbitration. Their decisions will no longer be enforced by physical means and will have a purely moral significance.'[18]

One does not need to follow Solzhenitsyn's account of the origins of the Gulag Archipelago to know that Bukharin's hopes were not fulfilled. When Bukharin himself was shot, shortly after playing a major role in the drafting of the 'most democratic constitution in the world' nothing could more powerfully highlight the advantage in simple terms of civil and personal liberty, of bourgeois right in the 'bourgeois doctrine of the separation of powers'.[19] Almost every dissident communist of the generation of '56 understood this simple truth, and that is why very few could be persuaded of the divine inspiration of such scriptures as *The State and Revolution*, which argues deliberately for the notion of a coalescence of administrative and executive functions. This would be an appropriate doctrine had the division of labour been finally overcome, but was a most dangerous one in the real, material and evolvingly wicked world.

Many of the more utopian neo-Leninist socialists seem to regard the separation of powers as simply itself an extension of the division of labour, and therefore retrogressive. The truth is the exact contrary: any democratic form in which the separation functions effectively will discover in it a powerful weapon against the atrophy of roles, and a constant stimulus to the erosion of particularised power-centres and fortified in-group interests.[20] So elementary is this truth that every workers' organisation applies it almost automatically. The simplest working-mens' clubs or associations elect a secretary, and then pace him with a separate treasurer whose job it is to stop him spending all the money, whereupon they immediately appoint separate auditors to control any lack of due public spirit in the conservation of the funds. Once an organisation is so clique-ridden that one caucus can determine the occupancy of all these offices without challenge, it is in danger, be it never so revolutionary. Of course, the bourgeoisie separated the judiciary from the executive, and imperfectly at that for a very long time, and then, after dividing the executive from the legislature, tended to cry halt.

But any transitional society which learns from Bukharin's awful fate will go far beyond the bourgeoisie in insisting on this crucial principle. This is why any statutory party monopoly is an abomination, for even if there is a juridical separation between executive and judiciary, if one caucus nominates both lists, justice will always be in danger. Bukharin's and Lenin's dream of the withering away of the state, and the overcoming of punishment by proletarian morality, might, or might not, have been a plausible short-term target if the judges in the USSR were even as imperfectly adjusted to humanist notions of penology as the vegetarian fringes of the modern English magistracy: but it was just not on with the party in effective control of the 'elections' for the judiciary. I doubt whether there is a single Russian judge today who doesn't think that both Bukharin and Lenin were completely mistaken in their perspective on crime and punishment. If I am seriously wrong, then there is sufficient genuine schizophrenia on the modern Russian bench to keep Soviet psychiatry honourably engaged for many happy years after it has been relieved of the problem of eliminating untoward opinions.

All this reasoning was much to be heard in the arguments which took place in the socialist forums of 1956 and 1957. It burst into life again in the Action Programme of the Czechoslovak Communist Party:

'The Communists in the government, too, must ensure as soon as possible that the principle of responsibility of the government towards the National Assembly covering all its activities is worked out in detail. Even under the existing practice of political management, the opportunity afforded for independent activity of the government and of individual ministers was not sufficiently made use of, there was a tendency to shift responsibility on to the Party bodies and to evade independence in decision-taking. The government is not only an organ of economic policy. As the supreme executive organ of the state it must, as a whole, deal systematically with the whole scope of political and administrative problems of the state. It is also up to the government to take care of the rational development of the whole state machinery. The state administration machinery was often underrated in the past; this machinery must consist of highly qualified people, professionally competent and rationally organised, it must be subject to a systematic supervision in a democratic way it must be effective. Simplified ideas as if such goals could be attained by underrating and decrying the administrative machinery in general were rather detrimental in the past.

In the whole state and political system it is necessary to create, purposefully, such relations and rules that would, on the one hand, provide the necessary safe-guards to professional officials in their functions and, on the other hand, enable the necessary replacement of officials who can no longer cope with their work by professionally and politically more competent people. This means to establish legal conditions for the recall of responsible officials and to provide legal guarantees of decent conditions for those who are leaving their posts through the normal way of replacement, so that their departure should not amount to a 'drop' in their material and moral-political standing.

The Party policy is based on the principle that no undue concentration of power must occur, throughout the state machinery, in one sector, one body, or in a single individual. It is necessary to provide for such a division of power and such a system of mutual supervision that any faults or encroachments of any of its links are rectified in time, by the activities of another link. This principle must be applied not only to relations between the elected and executive bodies, but also to the inner relations of the state administration machinery and to the standing and activities of courts of law.

This principle is infringed mainly by undue concentration of duties in the existing ministry of the interior. The Party thinks it necessary to make of it a ministry for internal state administration including the administration of public security. The schedule that in our state was traditionally within the jurisdiction of other bodies and with the passage of time has being incorporated into the ministry of the interior, must be withdrawn from it. It is necessary to elaborate proposals as soon as possible passing on the main responsibility for investigation to the courts of law, separating prison administration from the security force, and handing over of press law administration, of archives, etc., to other state bodies.

The Party considers the problem of a correct incorporation of the security force in the state as politically very important. The security of our lives will only benefit, if everything is eliminated that helps to maintain a public view of the security force marred by the past period of law violations and by the privileged position of the security force in the political system. That past period impaired the progressive traditions of our security force as a force advancing side by side with our people. These traditions must be renewed. The Central Committee of the Communist Party of Czechoslovakia deems it necessary to change the organisation of the security force and to split the joint organisation into two mutually independent parts—State Security and Public Security. The State Security service must have such a status, organisational structure, numerical state, equipment, methods of work, and qualifications which are in keeping with its work of defending the state from the activities of enemy centres abroad. Every citizen who has not been culpable in this respect must know with certainty that his political convictions and opinions, his personal beliefs and activities, cannot be the object of attention of the bodies of the State Security service. The Party declares clearly that this apparatus should not be directed and used to solve internal political questions and controversies in socialist society.

The Public Security service will fulfil tasks in combatting crime and in the protection of public order; for this its organisation, numerical state and methods of work must be adapted. The Public Security force must be better equipped and strengthened; its functions in the defence of public order must be exactly laid down by law and, in their fulfilment, the service will be directed by the national committees. Legal norms must create clearer relations of control over the security force by the government as a whole and by the National Assembly.

It is necessary to devote the appropriate care to carrying out the defence policy of our state. In this connection it is necessary to work for our active share in the conception of the military doctrine of the Warsaw Treaty countries, the strengthening of the defence potential of our country in harmony with the needs and possibilities, a uniform complex understanding of the questions of defence with all problems of the building of socialism in the whole of our policy, including defence training.

The legal policy of the Party is based on the principle that in a dispute over right (including administrative decisions of state bodies) the basic guarantee of legality is proceedings in court which are independent of political factors and are bound only by law. The application of this principle requires a strengthening of the whole social and political role and importance of courts of law in our society. The Central Committee of the Communist Party of Czechoslovakia will see to it that work on the complex of the required proposals and measures proceeds so as to find the answer to all the necessary problems before the next election of judges. In harmony with and parallel to that, it is also necessary to solve the status and duties of the public prosecutor's office so that it may not be put above the courts of law, and to guarantee full independence of barristers and solicitors from state bodies.'[21]

How was this argument received in the other Warsaw Pact powers? Walter Ulbricht gave a consensual view in his statement at the 20th anniversary of the founding of Walter Ulbricht Academy of Political Science and Law on 12th October 1968:

'Socialist democracy has nothing in common with the bourgeois "separation of powers" or with "separation and control of power". In the struggle of the working class for the establishment of its political power we have taken issue with the theory of the separation of powers not only once. This question was already on the agenda during the November Revolution. Also the Weimar Constitution proclaimed the separation of powers and even declared it to be a typical example of a parliamentary democracy, in which "the relations of the legislative, executive and judicial organs" should be based on their reciprocal independence and reciprocal control". But this so-called separation of powers really means nothing but the limitation of the rights of parliament and the guarantee of the class-biased independent activity of the majority of the civil servants and masters of justice educated by the bourgeoisie. The Social Democratic Party (SPD) was in government power for a long time in the Weimar Republic. But the result was not "democratic socialism" but undivided imperialist dictatorship, and the final result was fascism. Today West German imperialism marshalls its state monopoly rule in alliance with American imperialism and also calls it "marshalled rule". This new phase of state development is characterised by the emergency laws, the "internal state reform", "territorial and administrative reform", and "concerted action" of Messrs. Strauss and Schiller, the demands for strengthening and consolidating NATO and the concentration of the rule of the most aggressive forces of imperialism. There is not the least trace of a separation of power. Solely the decorative elements of certain plenary and committee meetings are left.

The slogan of the "separation of powers" is kept handy for the socialist countries, however. But with whom are the working people to divide power? Are they to divide power with the gentlemen in Bonn, the neo-nazis and Hitler generals or with the adherents of the forces of the exploiting classes deprived of their power, like those who crept out of their holes in Czechoslovakia and organised themselves in the various clubs in order to annul the achievements of socialism and restore the old conditions? This twaddle about the separation of powers originates from the veiled counter-revolution and is part of the programme of the global strategy of imperialism.

We have drawn the lessons from the history of class struggle that only one real guarantee of democracy exists: the working people must eliminate this system of bourgeois class rule inimical to the people, its basis of power in the economy under the leadership of the unitedly acting working class and take political and economic power into their own hands and set up their own democratic state. This state can only be constructed on the foundation of the complete concentration of power in the hands of the elected people's representatives and their close active relationship with the working people and their collectives. The democratic management of all administrative organs of the state and of justice is effected on the basis of this sovereignty of the people. That is also the reason why there is no room in our state order for administrative courts. These administrative courts existing in capitalist countries are only to replace the activity of parliamentary committees and increase the power of reactionary administrative officials.'[22]

In the juxta-position of these two views, we see a conflict which divides the entire socialist movement, without respect for agreement which may subsist on any lesser issues. Reformist or revolutionary, 'parliamentary' or 'soviet', every group of socialists includes those whose instinct is to concentrate power in the hands of the good and the just, and those whose instinct is to adapt institutions so as to prevent the abuse of power.

Of course, Ulbricht is quite justified in claiming that by itself the doctrine of separation of powers has no positive leverage for social transformation. Indeed, the doctrine as such will not even prevent injustice, which can only be thwarted when living and active men are prepared to make use of all the powers they have, and invent such new powers as they need, in defence of a cause. If one looks at the Czechoslovaks' *Action Programme* one sees that the Dubcek team wished to extend the doctrine of separation of powers to the development of cadres policy. This innovation would foreshadow many others. Was it not a form of separation of powers which uncovered the Watergate conspiracy in the United States? Is not the separation of the press from centralised control indispensable to a free society? Cannot the East German leaders recollect the impassioned appeals of the young Karl Marx for freedom from censorship? Is there nowadays some sinister theoretical principle which sanctifies proletarian censorship, while condemning all other forms? A careful reading of Marx would clearly establish that in his time he did not think so.

Ulbricht makes a convincing case that the doctrine of separation of powers has not undermined the bourgeois order, either in Germany or elsewhere. Why then should it undermine a proletarian order? Is Ulbricht telling us that proletarian rule is incompatible with autonomous ideas of justice? We invariably receive a similar type of response when leaders of established communist governments are asked why a genuine plurality of working class political parties cannot be allowed to contest within a socialist constitutional framework. Then we are always told that parties represent social classes, and that, since the communist party has preempted working class representation none other may exist without opening restorationist prospects. Yet, bourgeois states may secrete a diverse collection of parties, giving expression to an enormous variety of interests, all of which remain completely bourgeois. Is the working class less sociologically complex than the bourgeoisie? The notion is absurd.

David Widgery's instincts will all be ranged against Ulbricht, and in favour of rebellion. Yet the drift of his *argument* is painfully close to that of Ulbricht. He wishes to concentrate working class power in order to smash the capitalist state. Nowhere in his chosen readings do we see how the resultant power is itself to be dismantled.

We worried about this in 1956 and many of us worry about it still. It is possible to believe that the socialist transformation of our society is seriously overdue and yet to believe that there are urgent problems in the theory and practice of socialist democracy, the failure to resolve which must inevitably impede the development of socialism itself.

A collection of writings which was sensitive to this side of the problems discussed in the debate of the 1956 generation would lack some of the certainties of the Widgery version, but it would have far greater permanent value.

NOTES

1. *The Left in Britain*, 1956-1968, by David Widgery. Peregrine Books, Harmondsworth, Middlesex, 1976. (549 pp. £4.00).

2. See the introduction to the 20th Anniversary reprint of Khrushchev's report to the closed session of the XX Congress of the CPSU, by Zhores and Roy Medvedev, *Khrushchev's 'Secret' Speech*, Spokesman Books, Nottingham, 1976.

3. Almost the last words in this interview (and in Widgery's main text) are these:
   'If you look at my book on productivity I don't hide the fact at all that not one idea of it was created at the University, not one idea was created in the library, not one idea came from my own blooming brain.'
   Cliff is being somewhat overmodest about the provenance of the work in question. The fact is that large sections of it were copied out verbatim, and totally unacknowledged, from various writings of Tony Topham who would probably admit to getting at least some of Cliff's ideas from a library.

4. C. L. R. James' best-known books, on *World Revolution* and Toussaint L'Ouverture, *(The Black Jacobins)* were first published while he was still an active Trotskyist. The second of these works was reprinted in a revised version of the mid-'sixties, incorporating material presenting the author's changed views of politics.

5. Cliff's most original book is *Stalin's Russia—A Marxist Analysis*, which has appeared in various editions since it was originally published as an internal bulletin in the Revolutionary Communist Party. The work argues that the USSR is a 'state capitalist' society, governed by a new ruling class. Aside from purely terminological quibbles, the 'theory' involved in this, which is utterly eclectic and incoherent, allows its 'orthodox' followers to move parallel to an orthodox trotskyist analysis at one remove and more slowly, with occasional hiccups. The same 'theory' would admit anyone who took it seriously to do almost anything he liked, since its analytic power is nil and its predictive force no stronger. The authentic interpreters of the doctrine therefore face great difficulties when presenting their history. For instance, in March 1955, the editorial in Cliff's *Socialist Review* read in part:
   'A regime of bureaucratic state capitalism, with the terrific strain it imposes, needs the blood of a purge to make the wheels go round. The present set-up at the top is therefore temporary. . . The contradictions in Russian society are such that nothing could hold the system together except the iron hoops of totalitarian dictatorship.'
   By the time of the 22nd Congress of the CPSU, however, Tony Cliff could cheerfully write about the development of 'Welfare state capitalism' (*New Politics*, Winter 1962, pp. 51-65).

6. Healy's most distinguished theoretical article was a blistering attack on Jock Haston, who had rashly advised his little party to proceed 'empirically' on some matter or other. This brought on his head a strenuous denunciation, for had not Lenin written a whole book against 'empirio-criticism'? The longest text actually attributed to Healy was a pamphlet published in the Bevanite hey-day, which was actually written by George Novack, the American Trotskyist thinker,

nowadays accused by the WRP of being 'an accomplice of the GPU.' Another pamphlet on *The Coming World War* was actually written by Michel Pablo who has also since been fiercely denounced for his pains.

7. For an authoritative account of the CIA's involvement in this tragedy, see Peter Dale Scott's article in *Ten Years' Military Terror in Indonesia*, Spokesman Books, Nottingham, 1976.

8. Cf. Ruth First: *The Barrel of a Gun*, Penguin Books, Harmondsworth, Middlesex.

9. Neville Maxwell: *India's China War*, Penguin Books, Harmondsworth, Middlesex, 1972.

10. It could rot be, because it was never affiliated in the first place. Its relationship was based on a subsidy from Transport House, and a tight-rope walking dialogue with the Party's National Youth Officer.

11. Widgery could have found an accurate account of this case, by John Daniels and myself, in the *Socialist Review* for the relevant date.

12. Cf. Oxley, Pravda and Ritchie: *Czechoslovakia, The Party and the People*, Allen Lane, The Penguin Press, 1973.
Jiri Pelikan's *Ici Prague* will also be published, by Allison and Busby, during 1976.

13. The French 'events' did not unambiguously lend permanent support to 'soviets', either. The immediate result was a great reinforcement of the traditional organisations of Labour, including the (communist) CGT. See Andrée Hoyles: *Imagination in Power*, Spokesman Books, Nottingham, 1973.

14. The best documentary account of these movements is in Horvat, Markovic and Supek: *Self-Governing Socialism*, International Arts and Sciences Press, New York, 1975.

15. 'Popular Power' has crystallised around the new left movement and the candidacy of Otelo de Carvalho for the Presidency. After initially giving total support to this development, Widgery's co-thinkers quickly abandoned ship just before the November events, and then steadfastly failed to lift a finger in defence of Otelo throughout his confinement. The Russell Committee's report on these matters, edited by Jean-Pierre Faye, will be published in November 1976, by Spokesman Books.

16. A similar appreciation seems to be the view of Ernest Mandel, in *On the Current Stage of World Revolution* (Inprecorr, No. 53, 1976). Yet he explicitly excludes any long-range co-existence of 'workers' councils' with bourgeois-democratic governmental forms, which makes it difficult to see how the 'workers themselves' could ever 'experience higher forms of democratic freedoms on a broad scale.' If the movement for workers' control cannot establish real bases of power *within* the given structure, then only the prior destruction of that structure could bring them into being, by definition *de novo*, without prior 'experience'.

17. In this formulation, the word 'assimilated' is not to mean 'incorporated'. Both words are inadequate to express the reality which is sought after, which is visible where bodies like the National Union of Mineworkers, capable of provoking the fall of Governments, nonetheless sit in various official bodies and have an officially recognised representative status. 'Assimilation' in this sense does *not* imply any necessary abandonment of autonomous social objectives, while 'incorporation' in the normal usage, does.

18. University of Michigan, Ann Arbor Paperbacks, 1966, pp. 225-6.

19. See Stephen F. Cohen's important biography: *Bukharin and the Bolshevik Revolution*, Wildwood House, 1974.

20. Cf. in this connection, the most important treatment by Mihailo Markovic, in *On the Legal Institutions of Socialist Democracy*, Spokesman Pamphlets, 1976.

21. *The Action Programme of the Czechoslavak Communist Party*, Spokesman

Pamphlet, No. 8, p. 12.
22. Walter Ulbricht: *The Role of the Socialist State in the Shaping of the Developed Social System of Socialism*, Verlag Zeit Im Bild, Berlin, DDR, 1968.

MOVING ON

by Ralph Miliband

Twenty years after 1956, the main problem for the socialist left in Britain is still that of its own organisation into an effective political formation, able to attract a substantial measure of support and to hold out a genuine promise of further growth. A lot has happened in the labour movement in these twenty years, and much of this has been positive. But in organisational and programmatic terms, there has been no real advance. For different reasons, none of the organisations, old and new, which have occupied the stage in this period—the Labour Party, the Communist Party, the International Socialists, the Workers' Revolutionary Party, the International Marxist Group, etc.—constitutes an effective socialist formation or is in the least likely to become one. Such an organisation remains to be created. The present article discusses the reasons why existing organisations cannot fill the gap.

Inevitably, one must start with the Labour Party. There cannot now be many socialists in the Labour Party (and even fewer outside) who believe that most of its leaders are concerned with the task of effecting the 'fundamental and irreversible shift in the balance of wealth and power in favour of working people and their families' of which the Labour Manifesto spoke in 1974. But there are many socialists in the Labour Party who do believe very firmly that they can eventually and by dint of great pressure compel their leaders to adopt left-wing policies and even to translate these policies into practice; or alternatively that they can bring to the leadership of the Labour Party men and women who will want to adopt and put into practice such policies.

There is no point in rehearsing here arguments which have been endlessly canvassed as to whether this is a realistic prospect or not. That controversy has gone on for three quarters of a century, that is ever since the Labour Party came into existence; and insofar as it cannot be conclusively *proved* that the Labour Party will not in any serious sense be turned in socialist directions, the chances are that the controversy will go on for a long time to come, without leading anywhere. My own view, often reiterated, is that the belief in the effective transformation of the Labour Party into an instrument of socialist policies is the most cripling of all illusions to which socialists in Britain have been prone.[1] But this is not what I propose to argue yet again here. It will be more useful to take up some of the more important considerations which are commonly advanced by socialists for working in the Labour Party, whatever the odds, and for not looking farther afield.

One such consideration is that the Labour Party is 'the party of the working class' and that 'there is no alternative to it.'

It should be granted at the outset that there is indeed much strength in the claim that the Labour Party is 'the party of the working class.' Electorally, it is overwhelmingly *the* party of that major part of the working class which does not vote Conservative or Liberal, and now Scottish Nationalist and possibly soon Scottish Labour, and Welsh Nationalist. In electoral terms, whether at national or local level, the Labour Party occupies a crushingly dominant position in relation to other groupings on the left. Its nearest rival, namely the Communist Party, is in fact no rival at all; and such other left groupings as venture into electoral politics obtain even more derisory results. The new Scottish Labour Party may well do better, but must obviously be taken as a special case (although a significant one), which does not invalidate the general point.

At the level of membership, the Labour Party is also enormously stronger than any of its rivals on the left, with nearly 700,000 members as compared with the 28,000 or so members claimed by the Communist Party, and the two or three thousand members, on the most generous estimate, of the International Socialists and the Workers' Revolutionary Party, the few hundred members of the International Marxist Group, and the even smaller membership of a scatter of different sects.

Of course, 'membership' is a deceptive term, which tells one very little about levels of commitment. It has to be reckoned that a large and probably the largest part by far of the membership of the Labour Party is fairly nominal and mostly passive, except at election time. Its truly activist membership is unlikely to exceed 50-75,000 people. However, the same criteria must be applied to the Communist Party, and *its* activist membership is unlikely to exceed 5-8,000 members, the difference in proportion being due to the higher level of commitment which may be expected from C.P. members as compared with Labour Party ones. These estimates may be rounded off with, say, a few hundred activists for the Workers' Revolutionary Party and the International Socialists, and so on for the other groupings on the left.[2]

Still, when all such reckonings have been made and weighed up, it is evident that the only party of the left which can claim something of a 'mass' membership and a 'mass' basis is the Labour Party; and that no other party or grouping on the left even remotely approaches it. The membership of the Labour Party has tended to decline in the last twenty years and it is also worth noting that, at every election since 1951 with the exception of 1966, the number of votes and the percentage of votes cast for Labour have diminished. But whatever significance this may have, it still leaves the Labour Party as a 'mass' party and its rivals nowhere.

This major fact goes a long way to explain why so many people who belong to the socialist left cling to the Labour Party, notwithstanding all their disappointments and disillusionments. Here, and here alone, they argue, in the party of the working class and of organised labour; and here therefore is where socialists ought to try and make their influence felt, the more so since it *is* possible to fight for socialist policies inside the Labour Party, without nowadays much danger of expulsion or other difficulties.

There are some very large flaws in this argument. Thus to say that the Labour Party is the party of the working class is one thing, and as I have noted a very important one. But this affords absolutely no answer to the point at issue, namely that a socialist party is needed in Britain, and that the Labour Party is not it, and will not be turned into it. To say that it is the party of the working class is, on this view, to open the discussion, not to conclude it. It might be otherwise if there was any likelihood that the Labour Party *could* be turned into a socialist formation: but this is precisely the premise which must, on a realistic view, be precluded.

Nor can the argument that 'there is no alternative' to the Labour Party be taken as in any way conclusive. If it means that there is not the slightest chance of bringing into being an alternative *mass* party in the relevant future, and that the Labour Party will continue for a long time to be the major 'party of the working class', there need be no dispute about it, since it is so obviously true. But the idea is not to bring about all at once a mass party, which would very soon be able to supplant the Labour Party. This is a silly notion. What is at issue is something very different, namely the question of the possibility of creating a socialist party which would at first be necessarily fairly small but which would have a capacity for growth such as the existing formations on the left of the Labour Party do not have and are not likely to acquire.

There is also the question of the trade unions. Those who support continued work in the Labour Party and reject any exploration of an alternative to it also do so on the ground that the Labour Party has the support of the trade unions and that no other party of the left has any chance of attracting any such support in any time span that matters. Notwithstanding tensions and difficulties, the unions continue to see the Labour Party as their necessary political expression and their affiliation to it, in every sense, remains secure and all but unquestioned.

This too is not in dispute. But neither does it have much relevance to the question under discussion. A set of peculiar circumstances have created an organic link between the trade unions and the Labour Party that does not exist in most other countries with strong socialist movements; and there is no reason to think that such an organic link is an essential condition for the viability, growth and influence of a socialist party of a serious sort. Clearly, the support of *trade unionists* is vital for the purpose. But that is not at all the same thing as an organic and organisational link with trade unions. That such a link has been very valuable to the Labour Party is obvious. But there is no case for saying that it is essential for a serious socialist party. Such a party, to repeat, would need to include many trade unionists; and it would focus much of its work on the trade unions and seek to gain a hearing and influence in them. That would be enough to go on with, and the record of the Communist Party in this connection shows something of what is possible without organic links, and despite the marked hostility of trade union leaderships. In any case, the idea that the peculiar link between the trade unions and the Labour Party is an argument for accepting the latter's quasi-monopoly or that it sets a solid bar on the creation and growth of a socialist party of some substance is quite unwarranted. Not only is such a link unnecessary: it is in many ways undesirable.

There are socialists who work in the Labour Party not because they believe in its socialist potential, but in order, as they see it, the better to expose its leaders, to widen the gulf between these leaders and the militants in the rank and file, and generally to exacerbate the Party's internal tensions and contradictions. These endeavours, which have often formed part of a strategy of 'entrism' episodically favoured by this or that revolutionary grouping, have never come to anything much. They have produced ructions of various kinds, notably in the Labour Party's successive Youth organisations, but the Party leaders have always found it quite easy to cope with the problems which 'entrism' has created for them. As for those responsible for the ructions, they have generally passed on, and left little if any trace of their presence. It is not serious left-wing politics.

It is however one form of expression of a much more general aspiration, which has held generation after generation of socialists in its thrall, and which consists in the hope of 'capturing' the Labour Party for the adoption *and the carrying out* of socialist policies. The point is not here that this is an illusion but rather that it is the obverse phenomenon which has very commonly occurred, namely the 'capturing' of the militants by the Labour Party. This is not only true at the parliamentary level, though it is there that it has been most obviously true. But it has also occurred at the grassroots: people on the left who have set out with the intention of transforming the Labour Party have more often than not ended up being transformed by it, in the sense that they have been caught up in its rituals and rhythms, in ineffectual resolution-mongering exercises, in the resigned habituation to the unacceptable, even in the cynical acceptance and even expectation of betrayal. A new socialist formation should be able to attract at least some of these people.

But why a *new* socialist formation? Why not any of the existing alternatives on the left? Why not the Communist Party? And if not the

Communist Party, why not any of the other parties, groupings and sects on the left?

The Communist Party is the only party on the left of the Labour Party which has a genuine political and industrial implantation in the labour movement. It is small but not negligible. It is a Marxist party, of a sort, and many of its members are devoted and experienced activists. A good many of them are young and have been recruited in recent years. Some members of the Communist Party have acquired positions of responsibility and influence in trade unions; and whether this is because they are Communists or despite of it, the fact is that they are elected and re-elected and known to be members of the Party. The Communist Party has a daily newspaper, a fortnightly journal, a monthly theoretical magazine, a publishing house and printing presses. In quantitative terms, this is not very impressive— *The Morning Star* is reputed to print some 40,000 copies a day, a fair number of which are sold to the USSR and other Communist countries in Eastern Europe. But in comparison with all other organisations of the left, the Communist Party is obviously something of a force, particularly if account is taken of the fact that its influence has always been and is still much greater than its numbers would suggest. Many people who belong to the Labour Left and others who are generally speaking on the left have much sympathy for it, the more so since it has shed some of its most obnoxious characteristics in the period since 1956. The fact that the C.P. cannot elect a Member of Parliament and does not do well, to put it mildly, in local elections either, is a matter of political significance that must not be too easily dismissed, since it does indicate a real weakness and lack of popular resonance. But this is not, in the present context, to be taken as a conclusive proof of its inadequacy as an 'alternative' socialist party. Such an electoral criterion would be much too narrow—and in any case, *no* socialist party of any kind (except possibly in Scotland) could expect to do better for a fair while.

The reasons why the Communist Party is not the socialist formation that is needed lie elsewhere. There is first of all the fact that its main political perspective is to help persuade the Labour Party to adopt and carry out 'left policies'. It is very remarkable that the Communist Party appears to have accepted as a more or less permanent and irrevocable fact the Labour Party's domination of the labour movement. It wants to inflect the Labour Party's orientations in leftward directions; but it carefully refrains from any suggestion that the Labour Party must be dislodged, in however long-term a perspective, from the commanding position it occupies on the left if the notion of socialist advance is to acquire any serious meaning. 'Contrary to the ideas spread by some Labour leaders', the Communist Party Programme *(The British Road to Socialism)* notes, 'it is not the aim of the Communist Party to undermine, weaken or split the Labour Party.' 'As Communists', it declares, 'we sincerely desire the strengthening of the left trends within the Labour Party', and the Programme goes on to affirm the belief that 'the struggle of the socialist forces to make it a party of action and socialism will grow, and that the growth of the Communist Party will help this development.' It then follows that 'when (sic) the Labour Party rejects reformism, moves into the attack on capitalism, ends the bans and proscriptions against the left, it will ensure itself a vital role in the building of socialism. . .'[3]

When challenged, Communists tend to admit that this does *not* amount to a belief that the Labour Party will be transformed into the kind of socialist organisation required to assume the leadership of socialist advance in Britain; and many of the formulations of *The British Road to Socialism* are sufficiently ambiguous to allow diverse interpretations of what is involved when it speaks of 'Labour-Communist unity' and the like. But this is of no serious account. For all practical purposes, the Communist Party accepts the Labour Party's domination of the labour movement and places its hopes on the strengthening of the left in the Labour Party. What it wants is a Labour Party and a Labour Government that would pursue 'left policies' ('Our strategy', Gordon McLennan, the General Secretary of the Communist Party, told the 1975 Congress, 'is for the return of a Labour Government committed by the pressure of the mass movement to left policies'). Communists also proclaim that a strong Communist Party is necessary to enhance the pressure of the mass movement. But it is nevertheless on the Labour Party and on those who lead it that the pressure is to be exercised, for the effective translation of 'left policies' into actual measures to be carried out by a Labour Government.

But Communists also know perfectly well that the leaders of the Labour Party have absolutely no intention of embarking on the 'left policies' which the Communist Party advocates. This is why they are driven to attack the Labour Party's present 'rightwing' leaders, and to help foster the perennial hope that it will eventually be led by better, more 'leftwing' ones. Given their acceptance of the Labour Party's domination of the labour movement as a scarcely to be questioned datum, the Communists find themselves in the same box as the Labour Left, and seek to offer the same illusory way out of it.

At a more immediate level, the Communist Party tends to see the Labour Left as a bridge between itself and the rank and file of the Labour Party. What it fails to see is that the Labour Left has traditionally been and remains a bridge (and a much-trampled bridge at that) between the rank and file and the Labour leadership. The Labour Left does not, so to speak, open out leftwards but rightwards: it affords an important link between the activists and the leadership, and cannot as a constituent element of the Labour Party help but do so. It may be a nuisance at times; but it is nevertheless exceedingly useful to the Labour leaders. It helps to keep alive the myth of a transformable Labour Party. The Communist Party in its turn and at one remove is involved in the same enterprise.

This is not to suggest that the Communist Party should gratuitously and ridiculously proclaim itself as the alternative 'vanguard' party of the working class, or any such. Nor is the Communist Party to be reproached for seeking to put pressure on the Labour Party or on a Labour Government or for trying to influence the Labour Left or any other part of the labour movement. Any socialist party must try and make such connections and refuse to immure itself in self-righteous and sectarian isolation. But trying to make connections and open lines of communication and even cooperation is a very different matter from the pursuit of the politics of illusion in which the Communist Party has been engaged for more than forty years.

The fact that these policies should have been pursued for all this length of time without provoking at least vigorous debate in the Party is very significant, and suggests another and major reason for the inadequacy of the Communist Party. It is not after all as if these policies had brought it much success or even any success—if anything rather the reverse. Yet, and save for isolated mutterings here and there, there has not in all this time been any serious debate in the Communist Party on the absolutely central issue of the Labour Party and of the C.P.'s relationship to it. All that there has been is the endless reiteration of received policies, and that reiteration has now assumed the character of a traditional litany which makes its expected appearance in every pronouncement of the party—'left unity', 'exposing the Right-wing Labour leaders', 'strengthening the left in the Labour Party', 'the need for a strong Communist Party', and so on.

The reason for this lack of serious debate on this issue is very simple. It has to do with the fact that the Communist Party is an exceedingly *managed* party, in which the leadership is well able to reduce the scope and extent of debate; and to do so in the name of a 'democratic centralism' which is in fact a device for the oligarchic control of the leadership over its members.

It is quite true that a good deal has changed in the internal life and climate of the Communist Party in these last twenty years. So far as an outsider can judge, there is now much more 'tolerance' for divergent and dissident views, and these even find occasional expression in *The Morning Star* (mainly in the form of letters) and at Party Congresses. There is also now the possibility of serious and animated discussion *at branch level*. But between the rank and file in the branches on the one hand, and the leadership on the other, there is a thick layer of bureaucratic defences and devices which decisively *limit* the impact of rank and file debate, *defuse* opposition and *prevent* its organisation in the name of a sacrosanct 'ban on factions', and generally ensure that the right people—in other words the people of whom the existing leadership approves—remain in the key positions of party control and the wrong ones are kept out. The fact is that the democratic claims which the Communist Party regularly makes for its own internal organisation are a sham, save perhaps at the lower levels of the party. It has not yet begun to learn the meaning of the 'inner-party democracy' of which it boasts, and cannot do so as long as it continues to worship the sacred cows of 'democratic centralism' and the 'ban on factions'.

The result is that it is an extremely traditional and uncreative party, which exudes a very strong impression of intellectual paralysis, as a party, and of political conservatism. There is nothing about it which suggests any capacity for reinvigoration and renewal. This is not a matter of old hacks being in command, as is sometimes suggested. It is rather that its own rules of conduct make it inevitable that hacks, old *and* young, should be in command. In *this* respect, nothing much seems to have changed in the Communist Party over the years.

It is, not very paradoxically, the item of policy where change has been most obvious which also shows up in a cruel light the stiffness of limb of the Communist Party. This is the item which relates to its attitudes and pronouncements concerning the Soviet Union.

The Communist Party is now quite willing to do what would have been inconceivable before 1956 (and for some time after), namely express occasional criticism of certain Soviet internal and external policies—for instance the treatment of dissidents in the USSR and the invasion of Czechoslovakia in 1968. This has also been extended to include the occasional expression in Party publications of views suggesting that there are certain deep structural problems which the Soviet regime has not resolved. For anyone who remembers the totally unconditional endorsement of absolutely everything Soviet before 1956, however absurd or criminal, this is advance indeed.

But on other (and more appropriate) criteria, it is impossible not to note how cramped and constricted, how reluctant and limited, how laggard and uncreative the change has been. The point is not that the Communist Party should have turned itself into another agency of anti-Soviet propaganda and sought to emulate the capitalist and Chinese press in the denunciation of the USSR. It is rather that the Party never at any time in these two decades gave any sign that it could or wanted to produce a serious socialist critique of Soviet experience and Soviet policies, such as might have made a really useful contribution to a discussion which is crucial to the international socialist movement. Nor has the Communist Party shown any sign that it wanted to engage in a critical reassessment of the impact of Stalinism and the Soviet connection *on the British Communist Party*. It is after all not only on Stalinism in the Soviet Union that light needs to be cast: it is also on Stalinism in Britain and in the British Communist Party. If a party is to learn from its mistakes, as the Communist Party constantly says it wants to do, it must first be willing to identify what these mistakes were and to discuss them freely.

The Communist Party has proved incapable of any of this. Twenty years after the XXth Party Congress, the Party's former General Secretary, John Gollan, has produced a 20,000 words article in *Marxism Today* which must be taken, and has been taken, to represent the most important pronouncement of the Party to date on Stalinism and socialist democracy.[4] It is in fact a lamentable document, written in the familiar wooden style associated by long usage with such productions, mealy-mouthed, full of careful ambiguities and euphemisms, and generally content to repeat what have become the most commonplace formulas in the Communist movement concerning Stalinism and its consequences.

It must be taken as significant that an article such as this, on this subject, should be the best that the Communist Party is able to offer to its readers and to the labour movement at large. One is told that what matters is not what Gollan says but that he should have said it in *Marxism Today* and thus made possible a more thorough discussion than hitherto. But even if true, this is a sad comment on the state of the Communist Party. And the overwhelming chances are that it is not true, and that the discussion will proceed in the traditionally constrained ways which the nature and structure of the Party render inevitable. Nor is it to be overlooked that it will proceed, for the most part, on the assumption which is central to the thinking of the Communist Party's leadership, and which John Gollan expresses very well when he says that the problems of the socialist system which he takes the Soviet Union to be are 'essentially problems of growth and further economic and social development, including that of socialist democracy and its political institutions.'[5] This blandly complacent view of the Soviet system as a still-not-perfect version of socialism, but as a definite version of it nevertheless, is not conducive to serious discussion and appraisal.

What is at issue here is not an 'academic' discussion or appraisal but a political question of great practical importance, namely the attitude which a socialist party, of the kind which the British left requires, should have in relation to the Soviet Union. What may be said about it here is that this attitude cannot be that of the Communist Party, which continues to treat the USSR as the senior, if no longer as the dominant, member of a great international socialist family. It is no doubt a comfortable and comforting idea; but also a damaging and stultifying one. It renders more difficult, to put it too mildly, the exercise of an independence of judgment and a freedom of criticism in regard to *all* regimes which a socialist party, in the real world, absolutely must have; and which the Communist Party, given its past traditions and present stances, cannot have.

On the other hand, the Russian question is a deeply divisive one for the Communist Party. There is a part of the membership which now takes a very adverse view of the USSR and other Communist countries, on various socialist grounds. There is another part of the membership which is rather Stalinist in disposition: some of these members are the remnants of a bygone era who hanker for the certitudes which gave them strength and endurance. Others are newer and younger people who see the defence of the Soviet Union and of Stalin—indeed of Stalinism—as part of an affirmation of a socialist and revolutionary commitment which they see most of their own leaders as having lost in a 'revisionist' withdrawal. The fact that this is a very misguided way to affirm a socialist and revolutionary commitment is not here relevant. For the rest, there are all shades and nuances, with the leadership committed as described earlier, yet varyingly uneasy in that commitment. This is not a good situation for a socialist party. But the Communist Party appears unable to get out of it; and the issue wont go away.

Nothing has so far been said about the 'parliamentarism', 'electoralism', and the 'reformism' in general for which the C.P. is constantly denounced by its opponents on the left. This will be discussed presently. But whatever may be made of these strictures, they are of far less importance than the deficiencies discussed here.

The weaknesses of the parties, groupings and sects on the left of the Communist Party are different in several important respects.

All these organisations have one major characteristic in common: this is that they are all really very small and in some cases ridiculously small. This is no ground for their automatic rejection, but it is nevertheless an important and in some ways a crucial fact, all the more important because some at least of these groupings have been in existence in one form or another for a fair length of time and have not managed to achieve much or any growth. What is also notable about this failure is that it has occurred over a period of time when economic and political conditions have been sufficiently varied to suggest that their capacity for growth *under any circumstances* that it is reasonable to anticipate for the relevant future is very low. In short, there is no reason whatever to believe that any of them is going to be able to achieve any kind of political take-off, such as would turn it, say, into a party of ten thousand members and upwards. On the contrary, the signs are that the existing organisations on the left of the C.P. are facing difficult times, with divisions, splits, regroupings and the like—all without any grip on the political life of the labour movement.

This last point is the one which really matters. There is no inherent merit in numbers and size, and it would certainly be a great mistake to dismiss as of no account the growth, however modest, of 'ultra-left' groupings in the course of the last twenty years. Their presence on the left scene, much more notable than that of earlier such groupings, is one of the important developments of the last two decades; and their impact too has been many-sided and out of proportion to their actual membership. But a socialist party which wants to play a really serious role in the labour movement must have, or show signs of being able to acquire, a much more solid implantation than any of the groups concerned have been able to achieve or appear likely to achieve. And this must be taken as being particularly true under-bourgeois democratic conditions, such as have prevailed in Britain. No doubt, very small groupings may keep going more or less indefinitely, and make some sort of impact. But that is not the point. A socialist party requires a lot more than this, and this means a capacity to attract the kind of membership referred to earlier, and to go on attracting more people.

It is clearly necessary to ask why these groupings of the 'ultra-left' have not fared better—a good deal depends on the answer.

For the groupings themselves, there is no real problem. They explain their relative lack of success, in so far as they acknowledge it at all, in terms of a working class false consciousness engendered by the hegemony of the ruling class and its control of what Marx called the 'mental means of production'; by the weight of tradition; by the 'reformism' of the existing working class parties and their leaders, notably the Labour Party, and also the Communist Party.

The importance of any such factors in shaping working class consciousness is not here at issue. The point is rather that these factors do not explain why *none* of the 'ultra-left' groupings have been able to attract more people who do already have a genuine commitment to the socialist cause. The question is not why any of the groupings of the 'ultra-left' have failed to become mass parties or even large parties; it is why they have scarcely become parties at all. To this question, they themselves do not provide a worthwhile answer.

The answer which is usually provided by their critics on the left has to do with certain further characteristics which these groupings, for all their many ideological, programmatic and organisational differences, tend to share in varying degrees. This very prominently includes a narrow doctrinal sectarianism which in some instances assumes extreme and even grotesque forms; a marked tendency to believe that the final crisis of capitalism is more or less imminent, to which is naturally allied a strong propensity to adventurist sloganeering; and an internal rigidity of organisation which makes the Communist Party's 'democratic centralism' appear by comparison as a veritable model of inner-party democracy.

These are indeed unpleasant characteristics. But one may well ask whether they are not symptoms rather than causes; and whether the reason for the lack of attraction of the groupings of the 'ultra-left' must not be sought in much more deeply-rooted characteristics. I believe that this is the case; and that the main cause of their lack of attraction is not their sectarianism, dogmatism, adventurism and authoritarianism but their basic perspectives as to the ways of socialist advance in Britain. It is *this* which produces their isolation; and it is their isolation which at least in part if not wholly produces their unpleasant characteristics.

All these organisations have a common perception of socialist change in terms of a revolutionary seizure of power on the Bolshevik model of October 1917. This is their common point of departure and of arrival, the script and scenario which determines their whole mode of being. But this Bolshevik model has very little appeal in the working class movements of bourgeois democratic regimes in general, and virtually no appeal in the British working class movement. The context of a bourgeois democratic regime, in Britain at least as much as elsewhere, imposes upon revolutionary socialists a strategy of advance which has to include a real measure of electoral legitimation.

This is in no way to suggest that electoral legitimation is all that a socialist party needs to seek or that a socialist party which means business can afford to rely on such legitimation alone. On the contrary, there is no question that an attempt at the radical transformation of the existing social order in socialist directions will require a lot more than this, within a complex and diffuse scenario that must include many different forms of action, pressure and struggle.

But it also does need to include the attempt to achieve a measure of electoral legitimation at different levels and the achievement of a measure of representation in existing institutions. In the British context, as in the context of any other bourgeois democratic regime, this is an inescapable requirement for a socialist party, and needs to be treated as such, as a duty and as an opportunity, and not as a distracting and meaningless chore.

In *The British Road to Socialism,* the Communist Party speaks of the creation by the labour movement, and as a result of a many sided struggle, of 'the conditions for the election of a Parliamentary majority and government pledged to a socialist programme';[6] and it also suggests that 'when a socialist majority in Parliament is won it will need the support of the mass movement outside Parliament to uphold the decisions it has taken in Parliament. Conversely, the Parliamentary decisions will give legal endorsement to popular aims and popular struggles'.[7]

It is very reasonable to argue that formulas such as these place too great an emphasis on the parliamentary and electoral aspects of a strategy of socialist advance; and also that they offer much too cramped a view of the meaning of socialist democracy. This is what the 'ultra-left' groupings have always claimed. But they have usually tended to spoil a reasonable case by arguing in terms which had little if any relevance to the real conditions at hand. They have rightly been concerned to warn against the dangers of 'parliamentary cretinism'. But they have themselves easily succumbed to the temptations of anti-parliamentary cretinism and to the attractions of revolutionary phrase-mongering. There is no reason to think that this will change: it clearly answers the particular needs and wishes of a small and constantly changing but constant minority of militants on the British left. Nor is there any good reason to think that the Communist Party will eventually be able to fill the gap that exists on the left. In order to do so, it would have to transform itself so thoroughly as to become a new party: it is not a realistic expectation.

This is not a comfortable conclusion. For there are many formidable obstacles which stand in the way of political renewal on the left. Yet such a renewal is necessary if an effective challenge is to be posed to the domination which the Labour Party exercises over the labour movement: nothing much by way of socialist advance will be possible until such a challenge can be effectively posed. This requires the formation of a socialist party free from the manifold shortcomings of existing organisations and able to draw together people from such organisations as well as people who are now politically homeless. By no means the least of its purposes would be to provide a credible and effective rallying point to help in the struggle against the marked and accelerating drift to the right in Britain.

It is of course necessary to discuss the orientations, programme and organisation of such a party. Some of this has been suggested here by implication. But there is a large range of matters which need to be tackled and worked out. Socialists who believe that the time has come to move on should begin to explore seriously what can be done about it.

NOTES

1. See for instance the Postscript to the second edition of *Parliamentary Socialism* (Merlin Press, 1972); and for a critique of the argument, see Ken Coates, 'Socialists and the Labour Party', in *The Socialist Register, 1973*.
2. These are not of course the only organisations which include socialist activists of one sort of another—though most such activists are likely to be in one or other of the political organisations of the left.
3. *The British Road to Socialism,* third revised edition October 1968, p. 24.
4. John Gollan, 'Socialist Democracy—Some Problems', *Marxism Today,* January 1976.
5. Ibid., p. 5.
6. *The British Road to Socialism,* op. cit., p. 6.
7. Ibid., p. 48.

PART II

CONTROVERSIAL ISSUES IN MARXIST ECONOMIC THEORY

by Ben Fine & Laurence Harris

This article surveys critically the theoretical debates that have occupied Marxist economists in Britain during recent years.* In order to understand the debates it is necessary to clarify two things: how Marx saw the structure of the capitalist economy, and what is the structure of Marx's *Capital*. These will give us a benchmark for evaluating the contributions of the new Marxist economists.

1. *Marx's Economics*

In *Capital* (and, in particular, in Volume II) Marx repeatedly uses the concept of the circuit of capital to characterise the structure of the capitalist economy. In this circuit capital moves through several different forms. If we begin with *money capital*, M, this is exchanged for commodities C which consist of means of production MP and labour power LP—inputs into the productive process. These commodities are set to work under capitalist relations of production and at this stage of the circuit capital has assumed the form of *productive capital*. As a result of this setting to work new commodities C^1 are produced and owned by the capitalist, and in taking this form capital becomes *commodity capital*. The value of these new commodities is greater than the value of the commodities which enter as inputs into the production process; it is greater by the amount of surplus value which is produced in the production process. Finally, these commodities are sold for money (i.e. exchanged or realised) so that capital re-assumes the form of money capital, M^1. Since this money capital is greater than the money capital with which the circuit began, the surplus can either be consumed by capitalists (in which case simple reproduction occurs since the circuit merely repeats itself without expanding) or it can be accumulated by capitalists and the circuit of capital begins again on a larger scale (expanded reproduction). Marx divided this circuit into two spheres of

---

*As is apparent from the bibliography, the debates surveyed in this paper have been stimulated by the existence of the Conference of Socialist Economists and its *Bulletin*. Details of the CSE may be obtained from the authors at Birkbeck College, Economics Dept., 7-15 Gresse St., London W.1.

activity. The activity of setting to work means of production and labour power to produce new commodities, that is the activity from $C(MP,LP)....P....C^1$ on the circuit, takes place in the *sphere of production*. It is only here that surplus value is produced. The activity of selling the commodities for money and buying commodities as inputs, the activity from C^1——M^1——$C(MP,LP)$ takes place in the *sphere of exchange*. Although the two spheres are distinguished, the circuit of capital implies a unity of the two spheres so that capital can only be understood in terms of the circuit as a whole. (In mere symbols, the end of the sphere of production, C^1, is the start of the sphere of exchange, and the end of the latter, $C(MP,LP)$ is the start of the former.) The specific features of this unity are that surplus value is only produced in the sphere of production, not in the sphere of exchange, and that the unity of the two spheres in the circuit is a complex unity with its own dialectical contradictions. These features are relevant to several of the issues we discuss in the following sections.

An understanding of the spheres of production and exchange and their relationship is not sufficient for understanding the structure of the capitalist economy. In addition Marx introduces the concept of *distribution*. The distribution of values between the classes in the capitalist mode of production is a process which encompasses both the spheres of production and exchange. It can only be understood in terms of the unity of production and exchange.

The relation between production, exchange, and distribution is complex. As Marx states in the *Grundrisse* his conclusion is 'not that production, distribution, exchange and consumption are identical, but that they all form the members of a totality, distinctions within a unity. Production predominates not only over itself... but over the other moments as well... A definite production thus determines a definite consumption, distribution and exchange as well as *definite relations between these different moments*. Admittedly, however, *in its one sided form* production is itself determined by the other moments... Mutual interaction takes place between the different moments. Thus, to use language currently in vogue, production, exchange and distribution are to be seen as members of a structured whole. Production is determinant in the last instance, but the other spheres have a relative autonomy and each sphere has an effect on each other. We shall see that a fault common to many of the modern Marxist economists is an inability to grasp this complex structure as a whole.

The structure of Marx's *Capital* is closely related to his view of the structure of the capitalist economy. But there is not a simple identity between the two structures. *Capital* is best understood as the articulation of two structures. First, it is structured in terms related to the hierarchical relationships between the real world's production, exchange, and distribution. Thus Volume I, entitled *Capitalist Production,* is concerned with the sphere of production; Volume II, *The Process of Circulation of Capital,* is concerned with analysing the sphere of exchange on the basis of the already developed analysis of production (it is concerned with the circulation of capital through the two spheres); and Volume III, *Capitalist Production as a Whole,* is concerned with distribution as a moment of the articulated spheres of production and exchange. But it must be understood that this is a schematic view of the three volumes. Even in Volume I exchange must be present. Indeed, in the very first chapter, the fundamental concept of the commodity is predicated on the existence of exchange. In Volume II, similarly, distribution is present, but it is distribution considered only at a relatively high level of abstraction. The fact that no volume can simply exclude the other moments simply reflects the unity of the different spheres in reality. Moreover, it is to be noted that Marx's *first* volume is on production since this sphere is fundamental and the other two volumes can only be understood on the basis of it. Second, Marx's *Capital* is structured according to the level of abstraction of the argument. Marx elucidates in the *Grundrisse* his concept of scientific method wherein thought 'appropriates' reality in all its complexity, constructs out of this complexity the essential abstract concepts (corresponding to real abstractions) such as 'labour', and then takes the extremely significant step of reconstructing from these relatively 'simple' abstract concepts the complex concepts which parallel the complex phenomena of reality. This structure, from the simple abstract to increasingly complex abstract concepts, is found in *Capital.* Thus, Marx does not begin with 'capital' even though it is 'the all-dominating economic power of bourgeois society', he begins with commodities because in capitalist societies they are the form in which the most 'simple' abstract category, labour, is expressed. Note, however, that although Marx's *Capital* is structured according to levels of abstraction, it is by no means a simple structure following a unilinear development from simple abstract to complex abstract. For example, the relatively complex concept of the reserve army of labour (the general law of capitalist accumulation) enters well before the basis of the general law, the tendency of the rate of profit to fall, is constructed.

Thus, *Capital* must be understood as a structure of concepts or arguments which is itself an articulation of two structures: a structure according to the hierarchical relationship between production, exchange, and distribution, and a structure according to levels of abstraction. The two structures are not identical but they do overlap. Thus the relatively 'simple' concept of value is indispensible for the analysis of production so that both enter in Volume I while the 'complex' (hence observable) category of interest must primarily be considered from the point of view of distribution and therefore both are considered in Volume III. In what follows we shall employ this view of Marx's method as a standard of comparison for modern writers.

The protagonists in the debates can be classified into two schools of thought, neo-Ricardian and Fundamentalist, with some writers falling in between. Here we outline the distinctions between the schools and in Sections 2 and 3 we examine the specific issues which have been the object of debate.

For neo-Ricardians all analysis of the capitalist economy takes place in the spheres of exchange and distribution. Since both are only examined in isolation from the sphere of production the result is the antithesis of Marx's analysis, for the latter emphasises the dependence of exchange and distribution on production and the impossibility of understanding capital except in the complex unity of the three spheres. Moreover, and related to this one-sidedness, neo-Ricardians develop their conclusions only in terms of categories such as prices of production and market prices which exist at a relatively low level of abstraction. The ultimate theoretical justification for this approach is found in neo-Ricardianism's treatment of the transformation problem which Marx attempted (and failed) to solve in Volume III of *Capital*. Neo-Ricardians see the problem as one of deriving commodities' prices of production from the labour embodied in them and, concluding that prices of production can be quantified directly without quantifying values, they consider value theory to be an irrelevant diversion. Concomitantly, analysis of the sphere of production, for which value theory is necessary, is rejected. From this follows a rejection by neo-Ricardians of Marx's distinction between productive and unproductive labour, for the distinction between these categories is central to Marx's concept of the fundamental determining role of the sphere of production and it is only relevant within a view which takes as central the relations between the *three* spheres. There follows their conclusion that economic crises are to be explained solely in terms of class struggle over distribution in the sphere of exchange (but there is also an implicit denial of the concept of economic class struggle and economic crises as such and an identification of economic activity with political activity).

For Fundamentalists, the sphere of production is determinant. Indeed, it is the only sphere of economic activity that they analyse in a consistent manner. In doing so the Fundamentalists emphasize the significance of value theory, assert that the conclusions drawn by neo-Ricardianism from the transformation problem are invalid, consider important the distinction between productive and unproductive labour and locate the source of crises in the tendency of the rate of profit to fall. The source of this tendency is itself located in the nature of capital-in-general and it is treated as the development of capital's contradictions with the fundamental contradiction located in the sphere of production.

An understanding of the positions taken by these two schools and by the several writers who are identified neither with one nor the other, can only be gained by examining the specific issues over which debates have taken place. We make an heuristic division between the issues. In Section 2 we examine the essentially 'static' issues of the transformation problem and the productive/unproductive labour distinction. These bring to the fore the differences over the significance of the concept of value, over the relationship between values and prices of production, and over the relationship between production, exchange and circulation. In Section 3 we show how these differences are reflected in differences over 'dynamic' issues, the economic laws of motion of capitalism. We examine the disputes over the law of the tendency of the rate of profit to fall, over the concept of crises and over the role of the state in economic crises. Finally, in Section 4, we give a summary appraisal of the state of debate. Throughout, we discuss the methodological issues and the political implications involved in the debate.

2. Categorization and the concept of capital
Value, price and transformation problems

At the centre of controversies in Marxist economics has been the so-called transformation problem. Certainly, whilst it has been the object of the most frequent area of disagreement in Marxist economic theory, the disputes over the transformation problem have wider implications. Any treatment of the transformation problem embodies, at least implicitly, fundamental aspects of method, and it is differences in these that have to be recognised. For these differences in method, not surprisingly, are the source of further theoretical differences which appear to bear little or no relation to the transformation problem as such.

Marx's own treatment of the transformation of values into prices of production depends upon the formation of what we shall call the value rate of profit and label r. It equals the ratio of total surplus value produced S to total capital advanced $C + V$, $r = \dfrac{S}{(C + V)}$. Clearly this category r is calculated numerically in terms of the abstract production category of value, rather than the complex exchange category of price. However, Marx's motive for employing this average rate of profit was to develop the relationship by which surplus value becomes distributed to individual capitalists through exchange. The category r and the principle of distribution are not some ideal abstraction but reflect the real forces of competition that tend to equalise each individual capitalist's rate of profit to the average rate. The principle of distribution between capitalists is that each receives surplus value according to capital advanced. Each capitalist can be considered an individual share-holder in the joint-stock company that is the aggregate social capital. The significance of this is that the amount of surplus value appropriated by each capitalist does not depend solely upon the amount of surplus value produced in his individual enterprise. For, if social capital comprises two individual and equal capitals (each 100 say), they must, according to the principle of distribution, appropriate an equal quantity of surplus value. But, if each uses constant and variable capital in different ratios (say 60:40 and 40:60 respectively) then the one capital yields a different quantity of surplus value from the other. For example, if the rate of surplus value, $\frac{s}{v}$, is 100%, then the capitals individually yield 40 and 60 surplus value. This means that the average rate of profit $r = \frac{40+60}{60+40+40+60} = 50\%$, and the principle of distribution would yield 50 surplus value to each capital.

This is incompatible with the exchange of commodities at their values, for the respective values of the commodities are 140 (60+40+40) and 160 (40+60+60) and their respective costs of production (c + v) are both 100 so that if the commodities exchanged at their values one would yield a profit of 40% and the other 60% instead of both yielding the average rate of 50%. Marx integrated this theory of distribution with a theory of exchange (values) based on what he called modified values or prices of production. These were defined by marking up each individual cost of production by r. In our example, this would result in each having a price of production, or exchange value, of 150, and this conforms to the principle of distribution of surplus value according to capital advanced. But individual surplus value appropriated diverges from individual surplus value produced, and it appears in the qualitatively distinct form of profit. The distinction arises because distribution (profit) does and can only take place through exchange.

Marx's transformation of values into prices of production is situated towards the beginning of Volume III of *Capital*. The analysis of the earlier volumes of *Capital* is conducted at that level of abstraction for which commodities exchange at their values and this is so even though Volume II deals with the aggregate circulation of capital and commodities and consequently the articulation between production and exchange. What is clear from Volume III (and is universally agreed) is that Marx is concerned with moving to a lower level of abstraction for which commodities do not exchange at their values. But it would be an error to conclude that, in the context of the transformation problem, Marx was solely concerned with 'correcting' his earlier abstraction of the equality of exchange value with value. For he is also developing, against the background of Volume II's integration of production with exchange, a theory of distribution. This involves considering how surplus value created in production is distributed to capitalists through exchange. This is not simply a quantitative question (a question of the numerical relationship between values and prices) but requires an understanding of the qualitative distinctions between price exchange) and value (production) categories and in particular between profit and surplus value.

These remarks confirm the view that levels of abstraction do not correspond to some neat uni-dimensional scheme that constructs a stair-climbing process from the abstract at the bottom of the concrete at the top. In particular the articulation of production with exchange can be analysed on the basis that commodities exchange at their values. On the other hand, the articulation of production with distribution cannot proceed without being linked to a reconstitution of the articulation between production and exchange at a lower level of abstraction, where commodities do not exchange at their values. Second, and related to the first point, the transformation problem involves an analysis of the unity of production, exchange and distribution. Any treatment of it that fails to recognise this is bound to be one-sided and incomplete. This gives us a framework in which to analyse the various 'solutions' to the transformation problem.

Within this framework, Marx's transformation cannot be considered one-sided—neglecting one or the other of production, exchange or distribution in their unity. Nevertheless, Marx does make an inadequate integration of exchange with production and distribution. For, whilst values are modified to form prices of production in the movement from production to exchange, no such modification takes place for the movement from exchange into production. Values are transformed into exchange values in modifying costs $(c + v)$ into prices of production $(c + v)(1 + r)$, but no consideration is given to the transformation of exchange values into values as capital advanced in exchange becomes capital in production. Marx takes capital advanced in the form of value $(c + v)$, and has not transformed it from exchange value despite its movement from exchange into production. It follows that Marx's integration of production (and distribution) with exchange is one-sided, because production is united with exchange at one point in the circuit of capital but not at the other. This Marx recognises, for he observes that the value of capital advanced may diverge from the price of production of that capital, but he makes no effort to correct this discrepancy.

This omission on Marx's part has bred considerable controversy. It has led the neo-Ricardian school to reject value analysis altogether (see for example articles by Hodgson and Steedman). As we shall see this is not simply a conclusion of their theory but also their very starting point. For neo-Ricardianism bases its analysis on the *technical* relations of production. These comprise the physical and labour inputs necessary to produce any given set of commodities. For example, to produce a given commodity, quantities $x_1, x_2, \ldots x_n$ of certain raw materials (physical means of production) may be necessary as well as a quantity 1 of labour-time (not labour-power). Now if we impose on these technical conditions of production a system of exchange relations, in which every input has a price, then the cost of producing the commodity in question is simply $p_1 x_1 + p_2 x_2 + \ldots + p_n x_n + wl$ where $p_1, p_2 \ldots, p_i, \ldots p_n$ are the prices of the first, second, ..., ith, ... inputs and w is the wage-payment. In so far as this cost is less than the price of the commodity produced, there is room for profit, and this implies the existence of a rate of profit on costs advanced so that $p = (p_1 x_1 + p_2 x_2 \ldots + p_n x_n + wl)$ $(1 + r^1)$ where p is the price of the commodity and r^1 the price rate of profit. Clearly r^1 is a different concept from r, the value rate of profit. Later we shall see that it is also numerically different.

If we assume that the economy is competitive in the sense that the price paid for any input (including labour) is the same for any purchaser and that the rate of profit is the same for the production of any output, then it follows that we can write down similar equations as the one above for the production of every commodity. That is, the price of a commodity is determined by marking up costs of production since each input in the economy (except labour) is considered to be the output of some production process. This means that our technical relations of production generate a system of simultaneous equations. In these, prices in the economy are related to the wage rate and the profit rate. It is the solution of this set of equations which has been the major theoretical object of the neo-Ricardian school.

What they can show is that prices can be eliminated from the equations to leave an inverse relationship between the level of wages and the rate of profit. This is hardly a surprising result and corresponds to the inverse relationship between the value of labour-power and the value rate of profit, when everything else is held constant. It leads neo-Ricardians to conclude that distribution (in particular the rate of profit) in capitalist society is equally determined by economic class struggle for higher wages and the ability of productivity increases (i.e. development of the technical relations of production) to provide for higher wages (Gough (1975)).

This conclusion is deceptively appealing. Indeed, it has the air of tautology about it. It is further reinforced by what is considered to be a devastating criticism of Marx's transformation of values into prices of production. The neo-Ricardians observe quite correctly that Marx's value rate of profit depends upon the sectoral composition of output given the rate of surplus value $\frac{S}{V}$, unless either this is zero (along with r and r^1) or the organic composition of capital is the same in every sector. This is because the transfer of capital to a sector with a lower organic composition of capital (a low ratio of dead to living labour) will increase the surplus value produced as more living labour (the source of surplus value) becomes employed. In this case, r would rise because aggregate capital advanced C + V has remained constant whilst aggregate surplus value produced S has increased. An opposite movement of capital would decrease r.

In contrast, the neo-Ricardians argue that the price rate of profit r^1 is quite independent of the composition of output. It depends only upon the technical relations of production given the level of wages. It follows that Marx incorrectly calculates the price rate of profit, because he constructs the value rate of profit which can vary whilst the former remains constant. It can only be by a fortuitous composition of output that Marx calculates the rate of profit correctly, for it is only under exceptional circumstances that r and r^1 are always equal (i.e. no exploitation or equal organic compositions of capital in every sector).

However, even if Marx is lucky enough to calculate r^1 correctly by r, his subsequent calculation of prices of production is wrong. For Marx does this by marking up individual costs in value terms (c + v) by the rate of profit to obtain the price of production (c + v) (1 + r). This is illegitimate, for as we have already observed, the costs should first be transformed into prices of production prior to the mark-up by the rate of profit. The neo-Ricardians argue that without this prior transformation, Marx's determination of prices of production diverges from their own correct calculations of market prices based on exchange costs and the price rate of profit.

The neo-Ricardian critique of Marx's transformation of values into prices of production does not simply involve the conclusion that Marx fudges the transformation. This is because they pose an alternative theory of the determination of prices and distribution based on technical relations of production. Marx's transformation is not only wrong but superfluous because prices etc. can be obtained without any reference to value whatsoever. This conclusion has at its starting point the calculation of values from the technical conditions of production. The neo-Ricardian interpretation of value is based on consideration of equations of the type

$$W = W_1 x_1 + W_2 x_2 + \ldots + W_n x_n + 1$$

where W is the value of an output produced by the inputs $x_1, \ldots, x_n$ which have values $W_1, \ldots, W_n$ and 1 is the living labour input. To calculate the value of a commodity we add up the dead labour embodied in the physical inputs used to produce it (as measured by their values, W_1, W_2 etc.) together with the quantity of direct living labour. These value equations can be solved to find the labour-time necessary to produce any commodity and this constitutes the neo-Ricardian concept of value. This concept is simply a measure of labour-time embodied and bears no relation to the commodity form of production.

What is significant in this procedure is that the technical relations of production are the logical origin of their value equations, just as earlier they were the logical origin of the price equations. This leads the neo-Ricardians to the conclusion that it is quite unnecessary to proceed via values to the determination of prices. In effect the transformation of values into prices is an irrelevant stumbling block, because prices can be calculated directly without any reference to value. Since, for neo-Ricardians, the important object is the theory of prices and since they see their concept of value as unnecessary for this, they conclude by rejecting the relevance of value theory.

Not surprisingly, given its apparently destructive implications for Marx's theory, the neo-Ricardian theory has been subject to extensive criticism, although this is not always directed towards a consideration of the transformation problem. Typically neo-Ricardianism is identified with bourgeois economics for its preoccupation with exchange rather than production relations. This is a fair characterisation of the theory for it focuses on the articulation between distribution and exchange with only a token recognition of production (in the form of the specification of technical relations).

Yaffe (1975) for the Fundamentalists asserts that Marx's solution of the transformation problem is correct, not only quantitatively but also because of its reliance upon value categories and the priority this gives to capitalist production. In doing this he clearly recognises the distinction and unity between production, exchange and distribution, but he offers little in the way of argument to suggest why this makes Marx's solution correct. This results from Yaffe's inability to integrate production and exchange. Usually he is confined in the sphere of production, but for the transformation problem he analyses relations in exchange only, taking values as his original costs as a gesture of his former concentration on the sphere of production. Production and exchange are not theoretically integrated in the movement of capital. This error becomes most clear in a contribution by Howell (1975) who argues that far from transforming values into prices of production, Marx was concerned to transform (values expressed in) prices into prices of production. Therefore, Fundamentalists are forced into the position of thinking the transformation takes place only in the sphere of exchange rather than as something which expresses the contradictory unity of production, exchange and distribution.

Rowthorn (1974) has made a more extensive criticism of neo-Ricardianism in his discussion of vulgar economy. He argues that the neo-Ricardian method leads it to fail to comprehend capitalism as a specific mode of production. The class relations of production are entirely absent from the neo-Ricardian system which depends exclusively upon distributional relations based on property rights. In fact, the neo-Ricardian price equations fail to distinguish a capitalist system of wage-labour, from a system in which workers hire machinery for their own use from capitalists by a rent (profit) payment. This failure arises from the neo-Ricardian treatment of labour like any other factor input. This is quite explicit in their cost and mark up calculations where the labour costs wl enter equally with each $p_i x_i$: living labour has the same status as means of production (dead labour). This implies the use of the concept of the price of labour (the wage) and the failure to make the crucial distinction between labour and labour-power (but see Hodgson (1976) who claims otherwise).

It is arguments of this sort that Rowthorn uses to criticise the historically ambiguous concept of the capitalist mode of production that is implicit in the neo-Ricardian method. He particularly emphasises the inability of neo-Ricardians to demonstrate the coercive power of capitalists over labour in the production process. It is here that the classes of capitalist society confront each other on unequal terms. The exclusive preoccupation of neo-Ricardians with exchange gives ideological support to the bourgeoisie, for it is relations of exchange, and not production, that incorporate the bourgeois concept of equality *par excellence*.

Rowthorn's criticisms are significant but limited and that they are so is illustrated by the willingness of the less extreme neo-Ricardians to accept value analysis as a 'sociology of capitalist exploitation'. This reduces Marxism to a moral polemic rather than a science. Value can be seen by neo-Ricardianism as a category that simplifies the explanation of the form of exploitation in capitalist society. Marxism then becomes a sophisticated development of the theory of the natural right of labour. What is denied is that value is a necessary or even useful concept for uncovering the laws of motion of capitalism. This follows from the neo-Ricardian assumption that the necessary objects of analysis for such a study are the price categories that appear in exchange and which they alone calculate correctly.

Interestingly, neo-Ricardians have never really justified their view that prices are of such significance. Why is the price (rather than value) rate of profit, for example, a central concept for understanding capitalist development? Their explicit rationale for this is that their rate of profit is the central variable governing the behaviour (i.e. investment) of *individual* capitalists (and consequently capital as a whole), and that this price rate of profit is a central indicator of distributional struggle. These reasons are extremely weak, relying upon an aggregation of individual propensities independently of the coercion of underlying social forces and betraying a limited notion of the role of surplus in capitalist society (an absolute priority to distribution). Nevertheless, the neo-Ricardian assertion of the necessity for priority of distribution in the economic analysis of capitalism can only be met in analyses such as Yaffe's and Rowthorn's by the counter-assertion of the priority of production.

The barriers of dogma to which this situation led have begun to be broken down by the simple realisation that capitalist, indeed commodity, production is a unity of the processes of exchange and production. It is not a case of a theory of production versus a theory of distribution, but a theory of distribution linked to production through exchange. This method can restore the Marxist priority of production in determination but it need not suspend it in isolation from distribution. In this light, the neo-

Ricardian theory cannot offer an alternative because it does not contain a theory of *capitalist* production, the consequence of its rejection of value analysis. Indeed, neo-Ricardianism now appears as a poor imitation not so much of Ricardo as of Mill with the latter's emphasis on the natural laws of production and the socially determined relations of distribution.

The necessity of having a solution on this threefold unity is realised by Gerstein (1976) although he tends to subsume distribution in exchange. (See also Baumol (1974), Fine (1975a) and Fine (1975b)). His paper integrates the criticisms that have been made of the neo-Ricardian concept of value with a treatment of the transformation problem. In other papers, (Kay (1976), Pilling (1975), Williams (1975)) the neo-Ricardians have been shown to consider the category of value as simply a quantitative measure of labour-time to be calculated from technical relations of production. This is completely inconsistent with Marx's analysis of the twofold character of the commodity (exchange value and use value) and his criticisms of Ricardo. Marx's emphasis is on the form that value assumes for commodity production. For the production of use-values as commodities implies, through exchange, the social reality of the commensurability of different products and consequently the commensurability of different types of labour. This comparison of individual types of labour through market relations strips them of their individuality, in so far as exchange proceeds smoothly, and reduces the measure of exchange value to a standard based on undifferentiated labour-time or abstract labour. What is crucial is that this reduction cannot take place without the intervention of exchange, for it is based on the commodity form of production. On the other hand it is the quantitative application of labour in production that is the source and measure of value and this is merely expressed by exchange relations. In contrast, the false concept of value that the neo-Ricardians seek to reject can be constructed without reference to commodities and exchange at all, simply by forming the necessary mathematical equations which are derived from production considered merely as a set of technical relations.

Gerstein makes these criticisms of neo-Ricardianism explicit precisely because of his commitment to a concept of capital that embodies the unity of production and exchange. His own treatment of the transformation problem depends heavily upon the solution developed by Seton (1957), a contribution which has received relatively little attention from neo-Ricardians. Seton's difference from neo-Ricardianism arises because he does transform values into prices of production without reference to the technical relations of production that are so fundamental to neo-Ricardianism. This is simply done by setting up simultaneous equations between the price rate of profit and the ratios of prices of production to values. This involves correcting Marx's failure to transform the original costs of production from values into prices of production. Quantitatively the neo-Ricardian and Seton solutions must coincide, but their interpretation remains quite different. For the former, values are a detour in the derivation of prices and profits from technical relations of production whereas for the latter values are the starting point. Seton's solution can be seen as representing the unity of production and exchange. Only value categories enter *ab initio,* and the transformation explicitly constructs modified values based on the relations of distribution and exchange.

The uniqueness of Gerstein's contribution lies in his insistence that Seton's procedure is incomplete. This is because his solution to the transformation problem is only unique up to scale—it determines relative prices of production, the ratios of the prices of different commodities, and not absolute levels. This is a property in common with the neo-Ricardian determination of prices. Starting from a given wage level (corresponding to a given bundle of wage goods) prices of commodities are deduced. If we had set the wage level differently (for the same bundle of wage goods) then the level of prices would be correspondingly higher. There appears to be no rationale for choosing one *level* of prices rather than another. This is because the integration of production and distribution only requires a calculation of the *relative* shares appropriated by capital and labour. Gerstein, however, characterises the choice of the absolute level of prices as the central factor forging the link between the production and circulation of value. He argues that this requires a level of prices for which total value equals total price (rather than one where total surplus value equals total profit, which in general is incompatible with the other condition).

To us, whilst Gerstein is correct to emphasise the transformation of values into prices of production as an integration of production and exchange, this does not depend ultimately upon choosing an appropriate absolute level of prices. Indeed, the development of such an absolute level of prices is quite meaningless without the existence of a general equivalent i.e. money, and the direct intervention of money in the exchange process has been correctly absent from the analysis of the transformation. We have been treating value and surplus value as they exist in exchange but not explicitly as they exist in money form. At a lower level of abstraction, in moving from prices of production to money prices, i.e. from the circulation of (modified) values to the circulation of money, it will be necessary to relate the modified values of commodities to the modified value of commodity-money. Further development of the concept of market price depends upon the concept of fiat money and analysis of the credit system.

We conclude this section by considering the significance of the distinction between the value and price rates of profit. As has been noted, the correction of Marx's transformation leads to a divergence between the two rates. The neo-Ricardians argue so much the worse for the value rate of profit and any laws of political economy based upon it. This fails to recognise that the relationship between the price and value rate of profit is essential for understanding the unity of production, exchange and distribution. Such an understanding cannot be gained by discarding one or other of these concepts as neo-Ricardians do in rejecting the value rate (and Fundamentalists do in rejecting the price rate of profit). The neo-Ricardian method lends priority in determination to circulation and distribution, because the major determinant in capitalist society is considered to be the price rate of profit.

In contrast, we would emphasise movements in the value rate of profit as the critical indicator of the ability of capitalist society to create the conditions for a continued accumulation, free of economic and social crisis. It is in this context that the capitalist formation should be seen as an articulation of other economic and social relations with those of production.

Productive and Unproductive Labour

The importance of the distinction between productive and unproductive labour lies in the increasing significance in modern capitalism of those workers who might be classified as unproductive (e.g. state and commercial as opposed to industrial employees). Unproductive employees are not only distinct in the economic functions they perform for capital, but they are increasingly drawn into and hence hold a distinct position in economic, political and ideological class struggle. It is the movement towards an understanding of their role in these struggles and in capitalist society as a whole that makes the clarification of the concept of unproductive labour so potentially fruitful.

In an article that was the starting point for the debate, Gough (1972) summarised what was to become the neo-Ricardian interpretation of Marx's theory of productive labour; 'To conclude, productive labour is labour exchanged with capital to produce surplus value. As a necessary condition it must be useful labour, must produce or modify a use-value-increasingly in a collective fashion; that is, it must be employed in the process of production. Labour in the process of circulation does not produce use-values, therefore cannot add to value or surplus value. It does not add to the production of use-values because it arises specifically with commodity production out of the problems of realising the value of commodities. Alongside this group of unproductive labourers are all workers supported directly out of revenue, whether retainers or state employees. This group differs from circulation workers, however, in that they do produce use-values—all public teachers, doctors, etc. would be included in this category today.'

It is significant that this interpretation only bases itself on the circuit of capital in so far as labour is defined as productive or not according to what is done. It does not draw upon (and maintain) the distinction between production and exchange as separate but integrated spheres of economic activity (see Fine (1973)). This leads the neo-Ricardians to reject Marx's concept of unproductive labour (see Harrison (1973a) and Gough and Harrison (1975)). Their case for this is at its strongest in the case of commercial workers, although it is extended in various degrees to other unproductive and even to non-wage labour such as housework. It essentially consists of establishing that commercial workers labour under relations of production that are 'materially identical' to those of productive workers. This is because first, their labour-power and means of production are costs contributing to price, wage and profit formation; second, commercial workers are exploited wage-labourers and this is seen as a source of commercial profits; and third, commercial workers are subject to the control of capitalists over their labour process.

This reasoning conforms to the neo-Ricardian treatment of the transformation problem in basing analysis of the laws of motion of capitalism on technical relations of production (or more exactly labour activity). The effect of this is an eclectic aggregation of labour expended in both production and exchange to analyse the source of profit, the formation of the rate of profit and the potential for accumulation, whereas the major achievement of Marx was the demonstration that the potential for accumulation was created ultimately in the sphere of production alone. The neo-Ricardian conclusion is reached through examples which grant to each set of labour activities an absolute economic independence in their impact within the social formation. Treating the economy as a mixture of sectors of activity, they argue as follows for the effects of productivity increase sector by sector. For commerce, if productivity increases the rate of profit increases whilst real wages remain the same. In the state sector, the provision of any given level of goods and services can be achieved at a lower cost, allowing for resources to be released for accumulation and the raising of the rate of profit. This follows from the neo-Ricardian method of treating money wages and welfare services as commensurable and substitutable. The latter is a 'social-wage'. As long as workers' combined 'wage' remains the same, whether provided by exchange or the welfare state, profitability rises with productivity increase in the state sector. It only remains for this to be effected either by a reduction in the resources devoted to state activity, real output remaining the same, or by an increase in this activity, resources used remaining the same, whilst money wages are cut (for example through taxation) to 'compensate' for the increased 'social wage'. If luxuries are produced more cheaply, this does not affect the rate of profit, but it may release resources from capitalists' surplus consumption for capital accumulation. Finally, housework, because it is a source of use-values for the labourer, may be a source of reducing the costs of labour-power to the capitalist by providing wage-goods that would otherwise have to be purchased out of wages which would therefore have to be higher than they are if wives did not do housework *gratis*.

The major disagreement with the neo-Ricardians has been voiced by Bullock (1973) and (1974), a representative of the Fundamentalists. Basing himself exclusively within the sphere of production, he attempts to define as productive that labour which creates surplus value in a form that can be accumulated. This includes produced means of production and wage-goods (which can be exchanged against labour-power) but excludes luxury production. In effect, Bullock identifies productive labour with that labour that can produce relative surplus value. This places him in some embarrassment, because this definition of productive labour differs from Marx's (which includes luxury production). Bullock attempts to compensate for this by arguing that his definition is consistent with Marx's on (nebulous) methodological grounds. Appealing to the movement of theory between levels of abstraction, he considers that at the first level of abstraction, in simply elaborating the production of surplus value, luxury production does embody productive labour, and this is why Marx included this sector in the productive category. But at a lower level of abstraction, accumulation of surplus value is determinant and since luxury goods cannot be accumulated, he argues that the concept of productive labour must be modified to reflect this. This total emphasis on accumulation accompanied by a lack of clarity, a few terminological errors and a shifting of his position, yield to the neo-Ricardians a field-day of criticism.

However, the Fundamentalists have also been preoccupied with the nature of the wage-labour that educates and medically cares for the working class and in doing so modify their position (see Bullock and Yaffe (1975) and Howell (1975)). This they eventually classify as productive even if it is not employed by capital (for example, by the state instead), drawing the analogy between repair work on fixed capital and 'repair' and reproduction of the commodity labour-power. Because Marx categorises machine-repair as productive labour *sui generis*, it is argued that wage-labour reproducing the labourer is also of this genus and hence productive. This is a ludicrous mimicry of Marx's theory: for him repair work is not productive because it is of a unique type, but because it is undertaken by industrial capital. However, the error is symptomatic of a method confined to analysis of production, leading to a definition of productive labour according to the potential and contribution created for accumulation.

Fine and Harris (1976a) criticise Gough's (1975) neo-Ricardian assessment of the role of state employees. They argue that labour employed by industrial capital alone produces surplus value and this alone is the source of value upon which all labour-power and commodities that exchange with the capitalist economy ultimately depend. To suggest, as Gough does that state or any other unproductive employees can create surplus value through the transfer of their surplus labour by exchange is to construct a situation in which surplus value can be created without the use of capital except for 'conversion purposes'. Further, neo-Ricardians are quite wrong to argue that all wage-labour is by definition organised under 'materially identical' conditions. For, whilst productive labour is directly governed by the control of capital as exercised by individual capitalists through exchange relations and subject to the laws of motion of capitalist production, the immediate control of state employees lies in relatively autonomous political relations, even though these are determined by the economy. In particular, there need be no commodity production in the case of state employees, hence they do not create value and cannot be subject to the necessity of reducing socially necessary labour-time to a minimum as for capitalist production. In conclusion, the *ceteris paribus* arguments of the neo-Ricardians are quite wrong in granting different social activities an independence from capital. Productivity increases, changes in taxation, a relocation of the production of use-values etc. cannot be the starting point of any analysis. They must be situated relative to the forces that produce them and the forces that resolve them. In doing this, Marxist analysis must be based on capitalist production and analyse unproductive labour in its dependent articulation with capitalist production.

This criticism of the neo-Ricardian method can be extended to consideration of its strongest case for the rejection of Marx's concept of productive labour. . . commercial workers. Here, labour-power is employed by capital, exchange activity is subject to the coercive factors of competition that grind down socially necessary labour-time to a minimum, and labour expended in commercial activity is consequently commensurable with industrial labour. This means that the capital employed in exchange is subject to historical tendencies similar to those of industrial capital, concentration and centralisation for example, but it does not mean that production and exchange are subject to the same laws of motion as the neo-Ricardians imply. Capital must be understood as uniting production and exchange in a movement that grants relative independence to both but makes production determinant. The failure to distinguish productive and unproductive labour in the circuit of capital implies an inability to analyse the relatively independent movement of exchange in its dependence upon the laws of production. This anticipates our discussion of the theory of crisis, but it again reveals the essence of neo-Ricardianism. Interested only in the static formulation of the transformation problem and the calculation of the potential for accumulation, they misconceive both and therefore are unable to develop the laws of motion of capitalism and the contradictions that these create in society.

For Marx, the distinction between productive and unproductive labour only applies to wage-labour. So far we have examined the concept of unproductive labour according to whether it is directly under the control of capital (e.g. commercial workers) or not (state employees). Now we briefly consider the implications of various analyses for non-wage labour. In particular, debates have been generated over the nature and significance of housework.

Broadly theories of housework can be divided into two types—those for which the quantification of domestic labour-time is both meaningful and necessary and those for which it is not. Not surprisingly, the neo-Ricardian theory takes the first approach and seeks to discover the rate of exploitation of housewives (Harrison (1973b) and Gough and Harrison (1975)). They then argue that surplus domestic labour is quantitatively equivalent to surplus value and is appropriated by capitalists through the payment of wages that would be higher without the existence of domestic labour.

Although Seccombe ((1974) and (1975)) implicitly rejects the neo-Ricardian method of treating domestic and productive labour as equivalent creators of value, he measures the value he considers housework creates (embodied in labour-power) by the renumeration received by the housewife. The inevitable conclusion of any theory that measures housework in this, the neo-Ricardian, or any other way is that housework will be undermined and invaded by capitalist production. This follows from the action of the forces of competition which the capitalist sector exerts precisely because of its value commensurability with housework that cannot maintain the same levels of productivity increases. Housewives will be drawn into wage work, domestic use-values will be produced as commodities. The only obstacles are the political, ideological and other economic forces associated with the capitalist family.

This analysis owes more to a neoclassical theory of time allocation than to Marxism. It can only be rejected by realising that housework does not produce value (as properly understood—see above and also Gardiner (1975)), and its labour-time is not commensurable with value. Rather it is in their *dual* performance of domestic labour and wage that the analysis of the historical evolution of women under capitalism must be located (see Coulson, Magas and Wainwright (1975) and Gardiner, Himmelweit, and Mackintosh (1975)). There is not simply an evolution of one form of labour into the other.

Seccombe's economic analysis leads him to a one-sided political strategy for women. Drawn into industrial life, he sees women's campaign there for equality with men as primary, whilst having repercussions for raising the consciousness of women remaining confined to the home. Significantly, this channels women's struggles precisely along the lines that makes their division of labour most efficient for capital. Equal pay for women is a bourgeois demand for equality. In contrast, an emphasis on the dual nature of women's labour points to a political strategy based on the tension between the two. Women's ability to pursue equality in work and struggle is constrained by the duality of their labour. It is these constraints that must be the object of struggle, as much as equality in 'economic' life, and the failure of reformism to overcome them must be linked to the struggle for socialism. In this way, not only are the material interests of all women advanced within capitalist society by the socialisation of housework and the progress towards equality in the economy, but also women's participation in the revolutionary transformation of society becomes developed.

In Volume I of *Capital,* Marx perceived 'that the production of surplus value has at all times been made, by classical political economists, the distinguishing characteristic of the productive labourer. Hence, their definition of a productive labourer changes with their comprehension of surplus value. Thus the Physiocrats insist that only agricultural labour is productive, since... with them, surplus value has no existence except in the form of rent.' (p. 509) The Fundamentalists insist that only labour whose products can be accumulated is productive since with them, surplus value has no existence except in the form of accumulation. The neo-Ricardians insist that all labour that is exploited is productive since with them, surplus value has no existence except in the form of surplus product. Marx himself insists that only industrial labour is productive, since with him surplus value has no existence apart from production by capital. It is the maintenance of the distinction between productive and unproductive labour (and consequently non-wage labour) that is the starting point for understanding the role played by economic agents in the capitalist formation.

3. Laws of Development, Crises and State Intervention

In the previous section we have explained the significance of the debate over the transformation problem and the productive/unproductive labour distinction. Quite apart from the question of whether the positions taken are faithful to 'what Marx actually said' we have demonstrated the strengths and weaknesses of the different contributions in being able to develop an understanding of capitalist economic life as a whole on the basis of its hidden, inner characteristics. But the force of the arguments over these questions is best appreciated by examining them together with the debates over the economic laws of development of capitalism.

Law of the Tendency of the Rate of Profit to Fall

One debate on laws of motion has been central to much of British Marxist economics. It concerns the law of the tendency of the rate of profit to fall (TRPF). It is generally agreed that Marx in *Capital* and the *Grundrisse* put forward as a law of capitalism that the rate of profit has a tendency to fall: the laws of production and accumulation 'produce for the social capital a growing absolute mass of profit, and a falling rate of profit.' No one disputes that Marx considered this law to be of fundamental significance: it is 'in every respect the most fundamental law of modern economy, and the most important for understanding the most difficult relations. It is the most important law from the historical standpoint'. Beyond this there is no agreement. In order to appraise the neo-Ricardian and Fundamentalist interpretations of the law we begin by stating our own interpretation.

In the chapter on *The Law as Such* in *Capital* Volume III Marx considers the value rate of profit

$$r = \frac{S}{C + V} = \frac{\dfrac{S}{V}}{\dfrac{C}{V} + 1} = \frac{\text{rate of exploitation}}{\text{value composition} + 1}$$

and argues that if $\dfrac{C}{V}$ rises and $\dfrac{S}{V}$ does not rise sufficiently, the rate of profit will fall. For Marx, however, it appears in places that there is no 'if'; the law of TRPF appears as an inevitable aspect of accumulation. Our view is that this law is an inevitable concomitant of accumulation but the law must be understood as the law of the *tendency* of the rate of profit to fall; it is not a law which predicts actual falls in the rate of profit (in value or price terms). To clarify this, we must consider the structure of Marx's argument in terms of the different levels of abstraction which are employed in the three chapters (13 to 15) of Volume III, Pt. III entitled 'The Law as Such', 'Counteracting Influences' and 'Exposition of the Internal Contradictions of the Law'.

In the third of these chapters Marx is concerned with the effects on the surface of society of the law of TRPF, the counteracting influences and the contradictions between these. These effects take the form of 'overproduction, speculation, crises, and surplus-capital alongside surplus-population'. These are not simple effects of the law of TRPF or of the counteracting influences, but of both of these existing in a complex contradictory unity:

> 'From time to time the conflict of antagonistic agencies finds vent in crises. The crises are always but momentary and forcible solutions of the existing contradictions.'

The concept of crisis is, therefore, at a lower level of abstraction than the concepts involved in the law of TRPF and the counteracting influences: it is constructed on the basis of them.

Consider the law as such. It is constructed by abstracting from all distributional changes and from all changes in values except for those which immediately and directly result from changes in the technical composition of capital. To appreciate this one must understand the meaning of the three concepts of the composition of capital. The *technical* composition of capital is the ratio of means of production to living labour expressed in physical, material, terms (although clearly not measurable in such terms). The *value* composition of capital is the ratio of means of production to the paid portion of labour expressed in value terms; it is the ratio of consent to variable capital $\frac{C}{V}$. The *organic* composition is the same as the value composition expressed in symbols, it is $\frac{C}{V}$, *but* it is only equal to the value composition insofar as it *directly* reflects the technical composition. An example will clarify the distinctions. A rise in the technical composition (expulsion of living labour) is an inevitable aspect of capitalist accumulation. By definition this involves a rise in the organic composition, for this is the same thing as the technical composition expressed in terms of values where the value per unit of means of production and labour-power are the unit values which existed before the rise in technical composition. However, the value composition will not necessarily rise as a result of the rising technical composition since the latter has indirect effects on the ratio $\frac{C}{V}$ as well as its direct effect on organic composition. The indirect effects include the fact that the unit values of the commodities which enter into constant and variable capital are decreased, and not necessarily in the same proportion. These unit values decrease because the rise in technical composition is a rise in productivity and therefore less labour is embodied in each commodity than previously. The distinction between organic and value composition is made clear by Marx:

'The value composition, *insofar* as it is determined by its technical composition and mirrors the changes of the latter (is called) the *organic* composition of capital.' (Emphasis added).

whereas, in general,

'The altered *value* composition... only shows approximately the change in the composition of its material constituents.'

This distinction enables us to comprehend the meaning of the law of TRPF. For Marx specifies the law as the consequence of a rising *organic* composition. His method in deducing the law is therefore to abstract from the *indirect* effects of the rising technical composition of capital, to abstract from changes in the rate of exploitation and, since we are dealing with the value rate of profit, to abstract from the effects of price and wage changes on the rate of profit. With these abstractions it follows tautologically that the rate of profit in value terms falls. The significance of this proposition can only be seen when it is considered together with the counteracting influences and the complex effects which are produced. But even at the present stage it would be wrong to dismiss the law as a 'mere' tautology for it can already be seen that it is constructed on the basis of the concepts which come before it in *Capital*. It is the direct effect of the rising technical composition of capital and the necessity of that tendency itself follows from Marx's analysis of capital as self-expanding value, an analysis constructed from the concepts of the commodity, money, labour and value.

The law as such then is constructed by abstracting from many complications. The counteracting influences take account of these complications. Marx's presentation of the counteracting influences appears to be a rather arbitrarily delimited list of factors with analysis of the way in which each operates. The list is the same as that proposed by J.S. Mill and Marx prefaces it by the warning that 'the following are the most general counterbalancing forces' only. Those enumerated are chiefly concerned with the distributional effects which can only be understood in terms of the articulation of production, exchange, and distribution. Under this heading are to be considered increasing intensity of exploitation, depression of wages, foreign trade, increase in joint-stock capital, and relative overpopulation (which encourages low wages). As a result of these factors the effect on the rate of profit of increases in the composition of social capital will be counteracted through changes in distribution between labour and capital. In addition, Marx considers the cheapening of the elements of constant capital and the effect of relative overpopulation in encouraging the persistence of industries with low compositions of capital. These factors imply that the value composition of social capital will not rise as fast as the organic (and technical) composition thereby again counteracting the effects of the rising organic composition.

Thus, in considering the counteracting influences, Marx introduces accumulation's effects on distribution and on the value composition of capital. They are at the same level of abstraction as the law as such in the sense that the counteracting influences are not predicated upon the concept of the law—they are not the effects or results of the tendency of the rate of profit to fall. Instead, both the law of TRPF and the counteracting influences are equally the effect of capitalist accumulation with its necessary concomitant of a rising technical composition (reflected in Marx's analysis by a rising organic composition but a value composition which does not necessarily rise). As Marx puts it:

'the *same* influences which produce a tendency in the general rate of profit to fall, *also* call forth counter-effects' (emphasis added).

A more accurate name for Marx's theory would be 'the law of the tendency of the rate of profit to fall *and* of the tendency for counteracting influences to operate'.

Our interpretation of Marx's law has several implications which will become clear as we critically appraise other interpretations. One is worth stating immediately. The observable effect of the law cannot, on our interpretation, be a simple tendency for the actual rate of profit (in value or price terms) to fall. The effects of the law (which, being constructed from the law as broadly defined are at a lower level of abstraction) must be the effects of the complex contradictions between the tendency of the rate of profit to fall and the counteracting influences. One such effect is crises which are necessary at times to temporarily resolve the contradictions, another may in fact be actual falls in the rate of profit. But if the latter effect occurs it cannot be understood as a simple manifestation of the law, it is a manifestation of the complex internal contradictions of the law as defined above in the broadest sense. Hence the title of Marx's Chapter 15 where he considers the law of TRPF *and* counteracting influences is 'Exposition of the *Internal* Contradictions of the Law' (emphasis added).

Having set out our interpretation of the law of TRPF we are now in a position to consider the neo-Ricardian interpretation and critique of the law. That position is best represented in the writings of Steedman (1972), Hodgson (1974) and Himmelweit (1974). Many of the points they develop were already known in less developed form before the recent debates and had been summarised by Meek (1967) and Sweezy (1949). In essence, neo-Ricardian writers are concerned to demonstrate the invalidity of the law of TRPF (or, at least, their interpretation of it) by demonstrating that a rising technical composition of capital does not necessarily involve a rising value composition (or, as they call it 'organic composition'); that if the value composition of capital does rise this does not necessarily cause falls in the rate of profit and that the real source of falls in the rate of profit can only be wage increases, the result of class struggle over distribution in the sphere of exchange. (Since the models are generally constructed in terms of prices rather than values, wage increases are equivalent to falls in the rate of exploitation.)

The first point in the neo-Ricardian argument is that the value ('organic') composition is an irrelevant concept (Hodgson, Steedman). It is argued that the relevant concept is dated labour and this view inevitably follows from their concentration on a price of production model (their rejection of value theory which we explained in Section 2) for in such a model embodied labour is treated simply as a cost and prices are the sum of these costs multiplied by a factor which depends on the rate of profit and the date at which the labour was expended. In such a model there is no qualitative difference between dead and living labour, whereas for Marx there is such a difference and it is captured by the concept of value composition. This concept emphasises the distinction between constant capital (dead labour) which does not create value and variable capital which is a component of the living labour which does create value.

The second neo-Ricardian argument is that even if we accept the concept of the value ('organic') composition, a rise of the technical composition of capital does not necessarily imply a rise in 'organic' composition (Hodgson). The rise in technical composition will, since it raises the productivity of labour, lower the values of commodities: more commodities can be produced in a given number of labour hours. Assuming that the values of means of production fall in this process, then, depending on the rate of fall, the increasing mass of means of production may not involve an increasing value. The value of constant capital may rise, fall or stay unchanged, and therefore the value composition may not rise even though the technical composition of capital has risen.

A third strand in the neo-Ricardian critique is the idea that, even if the 'organic' composition does increase, the rate of profit will not necessarily fall. It is a proposition put forward in different ways by Hodgson (1974) and Himmelweit (1974). Hodgson's argument for this proposition is extremely weak since it reasons by a false analogy between neo-classical economics and Marx's theory. Himmelweit's argument is more worthy of consideration. She argues in a model expressed in terms of prices of production rather than values and she adopts $\dfrac{c^1}{v^1 + s^1}$, rather than $\dfrac{c^1}{v^1}$ as the measure of 'organic' composition (where the primes denote price rather than value quantification). Within Sraffa's neo-Ricardian model of prices of production it is easy to show that, given the state of technology there is a unique relationship between wages and profits: if wages go up, profits go down. Himmelweit argues from this that a rise in the wage rate is the sole cause of a fall in the rate of profit given the state of technology, and that a rise in the wage rate *brings about* a change in technology toward a higher organic composition as individual capitalists seek to offset the rise in wages by raising productivity. This rise in productivity actually *stems* the fall in the rate of profit which is being caused by rising wage rates (whereas Marx argues that the falling rate of profit and rising productivity are two manifestations of the same tendency). Therefore, the rise in the 'organic' composition slows or even reverses the tendency of the rate of profit to fall instead of being 'cause' of the fall. The capitalist class as a whole benefits from the fact that the new techniques introduced by individual capitalists for their own gain reduce the effects of rising wages whereas Marx argues that the competitive actions of individual capitalists in introducing new techniques are an aspect of the falling rate of profit and therefore harm the class as a whole. The contrast between Himmelweit's conclusions and Marx's, arises from the fact that the structure and status of each concept differs between the two writers. For Himmelweit a distributional phenomenon, the movement of the wage rate, is primary and the motive force (and this phenomenon is considered only as an exchange phenomenon).

For Marx, however, movements of wage rates are derivative from the accumulation of capital ('the rate of accumulation is the independent not the dependent variable; the rate of wages the dependent, not the independent, variable').

Marx begins with accumulation and the organic composition and productivity rise even without the prior stimulus of rising wages. When that happens, then even in Himmelweit's price of production model, the rate of profit will in general (although not in all circumstances) fall as long as wages rise. And in Marx's approach based on the law of value, wages *will* rise, since to maintain equality between wages and a constant value of labour power, wages must rise as labour productivity rises. For the rise in labour productivity means that the value embodied in each wage commodity falls; if the value of labour-power is constant and equal to wages, then wages must rise to allow more commodities and, hence, an equal amount of total value to be received by workers. This example illustrates the significance of value analysis since Himmelweit's concentration on price of production and wage rates diverts attention from the question of the value of labour power. More than that, it actually prevents an analysis which takes into account the articulation of the spheres of production, exchange and distribution with production as fundamental, for, as we have shown in Section 2, this articulation cannot be understood without value theory. Thus, Himmelweit is forced to consider matters from the one-sided exchange-based view of distribution.

What then is the conclusion of the neo-Ricardian critique of the law of TRPF? Hodgson and Himmelweit both argue that the element of truth in Marx's law is that a rise in the 'organic' composition, if it occurs, will involve a fall in the maximum attainable rate of profit—in the rate of profit which would be appropriated by capitalists if the wage rate were zero. The important point for neo-Ricardianism, however, is that the actual rate of profit is below its maximum since wages are greater than zero (and, indeed, only neo-Ricardians could in the first place conceive of an economy where wages are zero and therefore where profits exist without workers). As Himmelweit concludes, the fact that the maximum rate of profit will fall if the 'organic' composition rises says nothing about whether there is a tendency for the actual rate of profit to fall. What is emphasised is that changes in wage rates are the sources of changes in the profit rate. Class struggle over distribution in the sphere of exchange is everything (see Bhaduri (1962)). This is the theoretical basis for the empirical work of Glyn and Sutcliffe (1972) which we discuss below.

At the opposite extreme, the Fundamentalist interpretation of Marx's law of TRPF, as in Yaffe (1972) and Cogoy (1973), emphasises the immanent contradictions of capital as the basis of the law. In contrast to the neo-Ricardian approach, these are seen as being located within the sphere of production. Yaffe considers the problem in two stages: first, he argues that accumulation necessarily involves a rise in the technical *and* 'organic' (value) composition of capital and, second, he argues that this rise is not offset by increases in the rate of exploitation since there are definite limits to its rate of increase. Therefore, he concludes, there is a tendency for the value rate of profit to fall. The substance of his argument concerns the rising 'organic' composition: the inevitability of this tendency stems from the very nature of capital. The concept of capital implies a contradiction since capital is 'value in process'; it is self-expanding value which necessarily strives for expansion without limit, but its self-expansion is based on the labour of the working class and this is necessarily a limited basis since the population and length of the working day cannot be expanded without limit. As the resolution of this contradiction, capital therefore must make itself as independent as possible from its limited base by increasing the technical composition of capital, employing, that is, a greater proportion of machinery and raising labour productivity so that a greater amount of raw materials is worked up with a given amount of living labour. Furthermore, this must involve an increase in the 'organic' composition, the relative value of constant and variable capital employed. Why, we may ask, must this be so, for, as we have seen the increase in the use of machinery may itself cause a disproportionate fall in the value of machines and the value ('organic') composition may not rise? Yaffe concludes that the 'organic' composition must rise if the technical composition rises because new machines will only be installed if the labour embodied in the production of new machines (their value) is less than the value of the labour power (the paid labour) which is displaced by the machines. His argument is, however, impenetrable. On one inter- pretation, neo-Ricardians criticise it on the grounds that it is tautological since its conclusions follow immediately from the assumption about the rule for installing new machinery (Hodgson (1974), Catephores (1973)) and neo-Ricardians could argue that, in their terms, the rule for installing machinery is invalid since individual capitalists are not concerned with the labour embodied in constant and variable capital but with the price (or price of production) of these elements. Even if, however, one accepts that individual capitalists' decisions are taken on the basis of labour embodied, Yaffe's 'proof' of the rising 'organic' composition is flawed by mixing a theorem which concerns individual capitalists' behaviour with an equation which concerns aggregate values. Finally, as Catephores (1973) argues, Yaffe's 'proof' of a rising 'organic' composition contains an implicit assumption of competition (since it starts from the profit maximizing behaviour of an individual capitalist in introducing machinery) and this is a method which Yaffe claims to be avoiding. Yaffe's stated objective is to demonstrate that a rising organic composition is deducible from the concept of capital-in-general rather than the concept of many-capitals. Thus, neo-Ricardianism's thrust is that the idea of a rising organic composition cannot be the basis of the law of TRPF and that, instead, we should focus on changes in the rate of exploitation in price terms, changes brought about by class struggle over wages, as the source of a falling rate of profit. In contrast, the Fundamentalists argue that the law of TRPF stems from a rising organic composition and that the latter is inherent in the nature of capital. Both schools, however, suffer from the same weakness—a misinterpretation of Marx's method and the meaning of the law.

Neo-Ricardians and Fundamentalists alike consider the law to predict falls in the actual (value of price) rate of profit, falls which are the simple effect of a rising technical composition. Neo-Ricardians seek to disprove such a proposition by, among other things, emphasising the role of two groups of Marx's counteracting influences: the cheapening of the elements of constant capital which may prevent the value composition rising with the technical composition, and changes in distribution related to wage struggles. Fundamentalists seek to prove such a proposition by (unsatisfactorily) proving that a rising technical composition must involve a rising value composition. Fundamentalists recognise the existence of counteracting influences but treat them as secondary, transient factors so that the effects of the law of TRPF continually re-appear as actual falls preceding crises. The neo-Ricardian position is the reverse and is summarised by Hodgson's view that the counteracting influences may be considered as the law and the tendency of the rate of profit to fall as contingent. Both schools consider that what is a law and what a 'mere' influence is an empirical matter, a question of the frequency with which one is manifested rather than the other.

The burden of our own interpretation is that the existence of both the tendency of the rate of profit to fall and of counteracting influences has the status of a law in the sense that both are inevitable products of capitalist accumulation. One cannot preface the counteracting influences with the adjective 'mere'. The distinction between the law of TRPF and the counteracting influences is not one of their relative empirical or logical significance. It is a distinction based solely on the fact that Marx isolates and considers separately the different effects of accumulation; the concept of organic composition is employed to analyse the former and the concept of value composition to analyse the latter. The importance of the distinction between these two concepts has escaped neo-Ricardian and Fundamentalist writers; they use organic composition to mean value composition (and, in consequence, we have followed their terminology in describing their arguments but used quotation marks to denote our disagreement with their interpretation of organic composition).

Theory of Crisis

The debate over the falling rate of profit is not merely academic and technical. It has implications for the theory of crisis and this is undoubtedly the reason for its having aroused such interest. Fundamentalists see the tendency of the rate of profit to fall as the source of crises and the inevitability of the former ensures the inevitability of the latter. Neo-Ricardians see their attack on the law of TRPF as an attack on determinism and economism to which end 'we must bury the last iron law of Marxian politican economy' (Hodgson (1974)).

The neo-Ricardian position on crises is best summarised by Glyn and Sutcliffe (1972). For them, the recent economic crisis (and, implicitly, all crises) results from an actual fall in the rate of profit which is caused by a rise in wages, not a rise in value composition. The rise in wages is the result of a change in the balance of forces in class struggle—a rise in workers' militancy in the context of increased international competition so that capitalists cannot simply pass on and counteract rising wages by proportionate increases in prices. We therefore have an analysis where crises are not the mechanistic result of the faceless laws of economic practice. From the point of view of the economy, the rise in wages is purely contingent and this gives their theory both its strength and its weakness. Its strength because it emphasises that the 'subjective' actions of the working class have a role to play in capitalism's laws of development; its weakness because their theory implies that crises are accidental rather than the necessary concomitant of the complex contradictions between the relations and forces of production. The weakness in Glyn and Sutcliffe's position in that it emphasises distributional class struggle is compounded by Gough (1975) who emphasises class struggle in general. That is, he fails to distinguish accurately between political, ideological and economic class struggle and tends to reduce economic class struggle to political struggle; and to the extent that he refers to economic class struggle he is concerned only with distribution located in the sphere of exchange. This compounding of different types of class struggle has been criticised by Fine and Harris (1976a) on the grounds that it prevents an analysis of the links and contradictions between the different forms of struggle and it precludes any distinction between economic crises and the general crisis of a social formation. Neo-Ricardian writers, however, appear to think (erroneously) that it is necessary to concentrate on political and distributional class struggle as the source of crises in order to avoid the dangers of economism with its emphasis on a mechanistic determination of social events by the sphere of production. They implicitly adopt and misapply the slogan 'politics in command!'

Fundamentalists, on the other hand, locate the sources of crises in the law of the tendency of the rate of profit to fall which, as we have explained above, they analyse within the sphere of production and in terms of the concept of capital-in-general (i.e. attempting to abstract from competition). The position is best expressed by Yaffe (1972). The law of TRPF is seen as sometimes masked by counteracting influences and at other times comes to the surface in the form of an actual decline. When it does make this appearance it induces crises and these crises overcome the contradiction of capital for which the falling rate of profit is merely the form of expression; but in overcoming the contradiction, the barrier to accumulation, the crises remove it to a higher level. Economic crises is seen as *the* major counteracting influence to the tendency of the rate of profit to fall (although Marx considers it as the resolution of the contradictions of the tendency and the counteracting influences rather than a counteracting influence itself). Yaffe argues that the law of TRPF is located exclusively within the sphere of production, but that crises can only be analysed after competition and activities in the sphere of exchange are introduced. The processes by which the crisis counteracts the falling rate of profit the restores the conditions for accumulation include forces located within the sphere of production (e.g. restructuring of productive capital), those located within the sphere of exchange (e.g. depreciation of the prices of commodities) and distributional phenomena. In contrast to the neo-Ricardians, Yaffe is explicitly dealing with economic crises and succinctly makes clear that these cannot be reduced to general social crises whilst the latter, equally, cannot be reduced to economic crises. This analysis of crises is the opposite of the neo-Ricardians' it emphasises the priority of production rather than exchange and distribution based on exchange, it locates crises as necessary rather than contingent, and it distinguishes economic crises as a separate category. In this, Yaffe is closer to advocating Marx's theory of crises whereas neo-Ricardians can only be considered to be rejecting it. Yaffe's argument does have its faults. As we have seen, his treatment of the law of TRPF is not wholly satisfactory, but his greatest error comes when he introduces a problem not explicitly considered by Marx—the problem of the state's intervention in economic crises. Here, as we explain at the end of the present section, he falls into the same error as the neo-Ricardians and treats the state's intervention in the same way as it is treated by bourgeois Keynesian theory. A further weakness of Yaffe is that although he introduces competition and exchange in the analyses of crises he does not consider the relative autonomy of the spheres of exchange and distribution and, therefore, in his analysis their role can be reduced to the sphere of production. Itoh (1975) and Fishman and Ergas (1975) partially overcome this error.

Fine and Harris (1975a) and (1975b) develop the theory of crisis in a way which is closely related to that of Yaffe and suffers from some of the same weaknesses. They, too, consider the sphere of production as fundamental and locate the source of crises in the tendency of the rate of profit to fall (although they do not consider that the tendency must be manifested in an actual decline in order to precipitate crises). Moreover, as is made clear in Fine and Harris (1976a), they argue unlike the neo-Ricardians that a clear distinction must be made between economic crisis and political crisis if a proper understanding of society is to be achieved. The first particular feature of their work is their concentration on the forces through which crises lay the foundations for renewed accumulation. Here they emphasise the functions of crises in stimulating and establishing the conditions for the restructuring of productive capital, so that capital's concentration and centralisation and its internationalisation are stimulated, and new techniques with higher productivity are introduced. They argue that these forces are more fundamental than the distributional phenomenon (as understood by neo-Ricardians) of unemployment pushing down the level of wages. Indeed, such distributional phenomena can only be understood if one understands their relation to the sphere of production and the imperative restructuring of productive capital. The second, and most important, distinctive feature of Fine and Harris's work is their analysis of state intervention in crises. Neo-Ricardians and Fundamentalists both in their different ways, view the state in an essentially Keynesian manner in that they consider the state in the era of monopoly capitalism as having a commitment to maintain full employment. Fine and Harris argue against this view and, in doing so, stress the significance of the state's intervention in the restructuring of productive capital. The question of the state is central to modern analyses of crises and capitalism's economic laws of development. We now turn to consider it explicitly.

The State, Crises and Accumulation

Fine and Harris (1975a) (1976a) argue that to understand the state's economic role in accumulation and crises it is necessary to clarify the meaning of the relative autonomy of politics from economics—to understand the constitution of the two spheres as distinct but unified with the economy as fundamental. Thus, the state's position in capitalist society is to ensure the survival of capitalist relations in general and, since these relations have economic relations as their base, this specifically requires the maintenance of the economic conditions for capitalist accumulation. Since economic crises, whose ultimate basis is the operation of productive capital and the law of TRPF, are the necessary concomitant of capitalist accumulation the state cannot be considered to abolish crises. Instead, in its economic intervention the state is objectively forced to accept the necessity of economic crises, overproduction and unemployment. Bearing in mind that economic crises are founded in the sphere of production, rather than in exchange and distribution, that the primary recuperative force in crises is the restructuring of productive capital rather than the pushing down of wages, the state's intervention in crises must be located there. For the state does not passively 'accept' crises, it actively intervenes to ensure their fruitfulness for accumulation. This involves primarily increased nationalisation, financial aid to and supervision of private capital, restructuring of nationalised industries' capital, and cuts in state expenditure to release surplus value for accumulation; and the way in which these policies have operated in the current period of the British economy are analysed in Fine and Harris (1975b) (1976b). These are considered as the primary aspects of state intervention. Derivative is the fact that the state also intervenes in distribution through actions in the sphere of exchange (such as incomes policies). Moreover, for a complete analysis Fine and Harris consider it important that political class struggle and ideological tensions affect the extent to which the state can permit crises to develop at any given time and argue that the state can postpone crises, moderate their depth, and precipitate crises, but it can never abolish them. For it is ultimately bound by the laws of capitalist accumulation.

In this Fine and Harris are radically different from bourgeois Keynesian interpretations of state intervention. Such interpretations, accepting as reality the superficial appearance of the state as being above and outside of civil society; consider that the state has a real objective, the objective of abolishing crises and unemployment. It is able to do this because there exists a national interest (rather than antagonistic class interests) which the state represents and because economic crises result simply from capitalist anarchy and imperfect information having an effect in the, sphere of exchange and making the sale of commodities difficult at times. Thus, the state can abolish crises by economic planning and by increasing the demand for commodities when their sale becomes difficult. To the extent that there remains unemployment, Keynesian interpretations explain this by pointing to a conflict between the national interest's goal of full employment and the objective of balance on the balance of payments. The difference between this approach and that of Fine and Harris is transparent and, in particular, Harris (1976b) has argued that the idea of the balance of payments being an objective which conflicts with full employment cannot be accepted by Marxists.

Nevertheless neo-Ricardians, from a starting point different from that of Keynesians, finish by accepting the Keynesian view of the state. This is most clearly seen in the work of Gough (1975) who considers that the capitalist state had a commitment to full employment and in the period since World War II it has achieved this objective by maintaining aggregate demand and national planning. Gough's difference from bourgeois Keynesianism is found in two factors. First, the state has these full employment aims not because it represents some national interest but because the political strength of the working class (internationally and within each nation) since World War II has forced upon the capitalist states a rejection of unemployment. Second, to the extent that there is a contradiction in the state's full-employment policy this is not because of the balance of payments (although this purely Keynesian factor is considered by some neo-Ricardian writers), it is because class struggles over wages and profits, distributional struggles in the sphere of exchange, require the state to intervene on behalf of capitalists to create unemployment and push down wages. But these differences do not permit Gough to escape from Keynesian conclusions regarding the state's role as guarantor of full employment, they reinforce those conclusions.

As Fine and Harris (1976a) and Holloway and Picciotto (1976) argue, this error of Gough's results from a failure to identify the complex articulation of politics with economics. Fine and Harris consider that Gough's errors stem from an over-politicisation of theory, from viewing politics (and the state which Gough locates within the sphere of politics) as absolutely autonomous from economic laws. They also stem from a misconception of the economy, for Gough considers only exchange relationships and never the sphere of production. This emphasis on the sphere of exchange has important effects in the two parts of Gough's article, the part where he considers the sources of the long-term growth of state expenditure and the part where he considers the state's role in crisis. These effects are crystallised in his adoption of the neo-Ricardian position on productive and unproductive labour. In essence Gough in this rejects the significance of this distinction and therefore treats state expenditure on, or production of, welfare services as materially identical with the production of commodities by capital. He is therefore unable to satisfactorily explain the long-run growth of state expenditure on economic grounds, since in this scheme there is no valid reason why private capital rather than the state should not produce welfare services. Furthermore, Fine and Harris argue, this rejection of the productive/unproductive labour distinction is the necessary concomitant of Gough's emphasis on the sphere of exchange.

Holloway and Picciotto (1976) criticise Gough for reasons which are, in part, similar to those of Fine and Harris. They argue that Gough's separation of economics and politics permits him to imply incorrectly the existence of an absolute autonomy of politics and to fail to see the economic limits on the state's interventions. But whereas Fine and Harris argue that Gough's particular distinction between politics and economics is faulty with its implicit idea of complete separation and the primary of politics, Holloway and Picciotto argue that *any* separation of the spheres in theoretical work or in the tactics of class struggle is an error which must lead to the reformism of for example, those who envisage the possibility of transforming society by the mere capture of political institutions. We, however, consider that only through an understanding of the distinction between the spheres of economics, politics and ideology can the movement forge explicitly the unifying links between class struggle in the different spheres.

Although Fine and Harris's and Holloway and Picciotto's critiques of the Keynesian view of the state are primarily directed against its adoption in

Gough's neo-Ricardian framework, it is also the case that Fundamentalists adopt a Keynesian view of the state. This is clear from Yaffe (1972) (1973) but it is also clear that the state in his Keynesian conception plays a role different from that in the neo-Ricardian system. For Yaffe the law of the tendency of the rate of profit to fall gives rise to a tendency for crises. The state, because it has for political reasons a commitment to full employment, increases state expenditure in order thereby to increase aggregate demand and overcome the crises. In doing so it is producing a further contradiction or, rather, transforms the contradiction inherent in capital and expressed in the tendency of the rate of profit to fall. It transforms this because the growth of state expenditure itself further intensifies the tendency of the rate of profit to fall and the contradiction therefore takes the form of the state, in attempting to overcome crises, merely intensifying the source of crises and thereby underpinning their inevitability. This occurs because state expenditure must be financed by the taxation of surplus value produced by capital since state expenditure (except for the operation of nationalised industry) is itself unproductive of surplus value. An increase in state expenditure therefore must imply a reduction in the proportion of any given mass of surplus value which remains in the hands of capital and is available for accumulation: it must, that is, reduce the rate of profit in value terms. A similar view is adopted within the Fundamentalist framework by Gamble and Walton (1976), but for them the primary contradiction which results from the state's supposed commitment to full-employment is an intensification of inflation (and, therefore, of generalised social instability) rather than merely an intensification of the tendential decline in the rate of profit. The error in these approaches stems from the Fundamentalists' idea *faute de mieux*, that the state is committed to full employment.

It seems clear that the analysis of crises, the state and the relations between politics and economics must be, as Holloway and Picciotto argue, central to further development of the theory of capitalist accumulation. Not only is it the case that these phenomena dominate daily life in this era of monopoly capitalism and that state intervention is increasingly important, it is also the case that all the fundamental problems over which Marxist economists have fought in recent years are crystallised in these problems. The debates over values and prices of production, productive and unproductive labour, the articulation between the spheres of production, exchange and distribution, and the law of the tendency of the rate of profit to fall are all fundamental to the theory of crisis and the state. These debates, therefore, are relevant to an understanding of history and to the development of revolutionary strategy; the economists who contribute to them have a considerable responsibility.

4. Conclusion

The debates of Marxist economists in British journals have involved two polar schools with some writers (perhaps an increasing number) producing critiques of both schools. This polarisation is found, as we have seen, within all the major issues of 'high theory' and it has its effects on the analysis of concrete societies. Moreover, it is a real polarisation and separation. It is not that neo-Ricardians analyse the price phenomena which are on the surface of society while Fundamentalists complement that work by using value analysis to analyse the hidden forces. Marx's method involves understanding the different levels of abstraction as instances of a unified whole and there is no way in which the neo-Ricardian propositions can be united with those of the Fundamentalists in one whole.

The fact that the two schools cannot be regarded as complementary, two parts of a unity, is reflected in the differences between their (erroneous) methods. Consider the question of the role of contradictions in the analyses. Yaffe, for the Fundamentalists, has emphasised that *Capital* cannot be understood without an understanding of Hegel. Accordingly, a form of dialectical contradiction is central to his analysis. It takes the historical phenomena of capitalism, (falls in the rate of profit, crises, state intervention) as the simple expressions of one basic contradiction—that which is inherent in capital-in-general, its tendency toward unlimited expansion and the limited nature of living labour which is the basis of such expansion. Everything follows in a straight line of development from this one contradiction. For the Fundamentalists, the surface phenomena such as crises and state intervention are the simple forms, the appearances, assumed by the essential single contradiction. This essence is located in the sphere of production considered in isolation and appears to be thought of as the only reality. For neo-Ricardians, the laws of development are not seen as resulting from the internal contradictions of capital. The falling rate of profit, for example, is not thought of in dialectical terms but in terms of the simple mathematics of technical relations. Similarly, the transformation problem is not seen as a problem in specifying the contradictory unity of the spheres of production, exchange and distribution but as the problem of constructing a price system from technical relations. To the extent that dialectical reasoning enters neo-Ricardian analysis it is only implicit: it is the contradiction between the two great classes, proletariat and bourgeoisie, which determines the distribution of income and causes crises, but this contradiction is manifest only in the sphere of exchange (wage struggles) and at the level of politics. As we have made clear throughout, we consider that the methods of both Fundamentalists and neo-Ricardians are incorrect in this respect. What both in their different ways fail to see is that the structure of the economy (and the relation between economics, politics and ideology) must be understood as a complex structure. The laws of development are located within a structured relationship of contradictions. Thus, the law of TRPF and the counteracting influences are to be seen as contradictory effects of capitalist accumulation, they are contradictions of capital-in-general as has been pointed to by Yaffe. But crises do not result from the contradiction of capital-in-general as Fundamentalists argue, but from this in its relationship to the contradiction between the law of TRPF and the counter-acting influences and in its relationship to the other contradictions which are found in the articulation between exchange (and particularly credit) and production.

A second question of method which distinguishes Fundamentalists and neo-Ricardians concerns the proof of a theory's validity and the quantification of relationships. Neo-Ricardians such as Hodgson reject as metaphysical any theories which do not yield predictions concerning observable phenomena. Moreover, these predictions must be quantifiable so that they can be confronted by data in a proof or disproof. Fundamentalists, on the other hand, in concentrating upon the hidden essence of economic relations and treating them as the only substance of reality, would appear to deny the necessity of framing theories in a form corresponding to observable phenomena. Careful consideration of Marx's method lends little support to either of these positions. On the question of quantifiability, in particular, several points may be made. First, the law of TRPF (as an example) may not manifest itself on the surface of society as a fall in the actual price or value rate of profit when we bear in mind its existence in a structure of contradictions; its main observable effect is the crises which temporarily resolve the contradictions and which are not necessarily preceded by actual falls in the rate of profit. Second, observable effects need not be confined to quantifiable effects: the practice whose unity with theory is so central to Marxism is not limited to the practice of collecting statistics. Practice concerns the whole field of class struggle and the lessons learned from it; the collection and examination of statistics has some significance, but its role is limited and confined to illustration of theories rather than their proof in an empiricist manner. Finally, the direct use of statistics which are constructed within a non-Marxist framework is an invalid procedure for Marxist theoreticians, a point illustrated by Harris (1976a).

The debates surveyed here have occurred in the midst of turmoil in capitalism's economic and political relations, and several contributors take this as their point of reference. In this context in particular it is clear that the way forward for the economic debates is to clarify the relationships between economics, politics and ideology and to develop the analysis of the specific features of state monopoly capitalism. But for this to take place, the issues considered throughout this paper must be given more attention for neither neo-Ricardians nor Fundamentalists have produced theories of the capitalist economy which give a satisfactory basis for the analysis of capitalist society. They have asked questions, provided answers and enabled progress to be made, but neither has followed Marx's method and it is hardly surprising that a common view among Marxists is that the economists have failed to provide Marxist analyses of new problems.

BIBLIOGRAPHY
(CSEB stands for the Bulletin of the Conference of Socialist Economists)

Baumol, W., (1974)	'The Transformation Problem: What Marx Really Meant' Journal of Economic Literature (March).
Bhaduri, A., (1969)	'On the Significance of Recent Controversies in Capital Theory: A Marxian View' Economic Journal, Vol. 79.
Bullock, P., & D. Yaffe., (1975)	'Inflation, crisis and the Post-War Boom' Revolutionary Communist, 3/4 (November).
Catephores, G., (1973)	'Some Remarks on the Falling Rate of Profit', CSEB II.5 (Spring).
Cogoy, M., (1973)	'The Fall of the Rate of Profit and the Theory of Accumulation: A reply to Paul Sweezy', CSEB II.7 (Winter).
Coulson, M., B. Magas & H. Wainwright, (1975)	'The Housewife and her Labour under Capitalism— A Critique': New Left Review 89.
Ergas, H., and Fishman, D., (1975)	'The Marxian Theory of Money and the Crisis of Capital', CSEB IV.II (June).
Fine, B., (1973)	'A Note on Productive and Unproductive Labour' CSEB II.6 (Autumn).
Fine, B., (1975a)	'The Circulation of Capital, Ideology and Crisis', CSEB IV.12 (October).
Fine, B., (1975b)	'From Marx to Morishima', CSEB IV.12 (October).
Fine, B., (1975c)	Marx's Capital, MacMillan Student Text.
Fine, B., & Harris, L., (1975a)	'On the Problem of Analysing Current Economic History', mimeo.
Fine, B., & Harris, L., (1975b)	'The British Economy since March 1974', CSEB IV.12 (October).
Fine, B., & Harris, L., (1976a)	'State Expenditure in Advanced Capitalism: A Critique'. New Left Review, No. 98 (July/August).
Fine, B., & Harris, L., (1976b)	'The British Economy: May 1975-January 1976', CSEB V.14 (June).
Gamble, A., & P. Walton, (1976)	Capitalism in Crisis, MacMillan.
Gerstein, I., (1976)	'Production, Circulation, and Value: The Significance of the "Transformation Problem" in Marx's Critique of Political Economy'. Economy and Society, forthcoming.
Glyn, A., (1973)	'British Capitalism in 1972 and 1973', CSEB II.5 (Spring).
Glyn, A., (1975)	'Notes on the Profit Squeeze', CSEB IV.10 (February).
Glyn, A., & R. Sutcliffe,	British Capitalism, Workers and the Profit Squeeze, Penguin Books.

Gardiner, J., (1975)	'Women's Domestic Labour', New Left Review 89.
Gardiner, J., & Himmelweit, S., & M. Mackintosh (1975)	'Women's Domestic Labour', CSEB, IV.11 (June).
Gough, I., (1972)	'Marx's Theory of Productive and Unproductive Labour', New Left Review 76.
Gough, I., (1973)	'On Productive and Unproductive Labour—A Reply', CSEB II.7 (Winter).
Gough, I., (1975)	'State Expenditure in Advanced Capitalism', New Left Review 92.
Gough, I., & Harrison, J.,	'Unproductive Labour and House Work Again', CSEB IV.10 (February).
Harris, L., (1976a)	'On Interest, Credit and Capital'. Economy and Society, Vol. 5, No. 2, May 1976.
Harris, L., (1976b)	'The Balance of Payments and the International Economic System' in F. Green and P. Nore (eds) Economics: · An Anti-text (MacMillan, forthcoming.
Harrison, J., (1973a)	'Productive and Unproductive Labour in Marx's Political Economy', CSEB II.6 (Autumn).
Harrison, J., (1973b)	'The Political Economy of Housework', CSEB II.7 (Winter).
Harrison, J., (1974)	'British Capitalism in 1973 and 1974: The Deepening Crisis', CSEB III.8 (Spring).
Himmelweit, S., (1974)	'The Continuing Saga of the Falling Rate of Profit—A Reply to Mario Cogoy', CSEB III.9 (Autumn).
Hodgson, G., (1973)	'Marxist Epistemology and the Transformation Problem'—CSEB II.6 (Autumn), reproduced in Economy and Society 3.4 (November 1974).
Hodgson, G., (1974)	'The Theory of the Falling Rate of Profit', New Left Review 84.
Hodgson, G., (1976)	'Exploitation and Embodied Labour Time,' CSEB V.13 (February).
Hodgson, G., & Steedman, I., (1975)	'Fixed Capital and Value Analysis', CSEB V.13 (June).
Holloway, J., & Picciotto, S., (1976)	'A Note on the Theory of the State', CSEB V.14 (June).
Howell, P., (1975)	'Once Again on Productive and Unproductive Labour', Revolutionary Communist 3/4 (November).
Itoh, M., (1975)	'The Formation of Marx's Theory of Crisis', CSEB IV.10 (February).
Kay, G., (1976)	'A Note on Abstract Labour', CSEB V.13 (February).
Mage, S., (1963)	'The "Law of the Falling Tendency of the Rate of Profit": Its Place in the Marxian Theoretical System and Relevance to the U.S. Economy'. Unpublished Ph.D. Thesis, Columbia University.
Meek, R., (1967)	Economics and Ideology, and Other Essays, Chapman and Hall, London.
Pilling, G., (1972)	'The Law of Value in Ricardo and Marx', Economy and Society, Vol. 1, No. 3 (August).
Rowthorn, B., (1973)	'Vulgar Economy', CSEB II.5 (Spring). Reprinted in New Left Review 86, 1974.

Seccombe, W., (1974)   'The Housewife and her Labour Under Capitalism', New Left Review 83.

Seccombe, W., (1975)   'Domestic Labour—Reply to Critics', New Left Review 94.

Seton, F., (1957)   'The "Transformation Problem"'. Review of Economic Studies, 24.

Sraffa, P., (1960)   *The Production of Commodities by Means of Commodities'*, Cambridge University Press, Cambridge.

Steedman, I., (1972)   'Marx on the Rate of Profit', CSEB I.4 (Winter).

Steedman, I., (1973)   'The Transformation Problem Again', CSEB II.6 (Autumn).

Steedman, I., (1975a)   'Value, Price and Profit', New Left Review 90.

Steedman, I., (1975b)   'Positive Profit and Negative Surplus Value', Economic Journal (March).

Sweezy, P., (1949)   *The Theory of Capitalist Development*, Monthly Review Press, New York.

Williams, K., (1975)   'Facing Reality—a Critique of Karl Popper's Empiricism', Economy and Society, 4.3 (August).

Yaffe, D., (1972)   'The Marxian Theory of Crisis, Capital and the State', CSEB I.4 (Winter). Reproduced in *Economy and Society*, 2.2 (1973).

Yaffe, D., (1973)   'The Crisis of Profitability: A Critique of the Glyn-Stucliffe Thesis', New Left Review, 80.

Yaffe, D., (1975)   'Value and Price in Marx's *Capital*', Revolutionary Communist 1, (January).

MARXIST WOMEN VERSUS BOURGEOIS FEMINISM*

by Hal Draper and Anne G. Lipow

Introduction

The texts presented here are intended to revive acquaintance with a revolutionary women's movement which was undoubtedly the most important one of the kind that has yet been seen. Yet it has been so thoroughly dropped down the Memory Hole that even mention of its existence is hard to find.

Nowadays, references to Marx and Marxism show up rather frequently in women's liberation literature as a fashionable ingredient. This literature, however, seldom makes contact with Marx and Engels' real views on the issues involved, and takes even less notice of the fact that they helped to put these views into practice. By the 1890s, Engels together with a close disciple August Bebel helped to inspire and encourage a socialist women's movement that was militantly Marxist in leadership and policy.

The name associated with this women's movement is above all that of Clara Zetkin, its best political leader, organiser, theoretician, and publicist. After a quarter century or so of effective leadership in the women's struggle of the international socialist movement in its heyday, this same great woman also became one of the leading figures in the left-wing opposition to the First World War and eventually in the women's movement of the early Communist International. It would seem she did something. But try and find some notice of the great movement she led—either in contemporary feminist historical literature or in alleged histories of socialism! It is not impossible but very difficult.

I

The scene is Germany, and the time is the period of about three decades before the First World War.

There is no other country or period in which the issues of socialist feminism were so clearly fought out and worked out. This Introduction cannot hope to present a historical sketch of this movement or an adequate summary of all the issues involved. Fortunately, there is a work which

---

*This text is part of a forthcoming work, *Women and Class*, edited by Hal Draper and Anne G. Lipow.

partially provides this, W. Thönessen's *The Emancipation of Women*, and any reader who is at all seriously interested in revolutionary feminism must read it. Here we concentrate on the theme of this book: the class line that runs through feminism from the start, and in particular the relations between socialist feminism and bourgeois feminism. The German movement is especially instructive on the latter aspect.

The Marxist women of the German movement had to carry on a war on two fronts—just as all socialist leftists have always had to combat not only the direct enemy capitalism but also those reformers who offer substitutes for the socialist alternative. In the women's field, the direct enemy was, of course, the anti-feminism and sex oppression of the established powers and institutions; but alongside this conflict was the associated need to counteract the influence of bourgeois feminism.

For some preliminary light on this issue, let us start with what appears to be a problem in translation but which actually involves an important Marxist concept. The revolutionary socialist women of the German movement took over a favourite label for the bourgeois feminist types: *Frauenrechtlerinnen*. A more or less literal translation is 'women's-righsters.' Dreadfully awkward, obviously, though no more so than in German. The common translation 'suffragettes' is misleading and often downright wrong; 'bourgeois feminists' is usually better but misses the point. The significance of 'women's-rightsers', as the Marxist women used it, is that such feminists make women's juridical rights (under the existing social order) the be-all and end-all of their movement and programme, *by detaching the question of women's rights from the basic social issues, by making it a separate question.*

This is the characteristic which is the target of much of Zetkin's argumentation in the following sections. But it was made most explicit by Eleanor Marx, in the course of the first article she wrote for the Vienna socialist women (quoted in §5 below). She hits the nail on the head. It is so basic that we present the central passage here, even though it will be met later in its context. The Socialist International had recently voted complete equality for women as its programmatic aim, and Eleanor Marx explains why this programme has nothing to do with the 'women's-rightsers':

Just as on the war question the Congress stressed the difference between the ordinary bourgeois peace league, which cries, 'Peace, peace' where there is no peace, and the economic peace party, the socialist party, which wants to remove the causes of war—so too with regard to the 'woman question' the Congress equally clearly stressed the difference between the party of the 'women's rightsers' on the one side, who recognised no class struggle but only a struggle of sexes, who belong to the possessing class, and who want rights that would be an injustice against their working-class sisters, and, on the other side, the real women's party, the socialist party, which has a basic understanding of the economic causes on the present adverse position of workingwomen and which calls on the working-women to wage a common fight hand-in-hand with the men of their class against the common enemy, *viz.* the men and women of the capitalist class.

The analogy which E. Marx makes here, to bourgeois pacifism, is so close that still another point emerges. For there were not only bourgeois pacifists but also socialist pacifists, who likewise wanted to detach the question of war and peace from that of the overall social struggle. This is the strong tendency of all socialist reformism, part of its common ground with bourgeois reform. Much will be understood about the women's movement if this basic pattern is applied to it. Just as the issue of pacifism (pacifism understood in the above scientific sense) divided the socialist movement between right and left, so also the question of an attitude toward bourgeois feminism divided socialist women (and men) of the right and left wings.

This helps to explain why the Marxist women's movement that Zetkin led was also ranged, by and large, on the revolutionary left wing of the German Social-Democracy, while the reformists (Revisionists) tended to come out for accommodation with the bourgeois women's-rightsers. The first half of this statement is well known historically; for example, when the Social-Democracy collapsed at the onset of war in August 1914, the cadres and main leadership of the socialist women played an important anti-war role. Long before this, Zetkin had aligned herself strongly in the party debate on the side of the enemies of Revisionism.

The second half of the proposition is not as well known. This is what lends special interest to our §3 below, where we see a peculiar polemic launched by the party organ editors against Zetkin, precisely on the issue of attitude toward the women's-rightsers, shortly before Revisionism appeared as a public tendency.

Note that, in this exchange with Zetkin, the party editors—without as yet quite knowing how to define their uneasiness—are bridling above all at Zetkin's air of *hostility* toward bourgeois feminism. And down to the present day, this is the often amorphous form in which basic issues have been fought out. In various forms for most of a century, Marxists tried to pin the discussion down to politics and programme, while the liberalistic right wing preferred to keep the controversy in the airy realm of attitudes: *'Don't be so harsh on them; after all we agree on many things. . . It's the powers that be we should fight, not our friends the women's-rightsers. . . Don't be dogmatic, doctrinaire, rigid, unrealistic, and hard. . .'*

These half-truths were not peculiar to the women's question. On the contrary, the whole pre-1914 debate between Marxism and Revisionism was not usually favoured with clearcut argumentation about principles (such as tends to be the summary content of later histories) but rather with dreary polemics about attitudes, the function of which was to inculcate an attitude of soft accommodation to liberal capitalism. The Social-Democracy did not march into the arms of reformism; typically it backed into it. It stumbled backward as bogeys about doctrinairism and electoral realism were brandished before it.

So also with the question of the socialists women's *hostility* to the women's-rightsers of bourgeois feminism. The reformists did not have great objections to raising their hands in favour of Marxistical formulations in resolutions about the women's movement and socialism; it was another thing to concentrate hostility to bourgeois liberalism in practice.

This is how the right-left split on feminism stood by the 1890s, when Zetkin's work began to take effect. But it had looked very different at the inception of the German movement. Let us go back a way.

II

The German socialist movement was organisationally founded in the 1860s not by Marxists but by Ferdinand Lassalle and his immediate followers. The Lassallean tendency was essentially a type of reformist state-socialism, which persisted in the movement long after its surface Marxification. Perhaps the clearest expression of Lassalleanism was in Lassalle's secret negotiations with Bismarck, in which the would-be 'workers' dictator' (as Marx called him) offered to help the Iron Chancellor establish a 'social monarchy' (a presumably anti-capitalist despotism) using Lassalle's working-class troops as its mass base. Bismarck turned down the offer, and naturally headed toward a united front with the bourgeoisie instead; but this perspective remained the Lassallean trademark. The aim was the organisation of working-class cadres as an instrument of policy by leaders who had mainly contempt for the class on whose backs they sought to ride to power. Thus the Lassalleans developed as a 'working-class' sect, that is, one oriented toward a proletarian membership composition as its power base.

This is what helps to explain the position on the women's question first adopted by the Lassallean movement. It recruited its cadres from the first organisable workers, already conscious of their immediate demands, and it directed these demands into an interest-group programme. As an interest group, these organised workers, still a small minority of the class, were immediately threatened by the competition of cheaper female labour, used by capital to keep wages and conditions down. This posed the usual choice for self-styled socialists. Should they, in the teeth of pressing but short-range interests of (a part of) the working class, insist on the overriding need to 'always and everywhere represent the interests of the movement as a whole', as the working class passed through different stages of consciousness and struggle? Or should they go along with the immediate pressure of narrow group-interest demands, paying little attention to the needs of the class as a whole—which means, the long-range needs of the entire class, including its as yet unorganised sectors?

In 1867, four years after its founding, the Lassallean group came out directly against the industrial employment of women and in favour of measures to keep women out of the factories. The motivation was to reduce (men's) unemployment and keep wages up. While economically motivated, the demands tended to take on a high moral tone, for obvious reasons: arguments about preserving the family and defending female morals could appeal to circles beyond the interest group.

Was this movement to limit female labour due to something called 'proletarian anti-feminism', or was 'proletarian anti-feminism' the ideological form taken by the exigencies of the economic struggle? In fact there was the common intertwining of economic impulsions and ideological constructions, reinforcing each other in the short run. But the basic drive was evident as further developments changed the interest group's immediate perception of its own interests. For the number of women workers increased despite all moralising, and this created a new reality. The aim of keeping women out of the factories was not only reactionary but utopian, that is, unrooted in the real tendencies of social development.

Capitalism saw to it that female industrial labour went up by leaps and bounds, despite the outcries. In the 1870s the number of female workers passed the million mark, and a decade later was reaching six million. The immediate pressures changed on even the most shortsighted. There was a *fait accompli* to be reckoned with: if all workers' immediate interests were to be protected, these new workers had to be organised in trade unions too. If the women workers were to be included in the trade-union movement, then appeals had to be made to *their* interests. An interesting reversal now took place. The 'pre-feminist' employers, who had produced stalwart proponents of women's rights to work for a pittance (in the name of justice and equality), became alarmed at the Dangers to Morality that would result from women joining men's organisations (unions). The state responded to this new threat against public moral with laws that restricted women's right of association and assembly.

From the beginning in the 1860s, a fundamentally different approach came only from the first Marxist spokesmen, especially August Bebel and Wilhelm Liebknecht. In their view the interests of women as a sex and workers as a class were integrated. Their starting-point was the direct opposite of the shortsighted 'workerist' hostility to female industrial labour. Their first proposition was that women could be genuinely independent of men and equal in rights *only* insofar as they achieved economic independence. Economic independence meant not only the abstract right to work but the real possibility of doing so outside the home. This was the way to go, because it provided the only possible foundation for the whole long road to sexual equality. To the Lassalleans, the integration of women into industry was a scandalous abuse; to the Marxists, it was the first condition for progress. Here was the first right-left split on the women's question in the socialist movement.

In the Marxist perspective, the entrance of women into industry was not itself *the* solution; it merely posed the right questions for solution. It provided the necessary starting-point for struggle. The struggle had to include a fight against the abuses of female labour along with other working-class struggles. Once one saw the female half of the human race as an integral part of the great social struggle, everything else followed. Just as the Lassalleans had extended their rejection of women's employment to rejection of women's suffrage and political rights, so also the Marxists' approach pointed in the diametrically opposite direction, to the integration of women into every aspect of the social struggle, including the political.

III

Integration is the key word. As we have seen, this is what basically distinguishes Marxist feminism from *Frauenrechtlerei*, which divorces the demand for women's rights from the general struggle for social emancipation.

But integration does not mean that the women's question is simply swallowed up under the rubric socialism, any more than trade-unionism is. In general, Marxism seeks to integrate reform and revolution, to establish a working relation between immediate demands and 'ultimate' programme; it does not substitute one for the other.* There is a contemporary myth, widespread in feminist literature, that Marxism merely announces that 'socialism will solve the women's question' and that's that. It is a very convenient myth, since it is so easy to ridicule that it becomes unnecessary to get acquainted with what the founders of Marxism really advocated and how the Marxist women really organised.

The socialist women's movement led by Zetkin gave strong support to all the democratic demands for women's equal rights. But this movement differed from the bourgeois feminists not only in the programmatic context in which it put these 'democratic demands', but also—and consequently—in its choice of immediate demands to emphasise. It viewed itself, in Marxist terms, as a class movement, and this translates into *workingwomen's movement*. The immediate demands it emphasised corresponded to the needs of women workers in the first place. The socialist women fought for immediate economic gains for women workers, including legislative gains

---

*To be sure, there have been 'Marxist' sects that repudiated reforms on 'principle', even though Marx and Engels denounced this sort of sectarianism unmercifully. But such sects are irrelevant to everything, including our subject. The same goes for alleged 'Marxists' nowadays who apply this sectism to the women's question. One should read Rosa Luxemburg's *Reform and Revolution*.

to protect women workers' interests—just as every militant organisation of male workers did the same. But this simple fact produced a controversy which is as lively today as when it started, one that provides a touchstone of the class difference between socialist feminism and bourgeois feminism.

In the case of male workers, the question of 'special' protective legislation has been so long worked out that it no longer seems to be controversial. It is almost forgotten that, once upon a time, the legislative imposition of (say) a minimum wage was attacked within the labour movement on the ground that it would rebound against labour's interests. A common argument was that a minimum wage would tend to become the maximum wage, thereby hurting better-paid workers even if it improved the position of the lowest strata. There was a kernel of truth to this fear: this special protective legislation *could* be used by employers for their own purposes. In fact, there is no conceivable labour legislation which cannot be turned against workers as long as the labour movement is not organised to effectively police the way the law is used. In more modern times, experience has shown countless cases in which basic labour gains, painfully acquired by decades of struggle, have been latterly used by employers (and their allies in the trade-union and government bureaucracies) to discriminate against minority workers for the benefit of an entrenched job trust.

None of these real problems, past and present, would nowadays be used to argue openly that 'special' protective legislation for men workers has to be thrown out holus-bolus, turning the clock back a hundred years. The problems are met in other ways, especially when the particular devices have to be subjected to review and modification; but this is scarcely new or startling.

The picture is altogether different when it comes to special protective legislation for women workers. What is taken for granted on men workers' behalf is not accepted as a principle for women workers as well. Why? The difficulty comes not merely from employers (who are understandably reluctant to improve working conditions for any 'special' group) but also from the bourgeois feminists. Historically speaking, the reason for this state of affairs is quite plain. The hard core of the bourgeois feminist movements has typically been the 'career women' elements, business and professional strivers above all. Protective devices for the benefit of women workers in factories help to make life more bearable for them, but they are usually irrelevant to upper-echelon women trying to get ahead in professions. Worse, they may introduce restrictions which get in the way. At the very least, the 'pure' feminists demonstrate their social purity by rejecting the idea that the women's question has something to do with class issues. Protective legislation for *women* workers is, abstractly considered, a form of 'sex discrimination'—just as legislation for men workers is a form of 'class legislation' and was long denounced as such. The bourgeois feminists are . better served by making feminine equality as abstract an issue as possible, above all abstracted from the social struggle of classes.

To the socialist women, however, 'special' legislation for women workers is far more important than (say) opening up medical colleges to female students. This implies no hostility to the latter goal; the socialist women enthusiastically supported such efforts. But a law requiring (say) the installation of toilet facilities for women workers affected a mass of women, not merely a few aspiring professionals, even though it was unlikely to become the subject of a romantic movie. The socialist perspective on social struggle extended from the 'lowest' concerns to the highest, and integrated them. The few women who, rightly and bravely, aspired to crash into the medical profession were to be applauded for their striving; but at the same time one should not conceal that most of such types tended to look on the 'lower' interests of workingwomen as an embarrassment to their own high aspirations. Objectively, like most aspirants from the upper strata of society, they were quite willing to get ahead over the backs of the mass of their sisters; the *best* of them explained that as soon as they made it they would do some good for the less fortunate.

While the socialist women's fight for protective legislation for working-women could not be accommodated among the abstractions of the women's-rightsers, it integrated perfectly with the general social struggle of the working-class movement. Gains made by women workers often tended to become the opening wedge for the extension of similar gains to all workers. Thus the men in the factories were also beneficiaries.

The result was, and still is, that there are few questions in which the class struggle more nakedly inserts itself into abstract arguments about justice and equality. But the naked framework of class interests usually has to be clothed in more acceptable clothing—by both sides. One does not often find Ms. X arguing that the law which gives women farm workers a toilet in the fields has to be smashed so as not to get in the way of the strivings of women professors for full tenure. And on the other side, the argumentation for special legislation for women workers was often peppered with highminded appeals to morality in various senses.

Appeals to morality figured prominently in the 1860s in Germany. When the Lassalleans opposed the entrance of women into industry, it was convenient to prop up the economic demand with backward-looking rationalisations about 'women's place' in the home. The reactionary demand imposed a reactionary ideology as its justification. The working-women's movement often argued for special protective laws on the ground that they promoted social goods like the health and well being of working mothers as well as moral protection. Still, it was the relation of women to the working class that was the crux.

IV

The Marxist wing's position on the women's question won only a partial victory in 1875, when the Lassallean and semi-Marxist groups united at the Gotha Congress to form the German Social-Democracy. It was not until 1891 (at the Erfurt congress) that there was a complete programmatic endorsement of militant support to a consistent position for women's equality. This party, the nearest thing to a Marxist party that had been formed, was the first one to adopt a thoroughly pro-feminist position.

There was another unusual feature: the undisputed party leader, Bebel, was also its foremost theoretician of socialist feminism (until the socialist women's movement developed its own leadership). The publication of Bebel's great book *Woman and Socialism* in 1878 was, as Zetkin said (see below), an 'event' in itself, a revolutionary coup, with a tremendous impact that reverberated through scores of editions and translations for a half century and more. Six years later, Engels' *The Origin of the Family, Private Property and the State* came along to give a further impulsion. Both books put the immediate issues of women's rights in their context as part of a broad historical canvas of societal development, part of a social struggle in which were integrated the militant aspirations of an oppressed sex and an oppressed class.

The socialist women began to move toward self-organisation at the start of the 1890s. In 1890 a prominent socialist activist, Emma Ihrer, headed the effort to set up a propaganda centre in the form of a socialist feminist organ, *Die Arbeiterin* (The Workingwoman). When it foundered financially, Zetkin and Ihrer founded *Gleichheit* (Equality) in 1891, and this remained the centre of the movement right up to the end of the era marked by World War I and its aftermath.

The circulation of *Gleichheit* increased from a few thousand at the beginning to 23,000 by 1905; then it doubled in a year, and kept mounting steadily until it stood at 112,000 in 1913. This growth coincided with the recruitment of women to the trade unions and to the party. There were about 4,000 women in the party in 1905, but this number grew to over 141,000 by 1913. The contemporary reader must remember that this took place in a society where the very act of a woman's attending a meeting was not yet exactly 'respectable', even after it became legal.

The German Marxist women also became the main force in the international socialist women's movement, organisationally and administratively as well as politically.

This growth provided the context for the antagonistic tension, which we have mentioned, between the socialist women's movement and the reformist tendencies within the mass party. This antagonism was closely related to another one: that between the socialist women and the bourgeois feminist movement. It was the reformist ('Revisionist' from 1896 on) wing of the party that pressed for a soft attitude of collaboration with the women's-rightsers. The tendency of the reformists to avoid a clearcut political confrontation manifested itself here too. For one thing, it was easier and quieter to insert the right-wing line not as a viewpoint to be considered but as the 'practical' thing to do. When in 1896 Eduard Bernstein gave reformism its theoretical form as 'Revisionism', the party's org-bureau man, Ignaz Auer, told him he was making a tactical mistake: this sort of thing he wrote Bernstein, is not something to talk about but simply to *do*.

Similarly, the right wing's uneasiness about the course of the socialist women's movement was expressed by indirection; typically it did not attack but sniped away. One push against *Gleichheit* took the form of complaints that it was 'difficult to understand'—that is, that it was not written down to the level of the least-common-denominator woman. Zetkin's conception of the magazine was that its function was to educate and develop the leading cadres of women comrades, and that the important job of reaching down agitationally could be accomplished by other channels, including pamphlets and leaflets and pro-feminist material in the many Social-Democratic newspapers that reached a mass audience. By attacking *Gleichheit* for the higher level of its approach, the right wing was really saying that there was no need for any organ to deal with the women's question on this level; it implied the intellectual subordination of the women's movement.

But the party congresses voted down these sallies when they were clearly presented. In 1898 the party congress rejected the proposal that the ownership of *Gleichheit* should be transferred to the party itself and the editorship moved from Stuttgart to Berlin, where it could be controlled more directly. It was only after the world war had formally split the party into left and right that the new reformist party, the 'Majority Social-Democrats', was able to gut the contents of *Gleichheit* and then kill it.

Thönessen mentions another ploy of the reformists, more difficult to pin down. This was the use of 'malicious witticisms' in party discussions to trigger well-known stereotyped attitudes about women who meddle in 'men's affairs'. These attitudes were openly expressed everywhere else; in the party they could only be suggested by 'jokes'. It is Ignaz Auer who provides the examples for Thönessen. This device was still new because it was only just becoming necessary for sex-chauvinism to hide its face; and it was because the Marxist women were playing a new social role on a mass scale that innuendo had to be substituted for traditional derision.

There is another consideration which throws light on the difference between the reformist and Marxist wings. The women's question gave rise to articles not only in the women's press but also in the main party organs. Thönessen compares the articles which appeared in the theoretical organ of the more-or-less Marxist wing *Die Neue Zeit* and in the right-wing magazine

Sozialistische Monatshefte over a period of forty years, mainly pre-war. For one thing, the Marxist organ published about four times as many contributions on the subject as the other. The reformist magazine 'tended to provide relatively little concrete material on the real situation of women workers' and 'philosophical and psychological reflections on the nature of woman and her emancipation', along with vague speculations about the 'problems of women's life'.

Alongside all this was also the fact that in the general party struggle the outstanding women leaders were important advocates of the left. This was true of Clara Zetkin above all. In addition, the outstanding theoretician of the left was a woman, Rosa Luxemburg. Though Luxemburg's activity was not in the women's movement, one can be sure that the witty Ignaz Auer did not think it altogether funny that these rambunctious women were causing his comrades so much trouble.

In the following sections, the emphasis is on the attitude of the Marxist women toward the bourgeois-feminists, the women's-rightsers. To be sure, this did not occupy the bulk of the socialists' attention, but for us today it is of special interest. Above all, this is the side of Marxist feminism that has been largely ignored.

All of this material appears here in English for the first time, with the exception from Bebel in §1 (which, however, is given here in a new translation).

1
August Bebel
The Enemy Sisters

Bebel's epochmaking book Woman and Socialism *did not include a separate discussion of the feminist movement, which was not far advanced when the book was first published in 1878; but its introduction did make some germinal remarks on the differences between socialist feminism and the bourgeois women's movement. Following is a short passage from this introduction. It emphasises above all the principled basis for the counterposition.*

The phrase 'enemy sisters' (in the fifth paragraph below) became well known to the socialist women. How it jarred on some sensibilities may be seen, in a way, in the major English translation of Bebel's book, by the American socialist Meta L. Stern. This English version sought to dilute the impact of the phrase by rewriting the sentence a bit, so as to change 'enemy sisters' to 'sister-women': 'Still these sister-women, though antagonistic to each other on class lines. . .'

Our Introduction to Part II has already stressed Bebel's important aid to the women's movement. His encouragement came from four directions: from his writings, from his help as head of the party, from speeches in the Reichstag, and also from personal support. One of the leading people in the Austrian socialist women's movement, Adelheid Popp, relates in her autobiography how, one day, both Bebel and old Engels came to visit her mother to try to make the old lady understand what her daughter was doing, in order to help a promising woman militant.

If we assume the case, which is certainly not impossible, that the representatives of the bourgeois women's movement achieve all their demands for equal rights with men, this would not entail the abolition of the slavery that present-day marriage means for countless women, nor of prostitution, nor of the material dependence of the great majority of married women on their husbands. Also, for the great majority of women it makes no difference if some thousands or tens of thousands of their sisters who belong to the more favourably situated ranks of society succeed in attaining a superior profession or medical practice or some scientific or official career, for *nothing* is thereby changed in the *overall situation* of the sex as a whole.

The female sex, in the mass, suffers from a double burden. Firstly, women suffer by virtue of their social and societal dependence on men; and this would certainly be ameliorated, but not eliminated, by formal equality of rights before the law. Secondly, they suffer by virtue of the economic dependence which is the lot of women in general and proletarian women in particular, as is true also of proletarian men.

Hence it follows that all women—regardless of their position in society, as a sex that has been oppressed, ruled, and wronged by men throughout the course of development of our culture—have the common interest of doing away with this situation and of fighting to change it, insofar as it can be changed through changes in laws and institutions within the framework of the existing political and social order. But the huge majority of women are also most keenly interested in something more: in transforming the existing political and social order *from the ground up,* in order to abolish both wage-slavery, which afflicts the female proletariat most heavily, and sex-slavery, which is very intimately bound up with our property and employment conditions.

The preponderant portion of the women in the bourgeois women's movement do not comprehend the necessity of such a radical transformation. Under the influence of their privileged position in society, they see in the more far-reaching movement of the proletarian women dangerous and often detestable aspirations that they have to fight. The class antagonism that yawns like a gulf between the capitalist class and the working class in the general social movement, and that keeps on getting sharper and harsher with the sharpening of our societal relations, also makes its appearance inside the women's movement and finds its fitting expression in the goals they adopt and the way they behave.

Still and all, to a much greater extent than the men divided by the class struggle, the enemy sisters have a number of points to contact enabling them to carry on a struggle in which they can strike together even though marching separately. This is the case above all where the question concerns equality of rights of women with men on the basis of the present-day political and social order; hence the employment of women in all areas of human activity for which they have the strength and capacity, and also full civil and political equality of rights with men. These domains are very important and, as we will show later, very extensive. In connection with these aims, proletarian women have in addition a special interest, together with proletarian men, in fighting for all those measures and institutions that protect the woman worker from physical strength and capacity to bear children and initiate their upbringing. Beyond this, as already indicated, proletarian women have to take up the struggle, along with the men who are their comrades in class and comrades in social fortune, for a transformation of society from the ground up, to bring about a state of affairs making possible the real economic and intellectual independence of both sexes, through social institutions that allow everyone to share fully in all the achievements of human civilisation.

It is therefore a question not only of achieving equality of rights between men and women on the basis of the existing political and social order, which is the goal set by the bourgeois women's-rightsers, but of going beyond that goal and abolishing all the barriers that make one human being dependent on another and therefore one sex on another. *This* resolution of the woman question therefore coincides completely with the resolution of the social question. Whoever seeks a resolution of the woman question in its full dimensions must therefore perforce join hands with those who have inscribed on their banner the resolution of the social question that faces civilisation for all humanity—that is, the socialists, the Social-Democracy.

Of all the existing parties, the Social-Democratic Party is the *only* one that has included in its programme the complete equality of women and their liberation from every form of dependence and oppression, not on grounds of propaganda but out of necessity, on grounds of principle. *There can be no liberation of humanity without the social independence and equal rights of both sexes.*

2
Clara Zetkin
Proletarian Women and Socialist Revolution

The following short pamphlet contains Clara Zetkin's most general discussion of the class lines running through women as a social group and through their movements as ideological expressions. We therefore present in here first, although chronologically it was preceded by the discussion in §3. There is a connection between the two which must be mentioned.

In §3, Zetkin is taking aim at the weak position taken up by the editors of the party organ; it is already critical in tone, on the subject of the editors' soft attitude toward the bourgeois feminists. Less than two years later, Zetkin came to the party congress prepared to plumb this question in the movement. Her main statement was not presented in the resolution on the subject (which naturally had to be voted on) but in a speech to the congress which she made on October 16th, 1896. A motion was then made and carried that her speech be printed by the party as a pamphlet, and this was done. Thus her views appeared under the party imprint, but not as an official party statement.

The pamphlet was declaratively entitled 'Only with the proletarian woman will socialism be victorious!'—with the subtitle 'Speech to the Gotha Congress [etc.].' Here we have conferred a somewhat shorter title on it. It is translated from Zetkin's Ausgewählte Reden und Schriften *(Berlin, Bietz, 1957). Volume I.*

Zetkin's main concern in this pamphlet is social analysis. We can guess that most of it was presented with the pamphlet publication already in mind, not simply as a speech to the delegates. However, its latter part also presents some proposals on forms of propaganda which should be considered as more directly tied to the Congress's considerations of the moment.

Through the researches by Bachofen, Morgan and others, it seems established that the social subjection of women coincided with the rise of private property. The antagonism inside the family between the man as owner and the woman as non-owner was the foundation for the economic dependence of the female sex and its lack of social rights.

'In the family, he is the bourgeois; the wife represents the proletariat.'[*] Nevertheless there could be no talk of a women's question in the modern sense of the term. It was the capitalist mode of production that first brought about the social transformation which raised the modern women's question; it smashed to smithereens the old family economy that in pre-capitalist times had provided the great mass of women with the sustenance and meaningful content of life. Indeed, we must not apply to the old-time household work of women the conception that is linked with women's work in our own day, *viz.* the conception that it is something petty and of no account. As long as the old-time family still existed, within its framework women found a meaningful content of life in productive work, and hence their lack of social rights did not impinge on their consciousness, even though the development of their individualities was narrowly limited.

The age of the Renaissance is the Sturm und Drang period in the growth of modern individualism, which may work itself out fully in different ways. During the Renaissance we encounter individuals—towering like giants for good or evil—who trampled underfoot the precepts of religion and morality and looked on heaven and hell with equal scorn; we find women as the focus of social, artistic and political life. And nevertheless not a trace of a women's movement. This is especially distinctive because at that time the old family economy began to crumble under the impact of the division of labour. Thousands and thousands of women no longer found the sustenance and content of life in the family. But this women's question, far from coming to the fore, was resolved to the extent possible by cloisters, convents, and religious orders.

Then machines and the modern mode of production little by little knocked the bottom out of household production for use. And not for

---

[*]Engels, *Origin of the Family*, near end of Chapter 2.

thousands but for millions of women arose the question: Where are we to get the sustenance of life, where are we to find a serious content of life, an occupation allowing for the emotional side also? Millions were now told to find the sustenance and content of life outside in society. There they became aware that their lack of social rights militated against the defence of their interests; and from that moment the modern women's question was in existence.

As to how the modern mode of production operated to sharpen the women's question further, here are some figures. In 1882, in Germany, out of 23 million women and girls, 5½ million were gainfully employed; that is, almost a quarter of the female population could no longer find their sustenance in the family. According to the 1895 census, taking agriculture in the broadest sense, the number of women gainfully employed in it increased by more than 8 percent since 1882; taking agriculture in the narrower sense, by 6 percent; while at the same time the number of men gainfully employed decreased 3 and 11 percent respectively. In industry and mining, gainfully employed women increased by 35 percent, men by only 28 percent; in commerce, indeed, the number of women increased by over 94 percent, men by only 38 percent. These dry statistics speak much more eloquently on the urgency of a solution to the women's question than the most effusive orations.

But the women's question exists only inside those classes of society that are themselves products of the capitalist mode of production. Therefore we find no women's question arising in the ranks of the peasantry, with its natural economy, even though that economy is very much shrunken and tattered. But we do indeed find a women's question inside those classes of society that are the most characteristic offspring of the modern mode of production. There is a women's question for the women of the proletariat, of the middle bourgeoisie, of the intelligentsia, and of the Upper Ten Thousand; it takes various forms depending on the class situation of these strata.

What form is taken by the women's question among the women of the Upper Ten Thousand? A woman of this social stratum, by virtue of her possession of property, can freely develop her individuality; she can live in accordance with her inclinations. As a wife, however, she is still always dependent on the man. The sexual tutelage of a former age has survived, as a leftover, in family law, where the tenet 'And he shall be thy lord' is still valid.

And how is the family of the Upper Ten Thousand constituted so that the woman is legally subjected to the man? This family lacks moral premises in its very foundation. Not the individuality but money is decisive in its doings. Its law reads: What capital brings together, let no sentimental morality put asunder. ('Bravo!') Thus, in the morality of marriage, two prostitutions count as one virtue. This is matched also by the style of family life. Where the wife is no longer forced to perform duties, she shunts her duties as spouse, mother and housekeeper onto paid servants. When the women of these circles entertain a desire to give their lives serious content, they must first raise the demand for free and independent control over their property. This demand therefore is in the centre of the demands raised by the women's movement of the Upper Ten Thousand. These women fight for the achievement of this demand against the men of their own class—exactly the same demand that the bourgeoisie fought for against all privileged classes: a struggle for the elimination of all social distinctions based on the possession of wealth.

The fact that the achievement of this demand does not involve individual personal rights is proved by its espousal in the Reichstag by Herr von Stumm..When has Herr von Stumm ever come out in favour of individual rights? This man stands for more than a person in Germany; he is flesh and blood turned capital personified ('Very true!'), and if he has come forward as a friend of women's rights in a piece of cheap mummery, it is because he was compelled to dance before the Ark of capital. This same Herr von Stumm is indeed always ready to put the squeeze on his workers as soon as they stop dancing to his tune, and he would only grin complacently if the state, as employer, put a bit of a squeeze on the professors and academics who dare to get involved in social politics. Herr von Stumm strives for no more than a kind of entail on personal property with the right of females to inherit; for there are fathers who made fortunes but carelessly had only daughters for heirs. Capital makes even lowly women sacred, and enables them to exercise control over their wealth. This is the last stage in the emancipation of private property.

And how does the women's question manifest itself in the ranks of the small and middle bourgeoisie, and in the bourgeois intelligentsia? Here it is not a matter of property dissolving the family, but mainly the phenomena accompanying capitalist production. As the latter completes its triumphal progress, in the mass the middle and small bourgeoisie are more and more driven to ruin. In the bourgeois intelligentsia there is a further circumstance that makes for the worsening of the conditions of life: Capital needs an intelligent and scientifically trained labour force; it therefore favoured overproduction in proletarian brain-workers, and contributed to the fact that the previously respectable and remunerative social position of members of the liberal professions is increasingly disappearing. To the same degree, however, the number of marriages is continually decreasing; for while the material bases are worsening on the one hand, on the other the individual's demands on life are increasing, and therefore the men of these circles naturally think twice and thrice before they decide to marry. The age limits for starting one's own family are getting jacked up higher and higher, and men are pushed into marriage to a lesser degree as social arrangements make a comfortable bachelor existence possible even without a legal wife. Capitalist exploitation of proletarian labour power ensures, through starvation wages, that a large supply of prostitutes answers the demand from this same aspect of the male population. Thus the number of unmarried women in middle-class circles is continually increasing. The women and daughters of these circles are thrust out into society to establish a life for themselves, not only one that provides bread but also one that can satisfy the spirit.

In these circles the woman does not enjoy equality with the man as owner of private property, as obtains in the higher circles. Nor does she enjoy equality as a workingwoman, as obtains in proletarian circles. The women of these circles must, rather, first fight for their economic equality with the men, and they can do this only through two demands; through the demand for equality in occupational education and through the demand for sex equality in carrying on an occupation. Economically speaking, this means nothing else than the realisation of free trade and free competition between men and women. The realisation of this demand awakens a conflict of interest between the women and men of the middle class and the intelligentsia. The competition of women in the liberal professions is the driving force behind the resistance of the men against the demands of the bourgeois women's-rightsers. It is pure fear of competition; all other grounds adduced against intellectual labour by women are mere pretexts—women's smaller brain, or their alleged natural vocation as mothers. This competitive battle pushes the women of these strata to demand political rights, so as to destroy all limitations still militating against their economic activity, through political struggle.

In all this I have indicated only the original, purely economic aspect. We would do the bourgeois women's movement an injustice if we ascribed it only to purely economic motives. No, it also has a very much deeper intellectual and moral side. The bourgeois woman not only demands to earn her own bread, but she also wants to live a full life intellectually and develop her own individuality. It is precisely in these strata that we meet those tragic and psychologically interesting 'Neva' figures, where the wife is tired of living like a doll in a doll house, where she wants to take part in the broader development of modern culture; and on both the economic and intellectual-moral sides the strivings of the bourgeois women's-righters are entirely justified.

For the proletarian woman, it is capital's need for exploitation, its unceasing search for the cheapest labour power, that has created the women's question. . .* This is also how the woman of the proletariat is drawn into the machinery of contemporary economic life, this is how she is driven into the workshop and to the machine. She entered economic life in order to give the husband some help in earning a living—and the capitalist mode

---

*These suspension points are in the text.—*Ed.*

of production transforms her into an undercutting competitor; she wanted to secure a better life for her family—and in consequence brought greater misery to the proletarian family; the proletarian woman became an independent wage-earner because she wanted to give her children a sunnier and happier life—and she was in large part torn away from her children. She became completely equal to the man as labour-power: the machine makes muscular strength unnecessary, and everywhere women's labour could operate with the same results for production as man's labour. And since she was a cheap labour force and above all a willing labour force that only in the rarest cases dared to kick against the pricks of capitalist exploitation, the capitalists multiplied the opportunities to utilise women's labour in industry to the highest degree.

The wife of the proletarian, in consequence, achieved her economic independence. But, in all conscience, she paid for it dearly, and thereby gained nothing at the same time, practically speaking. If in the era of the family the man had the right—think back to the law in the Electorate of Bavaria—to give the wife a bit of a lashing now and then, capitalism now lashes her with scorpions. In those days the dominion of the man over the woman was mitigated by personal relationships, but between worker and employer there is only a commodity relationship. The woman of the proletariat has achieved her economic independence, but neither as a person nor as a woman or wife does she have the possibility of living a full life as an individual. For her work as wife and mother she gets only the crumbs that are dropped from the table by capitalist production.

Consequently, the liberation struggle of the proletarian woman cannot be—as it is for the bourgeois woman—a struggle against the men of her own class. She does not need to struggle, as against the men of her own class, to tear down the barriers erected to limit her free competition. Capital's need for exploitation and the development of the modern mode of production have wholly relieved her of this struggle. On the contrary; it is a question of erecting new barriers against the exploitation of the proletarian woman; it is a question of restoring and ensuring her rights as wife and mother. The end-goal of her struggle is not free competition with men but bringing about the political rule of the proletariat. Hand in hand with the men of her own class, the proletarian woman fights against capitalist society. To be sure, she also concurs with the demands of the bourgeois women's movement. But she regards the realisation of these demands only as a means to an end, so that she can get into the battle along with the workingmen and equally armed.

Bourgeois society does not take a stance of basic opposition to the demands of the bourgeois women's movement: this is shown by the reforms in favour of women already introduced in various states both in private and public law. If the progress of these reforms is especially slow in Germany, the cause lies, for one thing, in the competitive economic struggle in the liberal professions which the men fear, and, secondly, in the very slow and weak development of bourgeois democracy in Germany, which has not measured up to its historical tasks because it is spellbound by its class fear of the proletariat. It fears that the accomplishment of such reforms will advantage only the Social-Democracy. The less a bourgeois democracy lets itself by hypnotised by this fear, the readier it is for reform. We see this in England. England is the sole country that still possesses a really vigorous bourgeoisie, whereas the German bourgeoisie, trembling with fear of the proletariat, renounces reforms in the political and social fields. Moreover, Germany is still blanketed by a widespread petty-bourgeois outlook; the philistine pigtail of prejudice hangs close on the neck of the German bourgeoisie.

Of course, the bourgeois democracy's fear is very shortsighted. If women were granted political equality, nothing would be changed in the actual relations of power. The proletarian woman would go into the camp of the proletariat, the bourgeois woman into the camp of the bourgeoisie. We must not let ourselves be deluded by socialistic outcroppings in the bourgeois women's movement, which turn up only so long as the bourgeois women feel themselves to be oppressed.

The less bourgeois democracy takes hold of its tasks, the more it is up to the Social-Democracy to come out for the political equality of women. We do not want to make ourselves out to be better than we are. It is not because of the beautiful eyes of Principle that we put forward this demand but in the class interests of the proletariat. The more women's labour exerts its ominous influence on the living standards of men, the more burning becomes the need to draw women into the economic struggle. The more the political struggle draws every individual into real life, the more pressing becomes the need for women too to take part in the political struggle.

The Anti-Socialist Law has clarified thousands of women for the first time on the meaning of the words *class rights, class state* and *class rule;* it has taught thousands of women for the first time to clarify their understanding of power, which manifests itself so brutally in family life. The Anti-Socialist Law has performed a job that hundreds of women agitators would not have been able to do; and we give sincere thanks—to the father of the Anti-Socialist Law [Bismarck] as well as to all the government agencies involved in its execution from the minister down to the policemen—for their involuntary agitational activity. And yet they reproach us Social-Democrats for ingratitude! (*Laughter*).

There is another event to take into account. I mean the appearance of August Bebel's book *Woman and Socialism.* It should not be assessed by its merits or defects; it must be judged by the time at which it appeared. And it was then more than a book, it was an event, a deed. (*'Very true!'*) For the first time, in its pages it was made clear to the comrades what connection the women's question had with the development of society. For the first time, from this book issued the watchword: We can conquer the future only if we win the women as co-fighters. In recognising this, I am speaking not as a woman but as a party comrade.

What practical consequences do we now have to draw for our agitation among women? It cannot be the task of the party congress to put forward individual practical proposals for ongoing work, but only to lay down lines of direction for the proletarian women's movement.

And there the guiding thought must be: We have no special women's agitation to carry on but rather socialist agitation among women. It is not women's petty interests of the moment that we should put in the foreground; our task must be to enroll the modern proletarian woman in the class struggle. (*'Very true!'*) We have no separate tasks for agitation among women. Insofar as there are reforms to be accomplished on behalf of women within present-day society, they are already demanded in the Minimum Programme of our party.

Women's activity must link up with all the questions that are of pressing importance for the general movement of the proletariat. The main task, surely, is to arouse class-consciousness among women and involve them in the class struggle. The organisation of women workers into trade unions runs into exceedingly great difficulties. From 1892 to 1895 the number of women workers organised into the central unions rose to about 7,000. If we add the woman workers organised into the local unions, and compare the total with the fact that there are 700,000 women working in large industry alone, we get a picture of the great amount of work we still have to do. This work is complicated for us by the fact that many women are employed as home-industry workers, and are therefore hard to draw in. Then too, we have to deal with the widespread outlook among young girls that their industrial work is temporary and will cease with their marriage.

For many women a double obligation arises: they must work both in the factory and in the family. All the more necessary for women workers is the fixing of a legal working-day. While in England everybody agrees that the abolition of the homework system, the fixing of a legal working-day, and the achievement of higher wages are of the greatest importance in order to organise women workers into trade unions, in Germany in addition to the difficulties described there is also the administration of the laws limiting the right of association and assembly. The full freedom to organise which is guaranteed to women workers, with one hand, is rendered illusory by national legislation, with the other hand, through the decisions of individual state legislatures. I won't go into the way the right of association is administered in Saxony, insofar as one can speak of a right there at all; but in the two largest states, Bavaria and Prussia, the laws on association are administered in such a way that women's participation in trade-union organisations is increasingly made impossible. In Prussia in recent times, whatever is humanly possible in the way of interpreting away the right of association and assembly has been done especially in the governmental bailiwick of that perennial cabinet aspirant, the 'liberal' Herr von Bennigsen. In Bavaria women are excluded from all public assemblies. Herr von Feilitzsch, indeed, declared quite openly in the Chamber that in the administration of the law on association not only its text is taken into consideration but also the intention of the legislators; and Herr von Feilitzsch finds himself in the fortunate position of knowing exactly the intention held by the legislators, who died long before Bavaria ever dreamed of some day being lucky enough to get Herr von Feilitzsch as its minister of police. This doesn't surprise me, for if God grants anyone a bureau he also grants him mental faculties, and in our era of spiritualism even Herr von Feilitzsch received his bureaucratic mental faculties and is acquainted with the intention of the long-dead legislators via the fourth dimension. (Laughter).

This state of affairs, however, makes it impossible for proletarian women to organize together with men. Up to now they had a struggle against police power and lawyers' tricks on their hands, and formally speaking they were worsted in this struggle. But in reality they were the victors; for all the measures utilised to wreck the organisation of proletarian women merely operated to arouse their class-consciousness more and more. If we are striving to attain a powerful women's organisation on the economic and political fields, we must be concerned to make possible freedom of action, as we battle against the homework system, champion the cause of the shorter working-day, and above all carry on the fight against what the ruling classes mean by the right of association.

At this party congress we cannot lay down the forms in which the women's activity should be carried out; first we have to learn how we must work among women. In the resolution before you it is proposed to choose field organisers (Vertrauenspersonen) among women, who shall have the task of stimulating trade-union and economic organisation among women, working consistently and systematically. The proposal is not new; it was adopted in principle in Frankfurt [1894 congress] and in several areas it has already been carried out with excellent results. We shall see that this proposal, carried out on a larger scale, is just the thing for drawing proletarian women to a greater extent into the proletarian movement.

But the activity should not be carried on only orally. A large number of indifferent people do not come to our meetings, and numerous wives and mothers cannot get to our meetings at all—and it is out of the question that the task of socialist women's activity should be to alienate proletarian women from their duties as wives and mothers; on the contrary it must operate so that this task is fulfilled better than before, precisely in the interests of the emancipation of the proletariat. The better relations are in the family, and the more efficiently work is done in the home, so much the more effective is the family in struggle. The more the family can be the means of educating and moulding its children, the more it can enlighten them and see to it that they continue the struggle for the emancipation of the proletariat with the same enthusiasm and devotion as we in the ranks. Then when the proletarian says 'My wife!' he adds in his own mind: 'my comrade working for the same ideal, my companion in struggle, who moulds my children for the struggle of the future!' Thus many a mother and many a wife who imbues husband and children with class-consciousness accomplishes just as much as the women comrades whom we see at our meetings. (*Vigorous agreement*).

So if the mountain does not come to Mohammed, Mohammed must go to the mountain: We must bring socialism to the women through a systematic agitational activity in published form. For this purpose I propose to you the distribution of leaflets; not the traditional leaflets which cram the whole socialist programme onto one side of a sheet together with all the erudition of the age—no, small leaflets that bring up a single practical question with a single angle, from the standpoint of the class struggle: this is the main thing. And the question of the technical production of the leaflets must also be our concern... *[Zetkin here discusses these technical aspects in more detail]*...

I cannot speak in favour of the plan to launch a special women's newspaper, since I have had personal experience along those lines; not as editor of *Gleichheit* (which is not directed to the mass of women but to the more advanced) but as a distributor of literature among women workers. Stimulated by the example of Mrs. Gnauck-Kühne, for weeks I distributed papers to the women workers of a certain factory and became convinced that what they get from the contents is not what is educational but solely what is entertaining and amusing. Therefore the great sacrifices that a cheap newspaper demands would not pay.

But we must also produce a series of pamphlets that would bring women nearer to socialism in their capacity as workers, wives and mothers. We do not have a single one that meets requirements, outside of Mrs. Popp's vigorous pamphlet. Moreover, our daily press must do more than heretofore. Some of our dailies have indeed made an attempt to educate women through the issuance of a special women's supplement: the *Magdeburger Volkestimme* has taken the lead with a good example, and Comrade Goldstein in Zwickau has forged ahead along these lines with good fortune and good results. But up to now our daily press has been concerned mainly to win proletarian women as subscribers; we have pandered to their lack of enlightenment and their bad, uncultivated taste instead of enlightening them.

I repeat: these are only suggestions that I submit for your consideration. Women's activity is difficult, it is laborious, it demands great devotion and great sacrifice, but this sacrifice will be rewarded and must be made. For, just as the proletariat can achieve its emancipation only if it fights together without distinction of nationality or distinction of occupation, so also it can achieve its emancipation only if it holds together without distinction of sex. The involvement of the great mass of proletarian women in the emancipatory struggle of the proletariat is one of the pre-conditions for the victory of the socialist idea, for the construction of a socialist society.

Only a socialist society will resolve the conflict that comes to a head nowadays through the entrance of women into the work-force. When the family disappears as an economic unit and its place is taken by the family as a moral unit, women will develop their individuality as comrades advancing on a par with men with equal rights, an equal role in production and equal aspirations, while at the same time they are able to fulfill their functions as wife and mother to the highest degree.

3
Clara Zetkin
On a Bourgeois Feminist Petition

The special interest of the following material is that it is a controversy between Clara Zetkin and the editors of the central party organ Vorwärts, published in the columns of the party newspaper, hence a public intra-party argument—but the subject of the controversy is the socialists' attitude toward the bourgeois feminist movement.

The date, January 1895, precedes the invention of Bernstein's 'revisionism', for Bernstein was going to publish his first articles along those lines only the following year.

The issue that triggered this argument was, as often, minor in itself. German law prohibited meetings and organisations by women, and this anti-democratic restriction was one of the main targets of the socialist women. Full democratic rights for women had already been proposed in the Reichstag by the Social-Democratic Party deputies. To the socialist women's movement, the right to organise was above all bound up with the fight for workingwomen's demands. Now along came a petition sponsored by three individual women to ask for this right—in a framework which, in Zetkin's view, was entirely adapted to the bourgeois women's attitudes and unacceptable to the proletarian women's movement. She argues that socialist women should not give this petition their signatures or support. At first Vorwärts had also criticised the petition along the same lines, but then made a change of front (without consultation) and indicated that there was no reason why socialist women should not sign it. It was apparently enough for the editors that the petition's sponsors had included one Social-Democratic woman (not chosen by the socialist women themselves) and that they had stated they wanted socialist signatures. Zetkin argues that what is decisive is the political grounds given in the petition itself which deliberately ignores the point of view of workingwomen.

Vorwärts published Zetkin's protest in its issue of January 24th, 1895, and replied in a peculiar way. It did not append a systematic refutation but rather peppered Zetkin's article with editorial footnotes. These footnotes are not included with the article below but are discussed following it. Zetkin sent the paper a rejoinder the next day—that is, a comment on the editorial footnotes—and this, published on February 7th, was itself peppered with footnotes again.

On the publication of Zetkin's protest in Vorwärts, *Engels sent an ehtuusiastic hurrah to an Austrian comrade: 'Clara is right. . . Bravo Clara!'*

It is interesting that the more or less official biography of Zetkin published in contemporary East Germany, by Luise Dornemann, is rather apologetic about its subject's 'harshness' toward the bourgeois feminists—a bit like the Vorwärts *editors, rather, though Dornemann does not mention this 1895 polemic at all. Still, Dornemann's emphasis on the other side of the coil is valid, and we quote it to round out the picture. Dornemann writes:*

> *'If Clara's attitude toward the bourgeois women's movement, particularly at the beginning of the 1890s, was occasionally harsh, this was conditioned on the need to work on the class character and independent character of the socialist women's movement. Taking it as a whole, however, the bourgeois women hardly had a better helped than Clara Zetkin. There was no problem of the women teachers, or actresses, or women trying to study and work in medicine and law, that was not dealt with in Gleichheit, no significant literature which it did not take a position on. There were no congresses, campaigns, or big events organised by the bourgeois women that Gleichheit failed to report on.'*

Dornemann further emphasises that Zetkin had friendly relations with a number of bourgeois women's-righters, 'the best of them'; though, to be sure, 'she found more to criticise in the bourgeois women's movement than to approve.' In other words, Clara Zetkin was altogether willing to unite forces with the bourgeois women for common objectives, but not to subordinate the workingwomen's movement to the aims and style of the women's-rightsers.

We here present Zetkin's first protest to Vorwärts, *followed by a summary of the main points and passages in the subsequent exchange. The source of the text is the same as for §2.*

Last summer 22 women's rights organisations joined in an alliance which, in a petition to the kaiser, 'most humbly' implored the legal prohibition of prostitution and severe punishment of prostitutes, pimps, etc. by means of a cabinet order by the kaiser and allied princes. The lackey-like tone favoured in the petition was worthily complemented by its socio-political ignorance, redolent of a beggar's plea, and by the presumptuousness with which the organisations 'dared' to beg because their representatives would be accepted as 'authorities on women's affairs.'

New we find three whole women who ask in a petition for the right of assembly and association for the female sex. Three whole women have taken the initiative, on behalf of bourgeois women's circles, to win a right whose lack is one of the most significant features of the social subordination of the female sex in Germany!

The petition addresses itself to women 'of all parties and all classes.' Even the signatures of proletarian women, of Social-Democratic women, are welcomed.

I will not raise the question whether it is necessary for proletarian women to sign a petition for the right of assembly and association at a point when the party, which represents their interests as well as the male proletariat's, has introduced a bill to this end in the Reichstag. As we know, the Social-Democratic Reichstag group has proposed that the laws on association and assembly now existing in the individual states be recognised on a national legal basis, and that equal rights for both sexes be included in this reorganisation as well as legal guarantee of the unrestricted exercise of freedom to organise. So it demands not only what the petition requests but much more besides.

It may well be that to some people, perhaps even many, support to this petition by organised workers and its signing by proletarian women appears 'expedient'—expediency certainly smiles more sweetly for many in our party than principle does. Such a petition supported by a mass of signatures seems to them an excellent demonstration of favour of the Social-Democratic proposal, a proof that the widest circles of women as a whole feel the pressing need for the right of association and assembly.

From my point of view, even without the petition such a demonstration has been given once and for all; the proof that the reform demanded is a just one was given long ago, permanently and emphatically, in the form of the dogged and bitter struggle carried on for years against the rights of association and assembly by the allied forces of police and judiciary.

In this struggle the police actively showed the full vigour which has earned the highest respect for the German officialdom's loyalty to duty in the eyes of the possessing classes. The judiciary, for their part, show an interpretive skill which ordinary human understanding has not always been able to appreciate. One dissolution of a proletarian women's organisation follows upon another; one prohibition of a women's meeting follows upon another; the exclusion of women from public meetings is an everyday affair; penalties against women for violating the law on association simply rain down. From 1st October, 1893 to 31st August, 1894, proletarian women had to pay 681 marks worth of fines for such offences; and this only in cases that came to my knowledge. Despite all, new associations regularly rise in place of the organisations that were smashed; over and over again women throng to rallies, over and over again they organise new ones.

The proletarian woman, living in straitened circumstances if not bitter poverty and overburdened with work, continues to make the sacrifice of time and energy required by organisational activity; bravely she exposes' herself to the legal consequences and accepts the penalties that hang over her head 'in the name of the law.' These facts are to my mind the most indubitable proof that it is an urgent interest of life itself which makes the possession of freedom of association necessary for the proletarian woman and not a desire for political games or club socialising. If the Reichstag and the government do not understand the urgent language of these facts, they will bend their ears even less favourably to a petition.

Here it will perhaps be objected: 'Well, even if the petition is of no use, still it does no harm. It is a question of broadening the rights of the disfranchised female sex, therefore we will support it and sign it.' Very nice, I reply; but if this approach is taken, the petition must still somehow jibe with the bases of our proletarian viewpoint, or at least—to put it moderately—it must not stand in sharp contradiction with our viewpoint. This is not at all the case, on the contrary. The petition stems from bourgeois circles, it breathes a bourgeois spirit throughout—indeed, in many details, even a narrowly bourgeois spirit.

It baffles us, then, why Social-Democratic papers should push this petition and quasi-officially urge organised workers to support it and proletarian women to sign it. Since when is it the habit of the Social-Democratic Party to support petitions that stem from bourgeois circles and bear the marks of a bourgeois outlook on their forehead simply because such petitions ask for something valid, something the Social-Democracy also demands and has long demanded? Let us suppose that bourgeois democrats had put forward a petition whose purpose was the same as or similar to that of the women's petition under discussion, of the same character. The Social-Democratic press would criticise the petition but would in no way encourage comrades or class-conscious workers to trail along after bourgeois elements. Why should our principled standpoint with respect to the politics of the bourgeois world change because by chance an example of these politics comes from women and demands not a reform on behalf of the so-called social aggregate but rather one on behalf of the female sex? If we are willing to give up our principled attitude for this reason, we likewise give up our view that the women's question can only be understood, and demands raised, in connection with the social question as a whole.

In No. 7 of January 9, *Vorwärts* took a thoroughly correct attitude to the petition. It took notice of it, criticised it, and pointed out that it took up an old socialist demand. Unfortunately, and to my great amazement, *Vorwärts* changed its line overnight. Why? Because it was given to understand that the motivating preamble of the petition did not deserve the criticism made of it. That this assurance and an allusion to remarks in a 'communication' decided *Vorwärts* to make a change of front—this I must emphatically deplore. And in spite of the 'communication', the change made against the petition—that its motivating preamble is most defective— remains in full force. The 'communication' in fact has not the slightest thing to do with the petition and its preamble. It is nothing but an accompanying note, a circular letter to people whose signatures are solicited in support of the petition. It says: 'Among the "special interests" of women which are not detailed in the petition for the sake of brevity, the job situation of women especially requires a legislative bill in line with the petition.'

Should this passage be taken as a statement of advice on the value of freedom of association and assembly for proletarian women? We say thanks for this information but we don't need it. The proletariat recognised, much earlier that the authors of this petition, the value of freedom of organisation for all its members without distinction of sex. And in conformity with this recognition the proletariat fights for the conquest of this right. Should the passage be taken as an assurance that the maternal parents of this petition are themselves conscious of the significance of this right and its basis? We hopefully note this token of a socio-political comprehension that is commonly lacking among German women's rightsers. But this passage has no significance as far as the petition itself is concerned. As far as the petition and its possible consideration are concerned, it is not a matter of what its sponsors and signers had in mind for its preamble but rather what grounds they put forward in its favour. In the preamble of the petition there is not a word about the fact that for the interests of independently employed women the possession of the right of association and assembly is an imperative necessity. The petition lacks precisely the ground on the basis of which the proletariat espouses the demand. It lacks the ground which is so essential for this legislative reform that—according to uncontradicted newspaper accounts—in Bavaria Centre Party people will introduce a bill in the next session of the state Diet which will demand the right of association and assembly for the female sex out of consideration for women's economic situation.

There is an air of embarrassment in the statement of the accompanying note that the pertinent ground was not introduced into the preamble of the petition for reasons of space. Indeed—then why didn't the saving consideration of brevity prevent the preamble from making the special point that one of the effects of women on legislation due to freedom of association is urgently presented as being on the 'morality question'. What the bourgeois women want from the lawmakers under the head of the 'morality question' is made sufficiently clear by the abovementioned petition to the kaiser [on prostitution].

In my opinion, proletarian women, politically conscious comrades least of all, cannot sign a petition which on the pretext of 'brevity' passes over in silence the most important ground for the reform demanded from the proletarian standpoint, while regardless of 'brevity' it stresses a ground which would be laughed at from a halfway clarified socio-political viewpoint, as the product of a very naive ignorance of social relations. Proletarian circles have not the least occasion to pin a certificate of poverty on their own socio-political judgment by solidarising themselves with a petition of this content.

Still another reason makes it impossible for the socialist movement to come out in favour of this petition. The petition does not call on the Reichstag or a Reichstag group for a bill along the lines of the reform in question; it simply requests the Reichstag to send the plea for such a bill to the federated German governments. The petition therefore ignores the competence of the Reichstag to introduce bills on this subject itself and assigns it the modest role of a porter who opens the door for the petitioners to the higher government authority. The Social-Democracy cannot support such a procedure and cannot join in it. The Social-Democracy has at all times fought the duality of the legislative power as it exists in Germany thanks to the fact that our bourgeoisie has not broken the power of absolutism but made a cowardly deal with it. The Social-Democracy has to put up with the fact that this duality exists; indeed, that the legislative authorities—the government and the people's representatives—do not confront one another as factors of equal power but that the latter is subordinate to the former; whereas the Social-Democracy had always fought with every legal means at its disposal for the people's representatives to be what they should be. Among the few rights and powers that parliament possesses in the noble German Reich is the right to introduce proposals that make demands in the name of the people instead of addressing pleas to the government. The petition, however, avoids the only straight route to the Reichstag. Proletarian women can have nothing to do with this and don't want to. Anyway, at the very least, not at this moment when the governments are launching the sharpest battle against the organisational activity of proletarian women and when the federated governments have introduced the Anti-Subversive bill. Proletarian women who expect a reform of the laws on association and assembly in accordance with their own interests to come from our governments would try to pick figs from thorns and grapes from thistles.

If the bourgeois women wanted temporary collaboration with proletarian women for a common goal on behalf of the petition, then it is evident that the petition would be formulated in such a way that working-women could sign it without compromising themselves and their aims. Such a formulation would have been premised on a prior understanding with the representatives of the class-conscious proletarian women. As the sponsors of the petition well know, there is a [socialist] Commission on Women's Work in Berlin. Why didn't the petition's sponsors come to this commission with the following two questions: (1) Are you perhaps prepared to support the planned petition? and (2) How does this petition have to be put so that it can be supported and signed by proletarian women without abandoning their own viewpoint?

Such a mode of procedure should have been self-evident and would have been dictated by good sense and courtesy if one wanted the signatures of proletarian women. The formulation of the petition and its sponsors' mode of procedure are characteristic of the outlook of bourgeois women and their relationship to the world of proletarian women. One is humanitarian enough to do something for one's 'poorer sisters' under certain circumstances, and one is smart enough under all circumstances to accept their menial services, but to work together with them as if with a coequal power—well, that's an altogether different matter, you yokel.

The sponsors of the petition will refer to their 'good intentions' and insist they were very far from having any conscious antagonism to the outlook of the proletarian women. But that cannot induce us to take a different view of their mode of procedure. In the name of good intentions people have long committed not only the greatest crimes but also the grossest stupidities. And the fact that the thought processes of the petitions' sponsors instinctively and unconsciously ran in a direction diametrically opposed to the proletarian outlook is indeed a sign of the gulf that separates us from them.

I believe that I speak not only in my own name but in the name of the majority of class-conscious proletarian women when I say:

Not one proletarian signature for this petition!

The Editors' Reply and Zetkin's rejoinder:

The refutatory footnotes appended by the Vorwärts *editors had the advantage of telling the reader what was wrong with Zetkin even before the article itself was read. A footnote hung from the title announced: 'We are giving space to the following article without being in agreement with everything in it. We remark above all that we are as concerned about fidelity to principles in the party as Comrade Zetkin and* Gleichheit*. The sharp missiles hurled by Comrade Zetkin do not seem appropriate for the fight she is carrying on; they should be reserved for weightier targets.'*

This was in part the usual recommendation that leftists should go expend their energies on the capitalist class (only) instead of bothering party leaders. The injection of Gleichheit *was more malicious, for Zetkin had written in her personal capacity; in effect the editors indicated that they viewed* Gleichheit *as an oppositional organ. Zetkin took note of this at the end of her rejoinder.*

This first editorial note also adduced the information that one of the three petition sponsors was a Social-Democratic Party member and that the petition had been signed by some women party members before the offending Vorwärts *article was published. To this, Zetkin replied that*

... the fact that the petition was coauthored by a member of our party and that some comrades have signed it does not make it any better or above criticism. We do not form an opinion of a public question and especially not of a party question on the basis of individuals and their intentions but rather on the basis of whether or not it tallies in essence with our fundamental standpoint. That comrades have signed the petition is easily accounted for.

The special disfranchised position of the female sex, which is exacerbated for proletarian women because of the social subordination they suffer as members of the proletariat, leads one or another good comrade to assimilate the class-conscious female proletarian, the female Social-Democrat, with Woman. Far be it from me to cast a stone at her for that, but far be it from me likewise to approve her attitude, or, above all, to elevate this attitude to a level by virtue of which any criticism of the petition must not hurt a fly. I confidently leave it to the comrades of both sexes to draw the conclusions that would follow from generalising the standpoint from which *Vorwärts* here counterposes my article to the petition.

> *The last sentence points to the analogy with Social-Democratic Party attitudes towards bourgeois liberalism, on the general political scene.*
>
> *In their second note, the editors brought out the time-honoured 'step forward' argument. It is appended to Zetkin's most cogent passage on the basic politics of the whole thing, emphasising that 'the women's question can only be understood, and demands raised, in connection with the social question as a whole.' The editors answered: 'We cannot recognise the grave offence that Comrade Zetkin constructs here.' Women are entirely disfranchised; bourgeois women are politically untrained; 'hence every step toward independence is a step forward.' A minister, von Köller, had attacked the petition 'as a sign of growing "subversive tendencies"'; presumably, the minister's attack proved that socialists should support what he disliked, Zetkin replied.*

Certainly, every step by the bourgeois woman in the direction of independence is a forward step. However, the recognition of this fact must not, in my opinion, lead the politically developed proletarian women's movement to go along with the vacillating, inept and groping bourgeois women's-rightsers or even overestimate their significance. If Herr von Köller treated the petition as marking the growth of the danger of revolution and attributed a great significance to it, we have to put that down to a minister who is officially responsible for labouriously sweating to scrape together evidence of the growth of 'subversive tendencies.'

> *Perhaps the most significant admission came in the editor's attempt to answer one of Zetkin's most telling points. The petition sponsors gave brevity as their reason for omitting the motivating grounds important to workingwomen—namely, their economic situation; but, Zetkin pointed out, brevity did not prevent these women from including their own bourgeois considerations, like the 'morality question'. The editors replied in a footnote: 'We too criticised this, but we found that one excuse—even though not an adequate one—was the fact that the original authoress of the petition, on tactical grounds, did not want to forgo the signatures of bourgeois women, and [note this!] she would have had to forgo them if this had been the leading ground given in the petition as published.' So—bourgeois women would have refused to sign a petition which gave space to working-women's economic needs, even though it also emphasised their own motivations! Very class-conscious indeed. But the workingwomen, in contrast, were expected to be so alien to class-consciousness that they would sign even if their own considerations were nowhere included. Little else was needed to bring out the conscious class character of the petition. Zetkin commented:*

I quite understand that for the authors of the petition 'tactical considerations' with respect to bourgeois women were decisive in many ways. But why did they not let themselves be swayed by similar 'tactical considerations' with respect to proletarian women? Why did they make all concessions to the biases of bourgeois women, and why did they demand of the proletarian women that they give up their own views? What is right for the one must also be fair for the other if they wanted their support.

Zetkin's rejoinder summed up a number of questions as follows:

As for the sharp tone which I adopted and which *Vorwärts* objected to: I considered it necessary for a special reason. The appearance of the most recent tendency in bourgeois feminism, which I would like to call the 'ethical' tendency,[1] has here and there caused some confusion in the ranks of our women comrades. This new tendency raises more demands in the field of women's rights than its sister tendencies and does so more energetically, and in its social understanding, its recognition and critique of social wrongs and its espousal of certain social reforms, it stands a step higher than the others. And it is for this reason that there are various illusions in the socialist camp concerning the character of this tendency and its significance for our proletarian women's movement. Not long ago, indeed, I got letters from party circles saying that 'these women are essentially striving for the same goal as we are!' In view of the wobbliness that is spreading in our estimation of the abovementioned bourgeois tendency, the sharpness of tone seemed to me to be required. At present, I hope, all these illusions have once and for all been ended by [the bourgeois feminist] Mrs. Gizyeki's explicit protest against the report that she had declared herself in support of the Social-Democratic women's movement. (*Vorwärts*, 23rd of last month).

Since none of *Vorwärts* footnotes is directed against the actual, essential views of my article, but simply against incidental points, I believe I may take it that it too agrees with the gist of my exposition. In any case, in view of the present state of the matter, it would be a good thing if it stated clearly and forthrightly whether it recommends that women comrades sign the petition or not. With that the matter would be settled for me, at least as far as the petition is concerned.[2]

---

[1] At this point the editors appended a footnote protesting that 'No party paper has drawn the line of demarcation more energetically than *Vorwärts* between the ethical movement and the Social-Democracy which bases itself on the class struggle.' But Zetkin was explaining why some women comrades were being taken in by the new bourgeois feminists, who counterposed their broad ('ethical') non-class motivations to the 'narrow' class position of the socialist women, in the usual fashion.

[2] To this paragraph, the editors appended two footnotes (one to the first and another to the second sentence) in which, in effect, they threw up the sponge, without having the candour to say so. The first note read: 'We don't mind agreeing that Comrade Zetkin is right in principle, but we believe that she makes too much to-do

In conclusion, however, an important personal observation. My remarks consisted of nothing but a statement about *Vorwärts* change of front in the matter of the petition and the expression of my regret over it. No sharp attack. The only somewhat sharper passage against *Vorwärts* that was originally in my article was stricken by the editors. In my exposition I neither pointed to *Gleichheit* nor even mentioned it; in general, nowhere and never have I played *Gleichheit* off against *Vorwärts* as being specially faithful to principle. How did *Vorwärts* come to drag *Gleichheit* into the debate? And when and where have I, after the fashion of *Vorwärts,* given myself a testimonial in self-praise of my special fidelity to principle? The self-serving testimonial which *Vorwärts* confers on its own attitude I have duly given the same attention with which, out of a sense of duty, I follow all of *Vorwärts* pronouncements.

Whether, however, this attention has produced any change in my opinion, of *Vorwärts* is another story, but this is the least opportune time to write it and *Vorwärts* is the least opportune place.

4
Rosa Luxemburg
Women's Suffrage and Class Struggle

The following article by Rosa Luxemburg was published in 1912 in a collection on women's suffrage issued by her friend Clara Zetkin, on the occasion of the Second Social-Democratic Women's Day in May of that year. As the circumstances indicate, it was a question of a general propaganda article only. But the brief essay is of special interest to us for more than one reason.

It is one of the myths of socialist history that Rosa Luxemburg had no interest in the women's question. The kernel of truth is that Luxemburg certainly rejected the idea that, simply because of her sex, she 'belonged' in the socialist women's movement, rather than in the general leadership. In rejecting this sexist view of women in the movement, she performed an important service. Yet—without adducing a line of evidence despite the detailed nature of his two-volume biography—J.P. Nettl writes: 'Rosa Luxemburg was not interested in any high-principled campaign for women's rights—unlike her friend Clara Zetkin. Like anti-Semitism, the inferior status of women was a social feature which would be eliminated only by the advent of Socialism; in the meantime there was no point in making any special issue of it.' This statement about Luxemburg's views is quite

---

about a mere nothing.' The second note: 'It is self-evident that, in accordance with the statements of the Commission of Women's Work which *Vorwärts* published along with other papers, *Vorwärts* has no occasion to recommend signing the petition.' What was now 'self-evident' to the editors was that the women of the movement were against them, and that the *Vorwärts* position had no other party sanction. So Zetkin was right in principle and right in the specific proposal to boycott the bourgeois-feminist petition. Having exhausted their good nature in making this confession, the editors then appended a final Parthian shot to the last word of Zetkin's rejoinder: 'With this, we can and must leave Comrade Zetkin in peace.' This was simply a parting snarl—which, furthermore, would probably have been restrained if its target had been a male leader of the movement.

false. The fact is that Luxemburg herself made a 'special issue of it' on at least a couple of occasions when she wrote propaganda pieces for the socialist women; but it is not her own degree of personal participation that speaks of her point of view. Her friend Zetkin and others were taking care of the women's movement; it did not need her, and women were not required by their sex to confine their activities to it. We may also anticipate a side-point: it is true that 'Rosa never wanted either to claim women's privileges or to accept any of their disabilities' (Nettl) but in this she was no different from other revolutionary women of the time or today.

Another reason for the special interest of this piece is that it handles a question which, still in our own day, bedevils would-be socialist feminists sometimes, especially some who try to work out a Marxist analysis while under the impression that no one had ever contributed to it before. This is the question of the class position of women, particularly working women. Luxemburg's remarks on the 'unproductive' character of housework should be especially noted. Of course, attempts to put a separate-class label on women as a sex will not thereby be impeded, since most such efforts do not try to work with a rational definition of class, but we hope it will be harder to present such theorising as Marxist.

There is a nuance of difference between Luxemburg and (say) Zetkin which is directly traceable to Luxemburg's lack of personal participation in the women's movement and her lack of direct experience with its conditions and problems. This suggests another kernel of truth in Nettl's sweeping statement, particularly his comparison with the mechanical-Marxist attitude toward political issues (anti-Semitism in his example). Luxemburg, looking at the bourgeois women's movement from a great distance, grossly underestimated the appeals of abstract feminism. While this tinges the 1912 article given below, it is stated most plainly in a very short piece which Luxemburg wrote for International Women's Day in March 1914, published as 'The Proletarian Woman'.

In this 1914 piece, which has a mainly exhortatory tone, analyses are naturally not featured. Here Luxemburg's summary of the class situation of women is telegraphic: 'As bourgeois wives, women are parasites on society, their function consisting solely in sharing the fruits of exploitation. As petty-bourgeois, they are beasts of burden for the family. It is as modern proletarians that women first become human beings; for it is struggle that produces the human being—participation in their process of culture, in the history of humanity.' The thought which is telescoped here assumes that by the 'modern proletarian women', it is the woman militant that is understood, not simply any woman of the working class in any social situation. In any case, from this analysis Luxemburg goes on to assert: 'The bourgeois woman has no real interest in political rights because she exercises no economic function in society, because she enjoys the ready-made fruits of class domination. The demand for women's rights, as raised by bourgeois women, is pure ideology held by a few weak groups, without material roots, a phantom of the antagonism between man and woman, a fad.' This is an example of the abstract deduction of political analyses to which Luxemburg was sometimes prone; her greatest mistake of this sort was a similar dismissal of nationalism as a political issue. Zetkin did not make Luxemburg's mistake.

The article that follows (as well as the excerpts cited above from the 1914 piece) are translated from Luxemburg's Gesammelte Werke *(Berlin, Dietz, 1973) Volume 3.*

'Why are there no organisations of women workers in Germany? Why is so little heard of the women workers' movement?—These were the words with which Emma Ihrer, one of the founders of the proletarian women's movement in Germany, in 1898 introduced her book on *Women Workers in the Class Struggle [Die Arbeiterinnen im Klassenkampf]*. Hardly fourteen years have passed since then, and today the proletarian women's movement in Germany has developed mightily. More than 150,000 women workers organised in trade unions help to form the shock troops of the militant proletariat on the economic field. Many tens of thousands of politically organised women are assembled under the banner of the Social-Democracy. The Social-Democratic women's magazine has over a hundred thousand subscribers. The demand for women's suffrage is on the order of the day in the political life of the Social-Democracy.

There are many who, precisely on the basis of these facts, may under-estimate the significance of the struggle for women's suffrage. They may reason: even without political equality for the female sex, we have achieved brilliant advances in the enlightenment and organisation of women, so it appears that women's suffrage is not a pressing necessity from here on in. But anyone who thinks so is suffering from a delusion. The splendid political and trade-union ferment among the masses of the female proletariat in the last decade and a half has been possible only because the women of the workingpeople, despite their disenfranchisement, have taken a most lively part in political life and in the parliamentary struggle of their class. Proletarian women have up to now benefited from men's suffrage—in which they actually participated, if only indirectly. For large masses of women, the struggle for the suffrage is now a common struggle together with the men of the working class. In all Social-Democratic voters' meetings, the women form a large part of the audience, sometimes the preponderant part, and always an alert and passionately concerned audience. In every election district where a solid Social-Democratic organisation exists, the women help carry on the election work. They also do much in the way of distributing leaflets and soliciting subscriptions to the Social-Democratic press, this being the heaviest weapon in the electoral battle.

The capitalist state has not been able to keep the women of the people from undertaking these burdens and duties of political life. It itself was, step by step, forced to ensure and facilitate this possibility by granting the rights of association and assembly. Only the final political right—the right to cast a ballot, to directly decide on popular representatives in the legislative and executive bodies, and to be elected a member of these bodies—only this right does the state refuse to grant to women. Here only do they cry 'Don't let it get started!' as in all other spheres of social life.

The contemporary state gave ground before the proletarian women when it allowed them into public assemblies and political organisations. To be sure, it did this not of its own free will but in response to bitter necessity, under the irresistible pressure of an aggressive working class. The stormy thrust forward by workingwomen themselves was not the least factor in forcing the Prussian-German police-state to give up that wonderful 'women's section' at political meetings,* and to throw the doors of political organisations wide open to women. With this concession the rolling stone began to gather speed. The unstoppable advance of the proletarian class struggle pulled workingwomen into the vortex of political life. Thanks to the utilisation of the rights of association and assembly, proletarian women have won for themselves active participation in parliamentary life, in the electoral struggle. And now it is merely an inescapable consequence and logical outcome of the movement that today millions of workingwomen cry with class-conscious defiance: *Give us women's suffrage!*

Once upon a time, in the good old days of pre-1848 absolutism, it was commonly said of the whole working class that it was 'not yet mature enough' to exercise political rights. Today this cannot be said of proletarian women, for they have demonstrated they are mature enough for political rights. Indeed, everyone knows that without them, without the enthusiastic aid of the proletarian women, the German Social-Democracy would never have achieved the brilliant victory of 12th January [1912] when it got four and a quarter million votes. But all the same, the workingpeople had to prove they were mature enough for political freedom every time through a victorious revolutionary mass movement. Only when God's Anointed on the throne together the noblest Cream of the Nation felt the calloused fist of the proletariat on their eye and its knee on their breast, only then did belief in the political maturity of the people suddenly dawn on them. Today it is the turn of the women of the proletariat to make the capitalist state conscious of their maturity. This is taking place through a patient, powerful mass movement in which all the resources of proletarian struggle and pressure will have to be brought to bear.

It is women's suffrage that is in question as the goal, but the mass movement for this goal is not a women's affair only, but the common class concern of the men and women of the proletariat. For in Germany today women's disenfranchisement is only a link in the chain of reaction that fetters the life of the people, and it is very closely bound up with the other pillar of this reaction—the monarchy. In the contemporary twentieth-century Germany of large-scale capitalism and advanced industry, in the era of electricity and airplanes, women's disenfranchisement is just as reactionary a relic of an older and outlived state of affairs as the rule of God's Anointed on the throne. Both phenomena—the Instrument of Heaven as the dominant power in political life, and the woman sitting demurely at the domestic hearth, unconcerned with the storms of political

---

*In 1902 the Prussian Minister of the Interior had issued an ordinance requiring women at political meetings to sit only in one special section of the meeting hall, the 'women's section'.

life, with politics and the class struggle—both have their roots in the decaying social relations of the past, in the era of serfdom on the land and the guild system in the cities. In those days they were understandable and necessary. Both of them, the monarchy and women's disenfranchisement, have been uprooted today by modern capitalist development, and have become ridiculous caricatures of humanity. If they will nevertheless remain in modern society today, it is not because we have forgotten to get rid of them or simply because of inertia and the persistence of old conditions. No, they are still around because both of them—the monarchy and women's disenfranchisement—have become powerful tools of anti-popular interests. Behind the throne and the altar, as behind the political enslavement of the female sex, lurk today the most brutal and evil representatives of the exploitation and enserfment of the proletariat. The monarchy and the disenfranchisement of women have taken their place among the most important tools of capitalist class domination.

For the contemporary state, it is really a question of denying the suffrage to workingwomen and to them alone. It fearfully sees in them, rightly, a threat to all the institutions of class domination inherited from the past—such as militarism, whose deadly enemy every thinking proletarian women must be; the monarchy; the organised robbery of tariffs and taxes on foodstuffs, and so on. Women's suffrage is an abomination and a bogey for the capitalist state today because behind it stand the millions of women who will strengthen the internal enemy, the revolutionary Social-Democracy.

If it were a matter of the ladies of the bourgeois, then the capitalist state could expect only a real prop for reaction from them. Most of the bourgeois women who play the lioness in a fight against 'male privileges' would, once in possession of the suffrage, follow like meek little lambs in the wake of the conservative and clerical reaction. Indeed, they would surely be far more reactionary than the masculine portion of their class.

Apart from the small number of professional women among them, the women of the bourgeoisie have no part in social production; they are simply joint consumers of the surplus value which their men squeeze out of the proletariat; they are parasites on the parasites of the people. And such joint consumers are commonly more rabid and cruel in defence of their 'right' to a parasitic existence than those who directly carry on class domination and the exploitation of the working class. The history of all great revolutionary struggles has borne this out in a horrible way. After the fall of Jacobin domination in the Great French Revolution, when the cart carried Robespierre in fetters to the guillotine, naked prostitutes of the victory-besotted bourgeoisie shamelessly danced with joy in the streets around the fallen revolutionary hero. And when in Paris in 1871 the heroic Commune of the workers was crushed by machineguns, the wild-raving women of the bourgeoisie exceeded even their bestial men in their bloody vengeance on the stricken proletariat. The women of the possessing classes will always be rabid supporters of the exploitation and oppression of workingpeople, from which they receive at second hand the wherewithal for their socially useless existence.

Economically and socially, the women of the exploiting classes do not make up an independent stratum of the population. They perform a social function merely as instruments of natural reproduction for the ruling classes. The women of the proletariat, on the contrary, are independent economically; they are engaged in productive work for society just as the men are. Not in the sense that they help the men by their housework, scraping out a daily living and raising children for meagre compensation. This work is not productive within the meaning of the present economic system of capitalism, even though it entails an immense expenditure of energy and self-sacrifice in a thousand little tasks. This is only the private concern of the proletarians, their blessing and felicity, and precisely for this reason nothing but empty air as far as modern society is concerned. Only that work is productive which produces surplus value and yields capitalist profit—as long as the rule of capital and the wage system still exists. From this standpoint the dancer in a cafe, who makes a profit for her employer with her legs, is a productive workingwoman, while all the toil of the woman and mothers of the proletariat within the four walls of the home is considered unproductive work. This sounds crude and crazy but it is an accurate expression of the crudeness and craziness of today's capitalist economic order; and to understand this crude reality clearly and sharply is the first necessity for the proletarian woman.

For it is precisely from this standpoint that the workingwomen's claim to political equality is now firmly anchored to a solid economic base. Millions of proletarian women today produce capitalist profit just like men—in factories, workshops, agriculture, homework industries, offices and stores. They are productive, therefore, in the strictest economic sense of society today. Every day, the multitude of women exploited by capitalism grows; every new advance in industry and technology makes more room for women in the machinery of capitalist profit-making. And thus every day and every industrial advance lays another stone in the solid foundation on which the political equality of women rests. The education and intellectual development of women has now become necessary for the economic machine itself. Today the narrowly circumscribed and unwordly woman of the old patriarchal 'domestic hearth' is as useless for the demands of large-scale industry and trade as for the requirements of political life. In this respect too, certainly, the capitalist state has neglected its duties. Up to now it is the trade-union and Social-Democratic organisations that have done most and done best for the intellectual and moral awakening and education of women. Just as for decades now the Social-Democrats have been known as the most capable and intelligent workers, so today it is by

Social-Democracy and the trade unions that the women of the proletariat have been raised out of the stifling atmosphere of their circumscribed existence, out of the miserable vapidness and pettiness of household management. The proletarian class struggle has widened their horizons, expanded their intellectual life, developed their mental capacities, and given them great goals to strive for. Socialism has brought about the spiritual rebirth of the mass of proletarian women, and in the process has also doubtless made them competent as productive workers for capital.

After all this, the political disenfranchisement of proletarian women is all the baser an injustice because it has already become partly false. Women already take part in political life anyway, actively and in large numbers. Nevertheless, the Social-Democracy does not carry on the fight with the argument of 'injustice'. The basic difference between us and the sentimental Utopian socialism of earlier times lies in the fact that we base ourselves not on the justice of the ruling classes but solely on the revolutionary power of the working masses and on the process of economic development which is the foundation of that power. Thus, injustice in itself is certainly not an argument for overthrowing reactionary institutions. When wide circles of society are seized by a sense of injustice—says Friedrich Engels, the cofounder of scientific socialism—it is always a sure sign that far-reaching shifts have taken place in the economic basis of society, and that the existing order of things has already come into contradiction with the ongoing process of development. The present powerful movement of millions of proletarian women who feel their political disenfranchisement to be a crying injustice is just such an unmistakable sign that the social foundations of the existing state are already rotten and that its days are numbered.

One of the first great heralds of the socialist ideal, the Frenchman Charles Fourier, wrote these thought-provoking words a hundred years ago:

> In every society the degree of female emancipation (freedom) is the natural measure of emancipation in general. This applies perfectly to society today. The contemporary mass struggle for the political equality of women is only one expression and one part of the general liberation struggle of the proletariat, and therein lies its strength and its future. General, equal and direct suffrage for women will—thanks to the female proletariat—immeasurably advance and sharpen the proletarian class struggle. That is why bourgeois society detests and fears women's suffrage, and that is why we want to win it and will win it. And through the struggle for women's suffrage we will hasten the hour when the society of today will be smashed to bits under the hammer blows of the revolutionary proletariat.

5
Eleanor Marx
Workingwomen vs. Bourgeois Feminism

In this section we present some little-known articles by Eleanor Marx written for the Austrian socialist women's movement, with the direct encouragement of Engels, as part of a project to 'straighten out' the socialist women's attitude toward bourgeois feminism.

As we have seen, the German socialist women's movement got under way by the early 1890s. In spite of Zetkin's influence, it should not be supposed, of course, that its ranks were as consciously Marxist as most of its leadership. On the contrary, there was inevitably a considerable impact on its newly organised women by the bourgeois feminist circles outside. Later on, this was most clearly expressed within the socialist women by Lilly Braun, the leading Revisionist supporter among the women in the party. But in 1891-92 the Revisionist tendency had not yet taken open form.

The establishment of Gleichheit *in 1891 was a great help. The Austrian socialist women, too, planned to establish their own organ by autumn of that year, but in fact the first issue of their* Arbeiterinnenzeitung *(Workingwomen's Journal) did not appear till January 1892. During the preparatory months one of its important collaborators was Louise Kautsky (now divorced from Karl Kautsky but retaining the name), who was presently established in Engels' London house-hold as sort of general manager for the old man. Besides writing for the* Arbeiter-innenzeitung *herself, Louise together with Engels also worked at drumming up contributions to the paper from abroad.*

During the preparatory months of 1891, Louise worked at getting contribu-tions from two of the Marx daughters, Eleanor (London) and Laura Lafargue (Paris). From a letter by Engels to Laura, we see that the three women planned to use their contributions to the Vienna paper to clearly counterpose their own view of socialist feminism against the bourgeois-feminist influences of the day. Engels' letter of 2nd October, 1891 chortled that their articles 'will create a sensation among the women's rights women in Germany and Austria, as the real question has never been put and answered so plainly as you three do it.' German workingwomen, he added, were 'rushing' into the socialist movement, according to Bebel's reports, 'and if that is the case, the antiquated semi-bourgeois women's right ânesses [asses] will soon be ordered to the rear.'

All three did in fact write for the Vienna paper during 1892. Of greatest interest to us today were those written by Eleanor Marx. The most prominent issue all three addressed, in one way or another, was that of the bourgeois feminists' hostility to protective legislation for workingwomen. Then, as now, this gave concrete substance to the class differences in the movements for women's rights: which women? which rights?

The contributions of the three women were largely reportage, in form, not programmatic or analytical articles. Therefore they are best presented in the form of excerpts. Before getting to Eleanor Marx, we give an example from a piece by Louise Kautsky.

(1)
Louise Kautsky
The Women's-Rightsers and Reduction of the Working-Day for Women

Louise Kautsky here reports on an issue raised in the American feminist movement.

Although she was writing from Engels' household, as it were, and no doubt discussed it with him, it is well to stress that Louise Kautsky was her own woman. We know incidentally that Engels worked at getting her the materials, from a letter he sent to his chief American correspondent, Sorge. There Engels conveys a request from Louise for the Boston Woman's Journal, *which Louise will quote as her main source. Engels writes:*

> She needed it for the Vienna *Arbeiterinnenzeitung* (she, Laura, and Tussy [Eleanor], are the chief contributors) and she says it could never occur to her to force the drivel of the American swell-mob-ladies upon workingwomen. What you have so kindly sent her has enabled her to become well-posted again and has convinced her that these ladies are still as supercillious and narrow-minded as ever...

Louise's immediate subject was the bourgeois feminists' attack in Massachusetts on a bill to reduce the working-day for women factory workers.

The Women's Journal, which is published in Boston and for 22 years has successfully defended the rights of the women of the bourgeoisie, has a little article in its last issue (16th January, 1892) on the working-hours of female workers.

The reason these women concerned themselves with their proletarian sisters was a crying injustice done to them by the Massachusetts senate. A proposal was introduced there to reduce women's work-day in the factories while leaving the men to work the usual hours. 'There can be no doubt,' says the *Woman's Journal* writer, 'that the proposal's sponsor means well. But it is clear that the factory owner, who wants full use of his machines, will hire only workers who work the longest hours. If however the women's work-day is to be arbitrarily reduced, all the women will be thrown out on the street. Women who work in the factories work there because they are forced by necessity to earn a living, and they want to earn as much as possible. It would therefore be good, before anything is done, to ask the female Factory Inspectors to consult with the female workers.'

So goes the article. I am quite sure that the women workers acclaimed the reduction of the work-day, for they know from practical experience that, in every factory where men and women work together, the number of women is much bigger; hence the reduction of their work-day necessarily brings in its train the reduction of the men's hours too.

In England the first factory law protecting women workers over 18 dates from 7th June, 1844. In *Capital,* Vol. 1 [Ch. 10, §6], Karl Marx quotes a Factory Report of 1844-45, where it is said with irony: 'No instances have come to my knowledge of adult women having expressed any regret at their *rights* being thus far interfered with.'

The pained cries of the propertied women in America that their working sisters might not be ruthlessly exploited comes as a worthy close to the debate in the English lower house that took place on 24th February. It was on the second reading of a bill about all persons employed in retail stores.

Mr. Provand, the bill's sponsor, pointed out that the only law dealing with retail employees and regulating their working hours dates back to 1889 and applies only to young people, not adult women. His bill would include the women workers in those enterprises under the coverage of this law, *i.e.* limit their work-day to only 12 hours.

Louise Kautsky then relates that this mild proposal met with opposition—from a number of honourable supporters of women's suffrage, who rose to explain that, being for women's right to vote, they wanted women themselves to determine their working hours 'as they themselves wished, and without any legal limitations.' The hours bill would take away women's rights to do whatever they wanted to do; the opponents stood for freedom, of course. Viscount Cranborne said that a number of women had pointed out to him that the bill meant employers would hire men to fill women's jobs, and that these women were better off working hard than not working at all. It was further argued that it was unjust to reduce women's working hours before giving them the vote; the priorities were first women's suffrage, then cut hours.

The difference between the bourgeois women's movement and the working-women's movement is as clear as day. We are not hostile to the 'women's movement', but we also have not the slightest reason to give it support. . .

It is not my intention, and it would be absurd, to belittle the work burdens of women of the bourgeoisie, or to forget the difficulties with which Mrs. Garrett Anderson worked to open the medical schools to English women, or to forget the women who fought for women's rights in the courts and on the platform, and forced the abolition of many laws that put women in an inferior position. But all the benefits thus achieved always redound only to the privileged classes; the working-women get little or no profit out of them; they can be unmoved spectators to the   war of sexes in the upper class. But when these women use their preferential position to hamper the development of our working-women's movement, then we   are duty-bound to say: So far and no further.

(2)
How should we organise?

In the 5th February, 1892 issue of the paper, Eleanor Marx started a series of four articles, which began by posing the problem of how women should organise and then reported on how English working-women were organising in trade unions.

In their last session the 400 delegates to the International Socialist Congress in Brussels [1891] adopted the follwing resolution:

We call upon the socialist parties of all countries to give definite expression in their programmes to the strivings for complete equalisation of both sexes, and to demand first of all that women be granted the same rights as men in the civil-rights and political fields.

This resolution and this position on the suffrage gain even more meaning through the fact that in the first session of the Congress it was expressly declared that a socialist *workers'* congress had absolutely nothing to do with the womens-rightsers. Just as on the war question the Congress stressed the difference between the ordinary bourgeois peace league, which cries 'Peace, peace' where there is no peace, and the economic peace party, the socialist party, which wants to remove the causes of war—so too with regard to the 'woman question' the Congress equally clearly stressed the difference between the party of the 'women's-rightsers' on the one side, who recognised no class struggle but only a struggle of sexes, who belong to the possessing class, and who want rights that would be an injustice against their working-class sisters, and, on the other side, the real women's party, the socialist party, which has a basic understanding of the economic causes of the present adverse position of working-women and which calls on the working-women to wage a common fight hand-in-hand with the men of their class against the common enemy, *viz.* the men and women of the capitalist class.

The Brussels resolution is excellent as a declaration of principle—but what about its practical execution? How are women to achieve the civil and political rights it demands? For, so long as we do not soberly and realistically consider what must be done, nothing will come of theoretical proclamations on what-ought-to-be. It is not enough to point to the class struggle. The workers must also learn what weapons to use and how to use them; which positions to attack and which previously won advantages to maintain. And that is why the workers are now learning when and where to resort to strikes and boycotts, how to achieve protective legislation for workers, and what has to be done so that legislation already achieved does not remain a dead letter. And now, what do we women have to do? One thing without any doubt. We will organise—organise not as 'women' but as *proletarians;* not as female rivals of our working men but as their comrades in struggle.

And the most serious question of all is: *how* should we organise? Now, it seems to me that we must commence by organising as *trade-unionists* using our united strength as a means of reaching the ultimate goal, the emancipation of our class. The job will not be easy. In fact, the conditions of female labour are such that it is often heartbreakingly difficult to make progress. But from day to day the job will become easier, and it will begin to look less and less difficult in proportion as the women and especially the men learn to see what strength lies in the unification of *all workers.*

The Austrian working-women (Eleanor Marx went on to say) are showing why know how to organise, but they can learn from what their sisters are doing in

*other countries. In a series of articles reporting on women's unions in England,
three conclusions will emerge:*

(1) Wherever women organise, their position improves—that is, wages go
up, hours are reduced, working conditions are improved.

(2) It works to the advantage of the men at least as much as of the
women when the latter organise and their wages are regarded as real
workers' wages and not as little supplements to the general household
fund.

(3) Except in quite special trades, it is essential, in the case of un-
skilled workers especially, that men and women be members of one and
the same trade-union, just as they are members of one and the same
workers' party.

(3)
On The Workingwomen's Movement in England

*In her next letter Eleanor Marx started her account of women's trade-union
organisation in England and its problems.*

*The article begins with a summary of the progress made by women's trade-
unions since the start of the 'New Unionism,' marked by a match workers' strike,
the founding of the Gas Workers Union [of which Elearnor herself was an
organiser and Executive member], and the great dock strike, etc.*

Although we are happy to see this progress and also recognise the progress
made by the organisation of the workers, we cannot close our eyes to the
fact that women still remain considerably behind and that the results
actually attained by years of work are pitifully small.

*Even in the textile industry, the first site of women's trade-union organisation,
there are still great inadequacies. Firstly, in many cases women still remain unorganised, though this situation is becoming less frequent; for the unions see how
unorganised women workers become the employers' weapon against them. (Two
examples are given.) Secondly, the women unionists often have no voice in the
administration of their union:*

For example, in Lancashire and Yorkshire, where the women almost without exception belong to unions, pay regular dues and of course also draw
benefits from them, they have absolutely no part in the leadership of these
organisations, no voice in the administration of their own funds, and up to
now have never become delegates to their own union's congresses. Representation and administration lie wholly in the hands of the men
workers.

The main reason for this apparent indifference and apathy on the part
of the women can easily be discerned; it is common to a large part of all
women's organisations and we cannot ignore it here. The reason is that even

today women still have two duties to fulfill: in the factory they are *proletarians* and earn a daily wage on which they and their children live in large part; but they are also *household slaves,* unpaid servants of their husbands, fathers and brothers. Even before going to the factory early in the morning, women have already done so much that if the men had to do it they would consider it a right good piece of work. Noon hour, which promises the men some rest at least, means no rest for the women. And finally evening, which the poor devil of a man claims for himself, must also be used for work by the even poorer devil of a woman. The housework must be done; the children must be taken care of; clothes must be washed and mended. In short, if men in an English factory town work ten hours, women have to work at least sixteen. How then can they show an active interest in anything else? It is a physical impossibility. And yet it is in these factory towns that on the whole women have it best. They make 'good' wages, the men cannot get along without their work, and therefore they are relatively independent. It is only when we come to the towns or districts where woman labour means nothing but sweating work, where a great deal of *home work* [done at home for an employer] is the rule, that we find the worst conditions and the greatest need for organisation.

In recent years much work has been done on this problem, but I am duty-bound to say that the results bear no relation to the efforts made. However, the relatively small results, it seems to me, are not always due to the miserable conditions under which most of the female workers live. I think, rather, an important part of the reason is the way most of the women's unions have been established and led. We find that most of them are led by people from the middle class, women as well as men. No doubt these people mean well up to a certain point, but they cannot understand and do not want to understand what the movement of the working class really is about. They see the misery about them, they feel uneasy, and they would like to 'ameliorate' the conditions of the unfortunate workers. But they do not belong to us.

Take the two organisations in London that have worked hard to help build women's unions. The older one is the Women's Trades Union Provident League; the newer one is the Women's Trade Union Association. The latter's aims are somewhat more advanced than the former's, but both are organised, led and supported by the most respectable and ingrained bourgeois types, men as well as women. Bishops, clergymen, bourgeois M.P.'s and their even more petty-bourgeois-minded wives, rich and aristocratic ladies and gentlemen—these are the patrons of a large number of women's unions.

Such shameless exploiters of labour as the millionaire Lord Brassen and such 'ladies' as the wife of the arch-reactionary Sir Julian Goldschmid hold salon tea-parties to support the Women's League, while Lady Dilke utilises the movement for her husband's political interests. How little these people understand about labour is evidenced by their amazement that the women at one meeting 'revealed a very intelligent interest in. . . the wise counsels of their economic superiors!'

We hope and believe that working-women will take an equally 'intelligent interest' in their own affairs and that they will take them over themselves, and above all that they will form a large and lively sector in the great modern movement of the proletariat. To a certain extent they have already done so.

(4)
[A Women's Trade Union]

In two ensuing letters in this series, Eleanor Marx continued her sketch of the English working-women's movement, describing the impcat of the 'old unionism' and the 'new unionism', and a number of industries and situations involving women's activity. The following extract is from the fourth letter, published 20th May, 1892; it deals with an all-women's union:

The new Union of women cigarmakers, which I mentioned in my last letter, was founded about three years ago. Its members do not belong to the men's union, although the two unions work together. To the outsider it seems deplorable that the two unions do not wholly merge, albeit working together. The reason adduced by the men against amalgamation is that the women almost always view their work as a temporary thing and regard marriage as their real *trade*, one that frees them from the need to earn their own living. Of course, in the vast majority of cases marriage does not reduce the woman's work but doubles it, since she not only works for wages but also has to do hard unpaid 'household' labour into the unholy bargain. In spite of all this, the women unfortunately do look on their work as temporary all too often, and defend this attitude of the men, who regard their wage-labour as 'lifelong' and are therefore much more eager to improve the conditions they work under.

In London, explains the article, the women cigarmakers make 25-50% less than men, especially because they are kept in the lowlier kind of 'preparation work'; and men workers complain when employers give women better jobs at lower wages, thus undercutting the general wage-rate. The remedy, however, is not to oppose such jobs for women but to demand equal pay. After discussing the work of the laundresses' union against horrible conditions, Eleanor adds a comment on two kinds of bourgeois women. The Laundresses had sent a delegation to Parliament to demand coverage under the Factory Act—

It is worth while to make the point that immediately Mrs. Fawcett, the reactionary bourgeois advocate of women's rights (of the .rights of property-owning women), who has never worked a day in her life, along with Miss Lupton, an anarchist (likewise a woman of the middle class), sent a counter-delegation to protest against this intervention on woman labour!

To be just, I must mention another woman of the middle class, May Abrahams, the indefatigable secretary and organiser of the Laundresses Union. It is largely thanks to her that these women now clearly understand the urgent question of governmental limitation of the work-day.

(5)
Women's Trade Unions in England

> *This was a polemical reply to an article, which the* Arbeiterinnenzeitung *had reprinted from another periodical, bu a Mrs. Ichenhäuser, dealing with the above subject. Most of the long reply is a very factual exposure of the distortions and poor information in Ichenhäusen's account, which was mainly a glorification of the Women's Trades Union Provident League (which had been discussed in the second article of the series). In the course there is a trenchant picture of what it means when the lords, ladies and bishops of the charitable League hold their tea-parties for their working-women wards—We here excerpt passages in which the article generalises on the relation between bourgeois feminism and socialism.*

An old proverb says, 'The road to Hell is paved with good intentions.' Women workers can well understand the demands of the bourgeois women's movement; they can and should even take a sympathetic attitude toward these demands; only, the goals of the women-workers and the bourgeois women are very different.

Once for all, I would like to present my standpoint clearly, and I think I speak for many women. As women we certainly have a lively concern about winning for women the same rights as men, including working men, already possess today. But we believe that this 'women's question' is an essential component in the *general* question of the emancipation of labour.

There is no doubt that there is a women's question. But for us—who gain the right to be counted among the working class either by birth or by working for the workers' cause—this issue belongs to the general working-class movement. We can understand, sympathise, and also help if need be, when women of the upper or middle class fight for rights that are well-founded and whose achievement will benefit working-women also. I say, we can even help: has not the *Communist Manifesto* taught us that it is our duty to support any progressive movement that benefits the workers' cause, even if this movement is not our own?

If every demand raised by these women were granted today, we working-women would still be just where we were before. Women-workers would still work infamously long hours, for infamously low wages, under infamously unhealthful conditions; they would still have only the choice between prostitution and starvation. It would be still more true than ever that, in the class struggle, the working-women would find the good women among their bitter enemies; they would have to fight these women just as bitterly as their working-class brothers must fight the capitalists. The men and women of the middle class need a 'free' field in order to exploit labour. Has not the star of the women's rights movement, Mrs. Fawcett, declared herself expressly in opposition to any legal reduction of working hours for female workers? It is interesting and worth mentioning that, on this question, the orthodox women's-rightser and my good friend Mr. Base, the weak epigone of Schopenhauer's, both take absolutely the same position. For this women's-rightser as for this misogynist, 'woman' is just woman. Neither of them sees that there is the exploiter woman of the middle class and the exploited woman of the working class. For us, however, the difference does exist. We see no more in common between a Mrs. Fawcett and a laundress than we see between Rothschild and one of his employees. In short, for us there is only the working-class movement.

The articles make a short digression to pay tribute to a little-known woman. Eleanor relates that when her father wrote a reply to an attack on the International by a labour leader named George Howell, the 'respectable' magazine refused to print it—

... so my father had to turn to a working woman who at that time edited a little weekly freethinkers' paper. She was pleased to print Karl Marx's reply to Mr. George Howell. The connection between Ms. Ichenhäuser, my father, and the aforementioned Mrs. Harriet Law is not so far outside the scope of this article as it appears. Mrs. Law was the only woman who sat on the General Council of the International; she had already worked for years for her sex and class, long before the distinguished Mrs. Paterson who is credited by Ms. Ichenhäuser with starting the movement. Mrs. Law was one of the first to recognise the importance of a women's organisation from the proletarian point of view. Few speak of her today; few remember her. But one day when the history of the labour movement in England is written, the name of Harriet Law will be entered into the golden book of the proletariat.

Near the end of the article is another short summary passage. Eleanor has just made the point that the lords and ladies of the charitable Women's League are trying to 'mend the decayed and rotten conditions of today' whereas 'we stand on the class-struggle viewpoint.'

For us there is no more a 'women's question' from the bourgeois standpoint than there is a men's question. Where the bourgeois women demand rights that are of help to us too, we will fight together with them, just as the men of our class did not reject the right to vote because it came from the bourgeois class. We too will not reject any benefit, gained by the bourgeois women in their own interests, which they provide us willingly or unwillingly. We accept these benefits as weapons, weapons that enable us to fight better on the side of our working-class brothers. We are not women arrayed in struggle against men but workers who are in struggle against the exploiters.